Dead Run

DEAD RUN

The Shocking Story
of Dennis Stockton
and Life on Death Row
in America

Joe Jackson and
William F. Burke Jr.

Walker & Company
New York

Published by arrangement with Crown Business Books, a division of
Random House, Inc.

Original edition published in 1999 by Times Books, a division of
Random House, Inc., New York. First updated paperback edition
published in the
United States of America in 2000 by
Walker Publishing Company, Inc.

Published simultaneously in Canada by Fitzhenry and Whiteside,
Markham, Ontario L3R 4T8

Grateful acknowledgment is made to the Robbins Office, Inc., for
permission to reprint an excerpt from "The Genius of Death Row"
by Peter Boyer, which originally appeared in *The New Yorker,*
December 4, 1995. Copyright © 1995 by Peter Boyer. Reprinted by
permission of the author.

Library of Congress Cataloging-in-Publication Data
Jackson, Joe, 1955–
Dead run: the shocking story of Dennis Stockton and life on death
row in America / Joe Jackson and William F. Burke Jr.
p.   cm.
Originally published: New York: Times Books, 1999. With new
frontmatter.
ISBN 0-8027-7599-3 (pbk.)
1. Stockton, Dennis W., 1940–1995.   2. Escapes—Virginia—Case
studies.   3. Prisoners—Virginia—Biography.   4. Mecklenburg
Correctional Center (Va.)   5. Mecklenburg Six (Group)   I. Burke,
William F. Jr.   II. Title.

HV8658.S76 J33   1999
364.66'092—dc21
[B]   00-060022

Original book designed by Susan Hood

Printed in the United States of America
2   4   6   8   10   9   7   5   3   1

To Kathy, Susan, Laura, Nick and Alex

Life and death are before a man,
And whichever he chooses will be given him.

—*The Wisdom of Sirach,*
15:17

Contents

Preface

The guard at the prison gate was a stern, unsmiling woman who wore a curious name tag on her uniform: F. KAFKA; she greeted a newspaper editor from Norfolk and his colleague who had come to the Virginia penitentiary in Richmond that gloomy day in October 1986 to see a Death Row inmate, Dennis W. Stockton. The guard led the way through a labyrinth of corridors in the dungeonlike building, past other guards and through metal doors that clanged shut behind them. They descended to A-Basement, the site of Virginia's Death Row, where Stockton was now on death watch in a cell not far from the state's electric chair.

The meeting would take place in what seemed to be an old locker room. There were battered metal lockers and a bench where someone, guards probably, had left their lunch pails. A square "window" covered with heavy metal mesh was set in the wall opposite the lockers. Within minutes, Stockton's face filled the small square. He said he had passed the chair on his way to this room. It was hard to make out Stockton's features through the wire mesh as he talked, but there was one thing no visitor ever missed: his pale blue, probing eyes.

Now those eyes burned with anger and frustration. Stockton had grown convinced that the justice system would never give him a fair shake, so he let his appeals lapse, thus "volunteering" for execution later this week. The electric chair had won, Stockton told the editor. He was tossing in his chips. He wanted it to end.

The editor had come to interview Stockton for a story, but he had another mission that day. The court had appointed new lawyers for Stockton who thought they might be able to do what predecessors had not: prove Stockton's innocence, or at least get him a new trial. The editor hoped to convince the prisoner to renew his appeals, but convincing Dennis Stockton to do anything was no easy task. He was a stubborn man.

Stockton had been on Death Row since June 1983 following his conviction for murder-for-hire of a seventeen-year-old North Carolina boy, a crime Stockton insisted he did not commit. He noted that the man who allegedly hired him for the job was never prosecuted, and the state's only witness to the alleged murder deal later told several people that he lied at Stockton's trial. Stockton felt his former lawyers had not worked hard enough to get him a new trial; instead, they seemed bent on reducing his death sentence to life in prison. He wanted a new chance in court to prove his innocence, but since it did not look like that would happen, he'd decided to let the executioner have his way.

The editor had come to know Stockton in 1984, weeks after six condemned men fled the "escape-proof" Mecklenburg Correctional Center, about one hundred miles southwest of Richmond, an escape that remains the only successful mass escape from Death Row in American history. Stockton helped plan the breakout, but had not gone with the escapees. Instead, he stayed behind, hoping he'd made the right choice by not accompanying his friends. Meanwhile, he described the escape in the diary he'd begun when first arriving on Death Row. When the diary was published in the Norfolk newspaper a few months later, exposing the incompetence and corruption that allowed the escape, the state took revenge, locking Stockton in a prison considered by some experts as one of the most inhumane in the nation. It wasn't long before he grew tired of battling the system, tired of the abuse of guards and inmates alike. He was a forty-five-year-old man on Death Row with little hope, but his friends from Norfolk had come to change his mind.

"You don't want to just give up, Dennis," the editor told him.

"I just can't see much point in it no more, Bill," he said.

The editor had talked with a member of Stockton's new multi-lawyer defense team from a high-powered Washington firm that had taken the case pro bono. The lawyer was convinced Stockton might indeed be innocent of the teenager's murder, but Stockton had heard it all before. Lawyers never kept their promises, he said. It was all just words.

When the editor left, he had no idea what would happen next. The newspaper had followed Stockton's story for more than two years, and it always seemed there were last-minute twists and sudden surprises. Now it was gearing up for coverage of his execution, yet within hours of the final act Stockton relented, deciding to give the lawyers one more chance. He would renew his appeals, but he vowed this would be the last time.

• • • •

Every contact with an execution becomes a spiritual voyage. Although the event is steeped in ritual, it is the enormity of the walk to death itself that imbues the act with symbolism. An observer sees the effects in the face of the prisoner, aged beyond his years; hears it in the voices of his lawyers, hopeful in the days before the execution, tired and despondent when their efforts have failed; in the grief and complex anger of those who loved the murder victim, hoping perhaps the execution will ameliorate their pain; in the tension of state officials, hoping everything proceeds without embarrassment; in the silence of the witnesses to the execution, holding their breaths as the prisoner walks into the chamber, realizing that on some level they are watching a skewed reflection of their own journeys. Whatever their roles or stations, all are humbled by what they will see.

This book is about Stockton's journey, and those of other condemned men with him, from Stockton's arrival on Death Row in 1983 to his final scheduled execution in 1995. During this time, America's corrections system experienced enormous change. The nation's Death Rows were merely a part of this evolution. The changes included massive overcrowding, a shift in philosophy from rehabilitation and release to retribution and extended warehousing, amid growing concerns that innocent people might get executed. Stockton called it "the monster factory" and grew convinced that any reasonable person trapped in such a world would seek escape by every possible means.

As journalists covering these historic changes, we became involved in Dennis Stockton's story and that of his fellow Death Row inmates. Bill Burke was projects editor for *The Virginian-Pilot* of Norfolk

when the escape from Mecklenburg occurred in 1984. Through a series of events he "discovered" Stockton and his prison diary, directing
the effort that resulted in its publication. In 1994 and 1995, Joe Jackson was a justice reporter for *The Virginian-Pilot* investigating Stockton's claims of innocence. In the process he broke the story of a
recantation by the state's main witness against Stockton—a recantation that opened even more surprising lines of evidence and which
made many wonder whether, after all those years of claiming his innocence, Stockton had really been telling the truth. The journey is
told primarily from Stockton's point of view, using his diaries, journals, letters and unpublished works, as well as interviews with others
involved in the tale. Since we are just two of the many characters involved in the drama, we identify ourselves merely as "the reporter"
and "the editor." Slipping into first person would take away from the
fact that this is mostly Stockton's tale and that of his fellow prisoners,
not ours.

This book is an insider's vision of hell: the hopes, fears and murderous rages; the sights, smells and scams. People may ask how one
can base a book on the words of a convicted killer, and the question is
fair. It is, after all, the central question of all investigative journalism:
How can one trust a source when *every* source has his or her own bias,
agenda and point of view? Journalism's answer, of course, is independent verification—the accounts of other sources—and in this
realm Stockton proved himself repeatedly over the years. Whether it
was the Cadillac driven by a New York Yankees baseball scout, the
closing time of a lonely diner, the name of a guard in Mecklenburg
who sold contraband to inmates or last-minute affidavits supporting
his claims of innocence, Stockton's words kept getting verified by
others. We say when such verification was not possible.

As Stockton's scheduled execution in 1995 rushed upon him, questions of the truth and how it can ever be determined became more
and more important to all of those involved. "The only real distinction for a man is the death sentence," Stendahl wrote in *The Red and
the Black,* a distinction Dennis Stockton didn't want but could not escape. As he published journal entries in the Norfolk newspaper describing the process of walking to execution, some saw him as a
symbol for all the ironies and absurdities of the death penalty while
others saw him as an ice-cold killer using the media in a last-ditch at-

tempt to escape the executioner. In the end, justice itself was the heart of Stockton's story, its determination and limitations, its ultimate fairness—or lack thereof. Dennis Stockton labored long and hard in prison to remake himself as a writer, taking many wrong turns to find the right subject. He discovered, ultimately, that that short walk down a dark hall was the best story he ever told.

Joe Jackson
William F. Burke, Jr.
July 1999

Introduction

In the Commonwealth of Virginia, the locale of *Dead Run,* the execution of felons has had a long and sturdy tradition. In fact, as the authors point out, no state in the union can claim a greater number of confirmed executions; this is partly due, of course, to Virginia's status as the oldest political jurisdiction in America. But one has always had a sense that in the Old Dominion there exists a particularly strong lust for vengeance. Virginia's conservatism possesses real fangs. Growing up as a boy in the Tidewater during the 1930s and 40s, I was perpetually haunted by news stories, in the paper or on the radio, of condemned men trudging that Last Mile to the electric chair at the state prison in Richmond. Many of them were accused rapists and all of these rapists, without exception, were Negroes. It was not until I'd grown much older, and was able to regard Virginia's use of the death penalty from a critical perspective, that I understood that for more than half a century the state had convicted hundreds of white and black men for rape, but only the black men—fifty-one of them—had been executed. Rape as a cause for the death penalty was eliminated only as recently as 1977. But the rate of executions for homicides has in recent years accelerated at runaway speed, until the state has become the second leading practitioner of legal murder, after Texas.

Dead Run is a gripping, true narrative, remarkable for the manner in which it treats crime and punishment, and the issue of justice in this country, on a level that should trouble one's deepest conscience. At the focus of the story is Dennis Stockton, a sensitive and intelligent small-town white boy who somehow went wrong and fell into a career of petty crime; he became a chronic offender fated to spend most of his time in jail until finally, in 1983, at the age of forty-two, he found himself convicted of capital murder and was sent to Virginia's new Death Row in rural Mecklenburg County. What gives the tale much of its extraordinary fascination is its rendition of life on Death Row as seen through Stockton's eyes: the manners and mores of this repulsive dungeon with its incessant threat of violence, brutal guards, loathsome food, vermin, stabbing, homosexual rapes and other quotidian horrors. *Dead Run* presents one of the most vivid descriptions I've ever read of the wretched cauldron of prison life, its rage, its chaos and feral brutality. Yet there is no need to pity most criminals. Some of the convicts who joined Stockton as companions on Death Row were authentic monsters who committed monstrous crimes, and their deeds and fearsome personalities are scrutinized in detail; as Stockton himself sweated out his appeals, year in and year out, one after another of his fellow denizens shambled to the execution chamber, always providing a sinister foreshadowing of his own fate.

The centerpiece of this chronicle is an amazing mass escape—the only mass escape from an American Death Row on record—which was closely observed by Stockton, although he didn't participate in the breakout. Engineered by the two Briley brothers, vicious killers from Richmond who were joined by four of their colleagues, the ingenious getaway caused an uproar in Virginia and beyond, and focused attention not only on the security of this reputedly up-to-date prison but on the slick connivance and stratagem of the escape itself. There is a certain amount of grim humor in this account, and the kind of suspenseful writing that has an artful kinship with the best old-time Big House escape movies; it's hard not to admire the desperate skill of these men, pulling off such an unprecedented caper. All of the fugitives were eventually tracked down, but perhaps one of the most important outcomes of the episode was its joining together of the co-author of this book, William F. Burke, Jr., and Dennis Stockton, who informed Burke by letter that he had much to tell about the escape, and awful things to relate about Death Row.

In the cruel constellation of wrongs embodied by the death penalty, the cruelest wrong may be that it often claims the lives of the innocent. It appears virtually certain that Dennis Stockton was innocent of the crime for which he was convicted. Seven years after his death sentence the state offered Stockton a deal: abandon attempts to prove his innocence and he would be given life imprisonment. Stockton refused, preferring death to life in prison for a crime he did not commit. Such defiance is only profoundly suggestive, not conclusive proof, of a man's innocence. But certainly the evidence presented later in the text—a recantation by a witness (uncovered by co-author Joe Jackson) of crucial testimony that led to the original conviction, and three signed affidavits naming that witness as the real murderer—should convince the most skeptical observers, and perhaps even the most die-hard supporter of capital punishment, that Dennis Stockton was not guilty of the murder for which he paid with his life on September 27, 1995.

In the months before his execution, Stockton became a newspaper writer, contributing columns to the Norfolk *Virginian-Pilot* that tell—in a style colorful, ironic and cheerfully mordant—what it is like to exist in our society's closest approximation to hell on earth. He came to the writer's calling fairly late in life, and this straightforward and often pungently stoical record of his slow inching toward death was all he had to give us, before the state exacted its retribution for an illusory misdeed. It is a gift we should treasure, bearing witness as it does to Stockton's own appealing humanity, and the inhumanity of the law that destroyed him.

—William Styron
March 1999

Cast of Characters

Morris Mason (a multiple killer from Virginia's rural Eastern Shore)

Derick "Baylock" Peterson (one of the Mecklenburg Six)

Steve Roach (a young killer who became friendly with Dennis Stockton in 1995)

Dennis Stockton (convicted of the 1978 murder of Kenneth Arnder, Stockton chronicled the Great Escape in his diary and later wrote about the experience of approaching his execution; one of the original planners of the Great Escape, he chose not to run)

Lem Tuggle (one of the Mecklenburg Six)

Willie Lloyd Turner (the principal weapons-maker for the Great Escape, he chose not to run)

Alton Waye (one of the original planners of the Great Escape, he chose not to run)

Prison Personnel

Gary Bass (warden at Mecklenburg Correctional Center)

Nurse Ethel Barksdale (prison nurse taken hostage)

Officer Barry Batillo (guard who delivered the van used by the Mecklenburg Six in their escape)

Nurse Maud Boyd (prison nurse taken hostage)

Harold Catron (assistant warden at Mecklenburg)

Cpl. Harold Crutchfield (first hostage in the escape)

Lt. Milton Crutchfield (first ranking officer taken hostage)

Officer Donald Gentry (guard taken hostage)

Lt. Larry Hawkins (shift commander during the escape)

Officer Ricardo Holmes (guard in charge of Death Row's control booth)

Robert Landon (chief of the state Department of Corrections)

ON THE OUTSIDE

Kenny Arnder (young friend of Stockton's whose murder led to Stockton's arrest)

Wilma Arnder (Kenny Arnder's mother)

Randy Bowman (the witness whose testimony convicted Stockton)

Bill Burke (editor at *The Virginian-Pilot* who contacted Stockton after the Great Escape)

Timothy Crabtree (Randy Bowman's son)

Marie Deans (paralegal with the Virginia Coalition on Jails and Prisons who investigated conditions at Mecklenburg)

Russ Ford (Death Row chaplain)

Robert Gates (witness at the killing of Ronnie Tate)

Tony Giorno (Virginia Commonwealth's attorney who prosecuted Dennis Stockton)

Jay Gregory (Patrick County criminal investigator who later became county sheriff)

Joe Jackson (investigative reporter for *The Virginian-Pilot* who investigated Stockton's claims of innocence)

Anthony King (one of Stockton's last attorneys)

Tommy McBride (allegedly paid Stockton $1,500 to kill Kenny Arnder; conviction on this charge sent Stockton to Death Row)

Patricia McHone (Randy Bowman's ex-wife)

Gov. Charles Robb (Virginia's governor when the Great Escape occurred)

Steve Rosenfield (one of Stockton's last attorneys)

Ron Smith (Stockton's minister)

Ronnie Tate (friend who Stockton admitted killing, in self-defense)

Joe Wise (Stockton's friend and fellow condemned inmate at Powhatan Correctional Center)

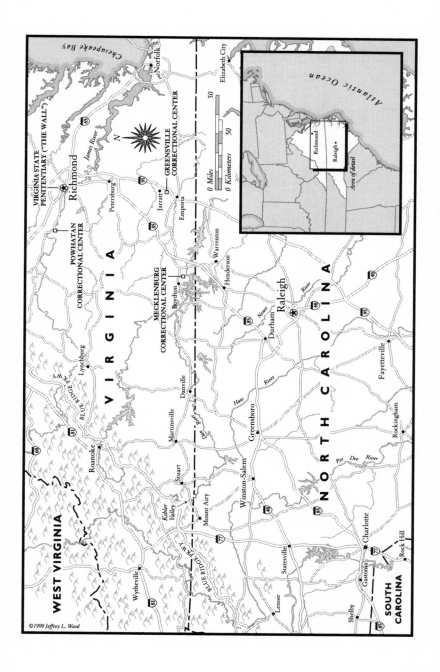

Part I

THE GREAT ESCAPE

"Let's do it."

—Gary Gilmore,
shortly before his execution
on January 17, 1977,
by a Utah firing squad

1

Dennis Stockton watched the rolling hills of Virginia's Piedmont scroll across the windows of the hot, sealed prison van. In his mind, the forest stretched forever like an immense green carpet, the shadows inviting and cool beneath the miles of sweet gum and pine. Although here at the forest's edge his view was blocked by secondary growth and kudzu, he'd escaped enough times during his prison career to know that deep inside there'd be perfect cover for dumping a getaway car and eluding pursuers. His thoughts drifted until he caught himself and smirked. Not that he expected to escape this time. Not from Death Row.

It was midafternoon on June 15, 1983, the temperature ninety-plus, humidity that seemed the same—typical summer weather in central Virginia. The heat dazzled up from the white slab; the whine of the tires grew hypnotic. The van's sides and roof were heavy metal; the rear doors had bar-covered windows that wouldn't open; the mercury inside topped that outside by several degrees. His brain throbbed from dehydration, while his prison-issue T-shirt and pants clung to him like a second skin. Up front, the three guards could watch his movements through a wire-covered portal. He asked them to crank open his window for relief, but they only laughed and told him to be patient. He'd be "home" soon.

He'd heard tales of this new home—the "escape-proof" Mecklenburg Correctional Center, less than ten miles north of the North Carolina line. As the van turned off the highway onto an asphalt track curving deep through thick woods and swamp, one of the guards tapped on the glass and pointed ahead to where the trees thinned. They rounded one last curve and he saw it: the double perimeter fence topped by billowing razor wire, the spaces between fences tangled with more scalpel-sharp coils. The four metal guard towers looming outside the fence. The lone guard manning each tower, a dark silhouette in the bright sunlight—each guard armed with an automatic rifle and told "shoot to kill" should an escapee get that far.

Not that anyone expected that to happen. The pride of Virginia's prison system, Mecklenburg began operations in March 1977 and was built in stages at a cost of $20 million. Regarded by penologists as one of the six most up-to-date maximum security facilities in the nation, it was also one of the most expensive to run. In 1983–84, the state spent over $29,000 a year on each prisoner at Mecklenburg, about double anywhere else in Virginia. While the statewide ratio of guards to prisoners was 1 to 2.47, the ratio in Mecklenburg was 1 to 1.29, making it one of the highest in the state, as well as the country.

The prison was a showpiece, yet for all its publicity Mecklenburg was just one part of an aging correctional machine that by anybody's estimate had grown huge and cumbersome. Virginia's Department of Corrections, known as the DOC, was a growth industry, its operating budget for the 1983–84 fiscal year $260.4 million, one of the largest of any state agency. That money ran 14 prisons and 26 road camps, housing a daily average of 9,454 convicts. Such logistics implied clockwork efficiency, an image DOC officials labored hard to maintain, and a new arrival's introduction to the machine began with his "processing." Prison officials checked his teeth, drew his blood, took his fingerprints, gave him a battery of psychological tests, cataloged his few possessions and prescribed any medications. Last but not least, he was given a prisoner number, making him a small yet identifiable part of the machine.

Stockton was processed the day before at the Virginia State Penitentiary, a deteriorating collection of brick and stucco buildings squatting on a hill in downtown Richmond. Established in 1800, the penitentiary was known to guards and inmates alike as "The Wall." Stockton noticed that much of Virginia's prison system seemed cast in absolute terms—The Wall, The World, The Man, The Law. The only thing that seemed to have its own proper name was Old Sparky, the state's seventy-five-year-old electric chair. Even after Death Row itself was moved from Richmond to Mecklenburg, Old Sparky remained behind, and it was here the condemned man returned to be executed. His last walk would be into a small room in a dank, cold basement with the chair placed in the exact center, a vision that even gave cops the creeps, much less the condemned.

Now Stockton, officially labeled Prisoner No. 134466, rode from old to new, past to high-tech present, in a dirty white van. He watched as they curved left past the administration building toward the main sally port gate separating the rest of the compound from The World. A fifth gun tower, smaller than the others, overlooked this gate, but no one manned it due to recent budget cutbacks. The van stopped and a chain was unhooked. His guards climbed out and were patted down by others, then all turned and peered inside at him.

They saw staring back an unsmiling man whose gaunt face was a study in sharp, dark planes: black eyebrows that nearly met, dark hair matted to his scalp, deep wrinkles defining the corners of his mouth and jowls. If they knew anything about him, it was that he'd been convicted of capital murder in March 1983 for the gruesome 1978 contract killing of seventeen-year-old Kenneth Wayne Arnder. The trial was held in the little town of Stuart, Virginia, in conservative farm country in the foothills of the Blue Ridge Mountains, a place that seemed as gentle and genteel as anyone could ever imagine. Prosecutors accused Stockton of accepting $1,500 in blood money to kill Arnder, then of shooting the teenager between the eyes in a remote picnic spot, hacking off his hands and dumping his body across the border near Mount Airy, North Carolina, hometown of Andy Griffith and prototype for TV's peaceful Mayberry. Stockton said he was innocent and the state had the wrong man, but the guards had heard *that* tale so often you'd think the prison was packed with innocent men. The jury didn't believe Stockton either and sentenced him to die.

Although Stockton claimed innocence of Arnder's murder, he never claimed to be an innocent himself. A sharp-eyed guard would see that Stockton wasn't some "fish," prison slang for a newcomer, the tip-off being the blue-green 6 on his right forearm. This was all that remained of "26," the number on the orange and white Ford driven by Curtis Turner, Stockton's first NASCAR hero. He'd had it tattooed when he was twenty, but this was no parlor special with sweeping lines and rainbow colors. No, this was a convict tattoo, carved freehand with jury-rigged tattoo guns patched together from melted toothbrushes, stolen sewing machine needles and cannibalized tape-player motors. Such tattoos were always blue green, the standard ink used in prison print shops. Now Stockton's racing idol was Dale Earnhardt, but the only way to erase all signs of his youthful hero-worship was to make a paste from salt and water, rub the skin until raw, then let it scar and rub again. Stockton had already erased the first digit and only its shadow remained. In time, he planned to erase the 6 the same way.

Now forty-two, Stockton was born in October 1940, and except for the few times he was free on parole or out on escape, he'd spent most of his adult life in a prison, work camp or jail. Yet Stockton was far from a common criminal. He was a talented left-handed pitcher scouted by the New York Yankees. His IQ was estimated between 130 and 160. Blessed with a sharp eye for detail and an exceptional memory throughout his life, he adhered to an angry habit of truth-telling that was often self-destructive. But more than anything else, it was his eyes that people remembered. They were deep-set and blue, separate somehow from the rest of his face, like the disembodied eyes that follow one in a dream. "It's not Dennis's fault he looked like Hitler," said one of his lawyers. "But it sure worked against him in trial." If anyone ever looked like a killer, this was the guy.

His prison education began in tenth grade, when two policemen dragged him from his high school near Mount Airy as his stunned classmates watched. A judge sentenced him to three to five years in prison on two counts of passing bad checks in his parents' names. He'd learned a lot that first time in prison, as if a criminal lifetime could be foretold in one short stint behind bars. Even then, in the late 1950s, prisons were overcrowded, and one weekend he and some others were housed in North Carolina's Death Row before being shipped elsewhere. The guards put him in an empty basement cell. It was dark in there, and spooky, with nothing to do but stare at the ceiling and walls. His only company was the guard carrying trays of cold food, his slow footsteps echoing down the hall. "Like it here, boy?" asked the guard, a squat man with a blond crewcut. "Think you'll be back? You fit in real well." He laughed at his joke and passed on.

That was twenty-four or twenty-five years ago. Stockton could still remember that long weekend spent alone in a cell that faded to darkness in the damp corners like a cave. He wondered about the other men who'd been there before him, what they'd done to deserve this life. They'd lain in this same bed, stared at the same ceiling, thought about the person or people they'd been accused of killing. It was like being buried alive. Is this what they think I'm worth? he'd wondered as a boy. Two forgery charges and I'm the same as a killer? A little shock treatment might do me good? Maybe other cons were right when they said that staying straight was a fool's game, that any misstep and your "friends" would turn on you like dogs.

Now he'd arrived at a different Death Row in a different state, but as his driver slid back behind the wheel Stockton couldn't help but wonder if the nightmare place would be the same. The van rolled forward slowly, guards walking alongside as it crunched up the gravel path to Building One, home of Virginia's condemned men.

Once inside the razor-wire fence, however, a new arrival might marvel at how Mecklenburg looked more like a small community college campus than a maximum-security prison housing the state's toughest convicts. The campus itself, shaped by the fence into a fat teardrop, rested in the center of a 189-acre clearing, this circled by thick pine woods. The five two-story buildings with high, narrow windows were built around a large, immaculately clipped oval lawn. Each building was an island to itself with four control rooms and three pods, or cell blocks; each pod housed twenty-four single-man cells, common areas the residents called "dayrooms," and eating and recreation facilities. Everyone came and went through computer-controlled sets of double doors operated by the control-room guards. A door slid open and the visitor walked into a sally port; the first door closed and locked behind him before the second unlocked. The control rooms also looked out over the cells and were separated from the dayrooms by thick Plexiglas plates. A control panel could electronically open and close all the cell doors individually or at once. If Mecklenburg did resemble a place of higher learning, it was the University of Hell.

The idea of prison as a place of rehabilitation and reeducation was an eighteenth-century Christian invention. The criminal was a person with an ailing soul: if sent to an isolated place to labor under austere conditions, he would do penance for his crimes and eventually be redeemed. Such places of redemption were dubbed penitentiaries— monasteries with chains and bars.

Mecklenburg too was a place of redemption, though in a much

narrower sense. It had a special mission: the development of better prisoners through behavior control. The state's most disruptive prisoners were sent there to become better citizens within the prison community, not the outside world. On passing through the double gates, they entered a "phase program" that rewarded good behavior with a series of increasing "privileges." Inmates started out in strict confinement in single-man cells, then steadily climbed the ladder of increasing freedom and privilege. Each building housed inmates at a different stage in the process. Successful completion of all phases was supposed to take two years. The final reward was simple: the inmate was shipped to another prison. It was the promised afterlife, a legal escape to anywhere but Mecklenburg.

Virginia officials believed they had designed a corrections model for the rest of the nation, the ultimate escape-proof prison that churned out better inmate-citizens. Unfortunately, the model prison was eroding from within. True, no inmate had successfully escaped since its opening in 1977, but this could not be credited to lack of effort. In October 1981, three female visitors tried slipping drugs, guns and ammo to condemned prisoners James Briley and Earl Clanton through a hole cut with homemade tools in the visitors' room partition. The attempt was spotted on security cameras and guards rushed in. The discovery assured officials their system was state-of-the-art and there were no more serious escape attempts in 1982 or 1983. Yet there was a wide gulf between the prison's "fail-safe" public face and reality. Mecklenburg was not a peaceable kingdom. The guards and inmates knew it, but prison officials placed so much faith in their design that they suffered from a *Titanic*-like syndrome, simply refusing to believe that disaster could occur.

The roots of Mecklenburg's weakness were built into its highly touted design. The prison was envisioned as *the* most secure facility in the state. It was the best penitentiary tax dollars could buy. By definition, it housed Virginia's worst criminals, including those who had escaped from other prisons time and again. A study by the National Institute of Corrections described "hostile, aggressive [and] highly dangerous" inmates who trashed the prison regularly and heaped abuse on staff and visitors alike. Part of the problem stemmed from a dearth of rehabilitative programs, an absence that resulted in inmate idleness. Such programs, which assumed an eventual return to society, had been supplanted by the "phase" programs, whose only goals were the creation of a more pliant inmate. The result: most convicts had plenty of time to sit and stew about privileges they didn't have, instead of working in hopes that they might win parole, beat the odds and never sin again.

Thus, the concentration of extremely dangerous inmates would prove one leg of Mecklenburg's eventual undoing. The second leg was the guards themselves. Although the state spent more on security at Mecklenburg than at any other prison, the money went into high-tech gadgetry and increased staffing levels, not into an individual's paycheck. In 1983, Virginia prison guards had a starting salary of $12,644, one of the lowest in the nation. Even campus police officers were paid more. Mecklenburg's guards were assaulted more often than in any other prison in the state. They were routinely cursed by inmates, spit on, hit and attacked with weapons. They had food, piss and shit thrown on them as they passed inmates' cells. In return, and not surprisingly, inmates regularly complained that the guards assaulted them. In the early 1980s, a jury awarded a prisoner $18,000 in damages after one such beating. During the same period, seven inmates filed a class-action suit with the help of the ACLU's National Prison Project claiming that Mecklenburg's rigid disciplinary system and overuse of solitary confinement bred a "hopeless and helpless atmosphere" that resulted in "physical and psychological deterioration." Alvin Bronstein, head of the Prison Project, said conditions at Mecklenburg were "out of control"; he called the prison one of the worst he had ever visited. The seven plaintiffs included two from Death Row.

Finally, the prison was plagued with drugs and other contraband, much of it smuggled in by low-paid guards trying to supplement their incomes. "With the stinking pay they give these officers for having their lives placed in constant danger, they shouldn't be surprised," one inmate explained. "A forty dollar ounce [of pot, at street rate] . . . costs an inmate 150 to 200 dollars to have an officer bring it to him. . . . Six inmates can get the guard $1,000 clear every two weeks, more than he makes from the state."

Thus, the cliché of a time bomb was too tame for Mecklenburg. The place was closer to Chernobyl on the eve of its meltdown. Yet in this world of violence and disorder, Death Row was a separate country, an almost tranquil land. Guards liked the assignment: it was an eye of calm within the circling storm, a wheel within a wheel. Indeed, it was a world that seemed deceptively peaceful next to the accepted cold brutality of general prison life—one ruled by an unnatural calendar where each resident knew the exact date, time and method of his scheduled demise. Most guards viewed it as just a job, but a few had turned philosophical: they wondered whether the quiet merely indicated surface tension. What lay hidden underneath? Guards and inmates alike remarked how strange it was the way death walked among them, ever so gently, as though its presence changed and soothed everyone entering its surreal domain.

The rules here were also markedly different than in the rest of Mecklenburg. Death Row had no phase program, no increments of beneficence doled out if one were good and did not sin. The state believed the condemned were beyond redemption. There were no classes, no entry into the prison job market, no mixing with other prisoners in any but the most fleeting ways. The men on The Row had their own gallows humor: the most repeated joke was that their keepers figured the only way to "modify" their behavior was by a trip to the electric chair.

By virtue of their sentence, they were the isolated and passed over—an infection kept in sight but out of bounds. Other prisoners watched from a distance: recreation, library visits, *everything* on The Row was self-contained. Even the building was separate, set at the back of the oval, a few yards away from the main sally port. The only other inmates with whom the condemned had any contact were those on segregation—inmates kept separate from the general population for a variety of reasons, including refusal to participate in behavior modification—and they too lived in Building One.

• • • •

The van stopped again, the doors were thrown open and Stockton was ushered inside. He was taken to the "strip room," where he was unshackled by several blue-shirted guards, these silently watched by a supervisor whose white shirt gleamed with gold tabs. Inmates could feel an occasional empathy for a blue-shirted "officer" if he was a decent man who treated convicts with common respect, but never for a "white shirt." He represented The Law. He was The Man.

A guard told Stockton to peel off his sweat-soaked clothes, then looked under his armpits, inside his mouth and at the bottoms of his feet. He was told to turn around and bend over, a prison ritual older than the draft board's "turn your head and cough." The guards threw him the regulation prison uniform: one blue jumpsuit, one white T-shirt, a pair of white socks, one pair of flip-flops, one pair of cotton briefs. On top was piled his linen: two folded sheets, one blanket, one pillowcase, one towel, one washcloth.

"How about a shower?" Stockton asked.

"Later," the guard replied.

Stockton's wrists and ankles were reshackled. As he carried his clothes and linen before him, three guards took him up the elevator to the second floor. They walked him slowly to The Row, one on each side, a white shirt behind. This was an important event in Building One, a solemn ritual, the arrival of another prisoner sentenced to die. Stockton was the sixteenth condemned prisoner sent here. Others would soon follow. The entourage moved in silence, except for the soft chiming of Stockton's chains and the click of the guards' heels. Inmates along the walk to Death Row stopped and watched. They wanted to check out the new guy; anything to break the monotony, every inmate's curse.

Death Row consisted of two sections: C-Pod right and left. All cells were identical, six upstairs, six down, twelve per section. The two sections were set at right angles and separated by walls or bars; they faced each other across the large dayroom where the condemned men mingled. A glass-enclosed control room was planted in the center; the guard on duty could see inside both sections and scan all cell doors with a turn of his head.

Stockton entered Death Row's sally port; the outer door closed behind him before the inner one opened, an airlock protecting The World from contagion. The guards watched; so did the other prisoners. Some sat around tables in the dayroom. Others stood up in their cells when they heard the inner gate slide back and watched from behind their doors. They stood there expressionless, framed by a thin strip of vertical glass. It gave Stockton the chills.

He was led across the dayroom and to Cell 67. The chains were taken off, the door shut behind him. The guards walked away.

He had been told that he would spend the next ten days locked in this cell for a period prison officials called "orientation," a ritual that was part observation, part initiation. Stockton looked around at his new home. The door was solid metal with two ways of looking out: a slot through which guards passed his food tray, and a narrow glass strip, two inches wide by thirty inches tall, that looked into the day-room. In one corner, a sink and commode had been blackened by fire. The inside of the commode was covered with rust. A steel bed, six feet long by two and a half feet wide, was welded to the wall; on that lay a pillow and a thin mattress, only about two inches thick. The walls and floor were filthy—they hadn't been washed in a long time. Across the cell was a closed window, and Stockton quickly cranked it open. If he stood on his toes he could see, in the distance, the forest's green curve.

Stockton heard a noise and turned. A guard pushed a tray of food through the door slot and walked off without a word. I really am in isolation, he realized: the guards didn't make eye contact, the other inmates had eyed him curiously but didn't speak. He looked at the tray. He wasn't hungry, but saw the two cups of tea that came with the meal. He gulped them down—his first drink since leaving The Wall.

He looked out his door and slowly grew amazed. The place seemed so relaxed, the inmates milling around the dayroom or sitting at one of three tables playing cards. They were dressed only in gym shorts—it felt like a hundred degrees in here, hot and humid—and their bodies glistened with sweat. A TV was set on a table pushed against the Plexiglas control booth. A guard and two prisoners sat before it, watching a baseball game. The guard's arms were crossed on his chest. No weapons hung from his leather belt, not even a night-stick. Just a pair of cuffs. He seemed unconcerned that he went un-armed among a bunch of killers. The inmates, in turn, acted like he wasn't there. Even the rules seemed relaxed: he knew that the doors to each cell were supposed to remain closed for better control and se-curity, yet some were open, even though the inmates were inside. If they weren't too obvious about it, he discovered quickly, inmates could visit one another's cells like neighbors in a sleepy small town.

Stockton's eyes drifted to the other section, where some of the men still stood behind their doors, gazing out like zombies. He realized that he would look the same to them, so stepped back and sat on his bed.

It was nothing like Carolina's Row of twenty-six years earlier, he thought. That was dark, this lit by fluorescent lights. That was still and empty, this filled with movement and sound. This reminded him more of that Jack Nicholson movie he'd seen in 1976, the one that took place in the mental ward. He'd liked that movie, though he'd been amazed how the movie house audience cheered when Jack Nicholson strangled the nurse. That wouldn't happen in real life, he thought. Yet the similarities still abounded between the movie reality and this place: supervisor watching behind a window, tiny rooms with patients staring out, common area where the residents milled around. In some ways, the dark Death Row of his past seemed more real.

With nightfall came a slight drop in the temperature. It would be many days before his sleeping pills, prescribed by prison doctors, arrived from Richmond. It was after 11 P.M. when a guard finally turned off the TV. The silence was instantly filled with the hollering of the men in their cells. Much later, the pod grew quiet. Stockton tossed and turned, thinking of family and friends, of people who believed he was a killer, of those who believed he was innocent. How could all this happen? he wondered. How could he keep from going crazy? Before dawn, exhausted, he dropped into sleep and fitful dreams.

2

Whether or not they knew it, Stockton and his neighbors were unlikely symbols in a deepening war of words. The right of government to decide life and death had become one of America's great moral and legal battles of the late twentieth century. The struggle grew more vicious the longer it continued. Both sides—death penalty supporters and "abolitionists"—steeped their arguments in the rhetoric of good and evil, claiming God and The Law for their cause. As in actual war, there were few, if any, protected bystanders. Beside the convicted killer and the victim, others littered the field. Lawyers, judges, ministers. Guards, wardens, other inmates. Families of both the condemned and the victims. Those chanting for death outside the chamber, as well as their opponents. Those who branded the killer evil, those who tried to bring him peace . . . even those who sought his love and strange blessing shortly before he died. Death was the great leveler, for some an even greater aphrodisiac. Like war, it was hypnotic and powerful, filled with ghastly beauty. Even those who survived got seared by the chair.

As the years progressed, only Texas and Florida would execute more inmates than Virginia, making the Old Dominion one of the nation's salients in this war. Ironically, this was also the state of Thomas Jefferson, who dreamt that all men and women should receive fair and equal treatment in The Law's grinding machine. Yet the tug-of-war between the present and traditions of the past made Virginia a crucible in the evolution of death-penalty law. The machine changed in ways Mr. Jefferson never dreamed. Condemned men like Stockton watched as the Supreme Court of the United States increasingly washed its hands of capital murder cases, turning from a sympathetic "court of last resort" to one reluctant to interfere even in cases where new evidence strongly suggested an innocent man would die. The condemned found themselves in a weird legal limbo where questions of guilt and innocence took a backseat to what judges called "the orderly processes of justice." Like many others, Stockton slammed against state laws prohibiting the introduction of new evidence after a set period of time: in Virginia, it was more than twenty-one days after conviction, one of the shortest in the nation. Designed to relieve pressure on the courts, such "procedural bars" also prevented the introduction of evidence illegally suppressed during the original trial. In most states with the death penalty, judges and advocates of the condemned found ways to override the bars, but Virginia's penalty, among the nation's most rigid, was rarely challenged by higher courts. Opponents claimed the issue had become less one of individual justice, more that of power over life and death, and revenge.

In such a world, the natural response was escape, yet in the escape-proof Mecklenburg a resident focused on more mundane concerns. During Stockton's second day on The Row, he griped about the filthiness of his cell. He complained so loud and long that the guards finally moved him to a cleaner one, Cell 71. He asked for soap and a scrub brush and they brought these too. The guards joked about the new guy who seemed more worried about death by germs than by the electric chair, who'd go down on his knees to scrub the cell from floor to ceiling when he should kneel and pray. A prison psychologist would later call his behavior obsessive-compulsive, but for Stockton it was stay busy or rot, keep occupied or brood about his fate. Brooding only made him want to pound the walls. Besides, he just didn't like a dirty cell.

Stockton was still scouring the floor that day when he heard a rap at his door. Glancing over, he saw his new neighbor, a medium-sized black man in his late twenties with a small mustache, goatee and long sideburns. A diamond stud glinted in his left ear; his hair, worn long in the back, was closely cropped and beginning to thin on the sides. This was the first person to acknowledge Stockton's existence since his arrival, but Stockton had already noticed him while observing this strange new world. He'd watched the other inmates defer to the stranger, noted that even the guards treated him well. Unlike others, the man almost seemed at peace with the off-white walls of his captivity, able to sit for long periods playing cards or watching TV. He listened with a slight, bemused smile when others talked, his eyes half-closed as if his thoughts were a hundred miles away. Now he placed a chair outside Stockton's door, pushed two packs of cigarettes through the slot like he was from the Welcome Wagon and introduced himself in a soft, fluid voice. "I'm Linwood Briley," he said.

Stockton jerked in surprise. Everyone knew of the Brileys: Linwood and his younger brother James, known as JB. The two were the most notorious killers in modern Virginia history, said to have slaughtered anywhere from eleven to twenty people in their combined careers. Most of the victims died during a ten-month robbery spree in Richmond, the killings usually an afterthought to leave no witnesses. The courts convicted them of eight slayings and hustled them off to Death Row, where they arrived little more than a month apart. Officials put them in the same section of C-Pod, instantly establishing a core of power that couldn't be broken.

The Brileys were a unit, their fates bonded like glue. Linwood was the leader, a diplomat who led by example, while JB was the enforcer, someone to fear. A prosecutor called them "killing machines," and indeed the Brileys went beyond any other Death Row inmate in the scope of their crimes. They killed strangers, neighbors, old friends, even a five-year-old boy. Killing styles are personal, like windows to the soul, but with the brothers the boundaries overlapped. The rage of one fueled the calculation of the other. What emerged had a life of its own.

From March to October 1979, Linwood, JB, their younger brother Anthony and teenage neighbor Duncan Meekins cruised Richmond and its surrounding counties, looking for isolated victims who seemed easy to rob. The first known attack came on March 12, when Linwood knocked on the door of Henrico County couple William and Virginia Bucher and asked to use the phone because his car had broken down. When the Buchers let him in, Linwood pulled a gun and opened the door for Anthony; he tied them up, ransacked the house, doused several rooms with gasoline and set the home ablaze. They loaded the Buchers' car with a TV, police scanner and some jewelry and sped off as the flames lit the night sky. But William Bucher freed himself and his wife and the two escaped, the only known survivors of a Briley attack. When police later arrested Linwood, they found Bucher's scanner in his car.

The last attack came on October 19, 1979, seven months and eleven victims later. During this time the gang refined its technique, watching and waiting until sure they had a lone victim who couldn't get away. They literally hunted humans, stalking their prey until the time was right to spring. On April 9, they followed their third victim, seventy-six-year-old Mary Gowen, across town from her babysitting job, then raped, robbed and shot her outside her home. The sixth victim, sixty-two-year-old Mary Wilfong, was followed on September 30. They broke inside her apartment, took her purse and JB crushed her skull with a baseball bat.

Linwood earned his death sentence with one such crime. Unfortunately for the brothers, this fifth victim was well known and his murder highly publicized. On the night of September 14, 1979, Richmond disc jockey John "Johnny G." Gallaher's band was playing at a Southside Richmond nightclub. Gallaher stepped out the back door for some air between sets; the gang was posted in the bushes outside, awaiting promising prey. Meekins later testified that the four had gone prowling that night but without luck, so they waited outside the club like predators around a watering hole. When Gallaher stepped out, Linwood jumped him; they stuffed him in the back of his Lincoln Continental and drove to a deserted paper plant on Mayo Island in the James River. Gallaher probably knew he was doomed: he started struggling as he was forced from the car. Linwood shot him in the neck and dumped the body in the river, where it was found two days later. When Linwood was arrested, he still wore Gallaher's ring.

But the killings weren't always so cold and calculated and both brothers were capable of blood rage. On July 4, Linwood killed seventeen-year-old Christopher Phillips when he found the teen breaking into his car. The gang was scouting for victims when they came back to their car and discovered Phillips there with another boy. When Phillips said the car belonged to a friend, the gang dragged him into a backyard. He screamed for help. As the other boy fled, Linwood lifted a cinder block and dropped it, crushing Phillips's head.

Then came October, the bloodiest month of all. By now, they'd grown reckless and had fouled their own backyard, a violation of one of crime's first rules. On October 6, they visited a seventy-five-year-old invalid on their block to sell stolen CB radios; when they left, she was beaten to death with a pipe and her fifty-nine-year-old boarder had seven knives sticking from his body, many broken off at the hilt. Eight days later, they got into a fight with a Vietnam veteran and shot him with a rifle. Five days after that, the Brileys went calling on a childhood friend.

It was October 19, 1979. That morning, JB promised a Richmond judge that he would do whatever it took to stay off the streets and stay straight after his parole for the 1973 robbery and attempted murder of a policeman. That evening, he broke his vow. He and the others visited Harvey Wilkerson, who had grown up with the Brileys. Wilkerson now lived with his wife, twenty-three-year-old Judy Barton, five months pregnant, and her five-year-old son. The Brileys knocked and Wilkerson nervously let them in, apparently aware of the rumors surrounding the gang yet even more afraid to cross them. His fears proved true: the gang overpowered the adults, binding and gagging them with electrical tape. Then Linwood dragged Barton into the kitchen and raped her within hearing of the others. Meekins raped her next. Linwood dragged her back into the room with her son and husband, rummaged through the house and left.

Without Linwood, the others seemed at a loss for what to do. Worse, the five-year-old wouldn't stop crying. They covered the adults with sheets; there were four shots. When Meekins looked over, JB stood above the bloody sheet covering Barton. "You got to get one," he said.

Meekins stuck a pistol to a pillow, put it to Wilkerson's head and fired. JB shot the boy.

By now, police were frantically seeking the Brileys to end the murders. They'd tracked them to Wilkerson's, heard the shots and watched the four run off, but were unsure from where the shots originated. They would not realize that a triple murder had occurred until two days later when the bodies were found. The day after that, police picked up Linwood and Meekins, and within an hour, Meekins broke down. He laid out every act in the seven-month spree.

Linwood arrived on Death Row on January 28, 1980, for John Gallaher's murder. JB arrived on March 4 for the murders of Judy Barton and her son. Anthony Briley and Duncan Meekins received several life terms. Anthony was sent to a cell in Mecklenburg within sight of Death Row, while Meekins went to a prison across the state for his own protection. Sometimes Anthony could peer out his window and see Linwood and JB practicing karate in The Row's small recreation yard. They were up to something, he thought, smiling to himself. The Man might underestimate his brothers . . . but not him.

Even though prosecutors successfully portrayed the two as monsters, their true natures remained a mystery. Some of their lifelong neighbors called them bright, personable and reserved. Their teachers in elementary and secondary school seemed divided on whether they were good or problem students. Friends said they had plenty of girlfriends and loved fast cars; others called them "nice guys." Lawyers, preachers, even prison officials called them dignified.

Yet by the time they were teenagers, it was obvious something was seriously wrong. Linwood was fifteen when he was charged with his first killing, the shooting of an elderly neighbor. Although his lawyer said he aimed at birds, Linwood—who quipped the woman had heart problems and would have died anyway—was convicted of manslaughter and sentenced to a year in a juvenile institution. JB entered prison at sixteen for robbery and attempted murder. When police searched the Brileys' two-story house in 1979, they found among their pets a boa constrictor, piranhas and a tarantula. Their father had a lock on his bedroom door.

The key to the Brileys' charisma seemed an innate genius for control, especially by Linwood. One of the best accounts of Linwood's style came from Reverend Odie Brown, who served as the elder Briley's prison chaplain in 1984 as he approached execution. Brown recalled once waiting for Linwood to complete some ritual before his presence was even acknowledged:

> For example, the days that he took a shower, sometimes I was down there. He would come out of the shower, would dry himself off— he was very fond of his hair. He would towel dry his hair; he would comb his hair. And not saying too much to me. He would plait that hair in the back and put his stocking cap on. And what was interesting, he always rubbed down in cocoa butter. After that he would say, "Guard, I'd like to have one coffee, two sugars and a cigarette." And *then* he'd talk to me. I think he was so much in control of himself and of other people around him until he just knew you'd be there.

Another time, Brown told Linwood, "You know, you got me hypnotized." Linwood smiled. "Yeah, I can do that to people," he said.

None of the viciousness was evident now, just an easygoing confidence as Linwood slid a hand-rolled cigarette through the slot. Expecting tobacco, Stockton lit up and was in for another surprise. It was Colombian reefer. Halfway through the joint, he was stoned.

"Is getting high a regular thing here?" Stockton asked between tokes.

Linwood grinned and nodded. "Some people" brought him reefer, though he didn't say who. "And we got some mash working off." Five gallons ought to be ready this weekend, he said.

This was crazy, Stockton thought. "Mash," slang for home-brewed wine, was a prison standard, but wasn't The Row supposedly more secure?

"How do you keep the guards from smelling it?"

"They don't care. They'd rather see us doing that than sawing on the bars."

That made sense. After watching the routine in the dayroom, Stockton had already guessed that a truce existed between the guards and the condemned. In most places, guards and prisoners split into hostile camps. Here, there was a kind of agreement: the inmates drank home brew, played cards and didn't fight, and in return the guards looked the other way on many of the rules. For example, they rarely dumped the mash, even though the sweet yeasty smell of fermenting fruit drifted from the cells. He'd seen the rule prohibiting inmates from entering another's cell broken twice more since yesterday. Maybe the guards hoped they could get on the inmates' good sides and get less trouble by being a little lenient. If so, it seemed to be working.

Stockton asked Linwood about retrieving his legal papers and other property that had been left behind in the Richmond penitentiary. Linwood said he'd see what he could do, strolled downstairs to the control booth and chatted with the guard inside. He came back up and smiled. "They're calling about your stuff now," he said.

Stockton began to suspect that his new friend was a power here. He'd also gotten a crazy idea. Reefer was available, but it sure didn't come free. Why not grow it from seed, right in their cells? All he needed was dirt and a big container. If Linwood had so much pull, maybe he could get the container, and if he could, Stockton could scoop dirt from the rec yard once his orientation ended. He'd set the plant in his window for sun and grow his own weed.

Now Linwood was surprised. "You could do all that?" he asked.

"Sure, all you need is a container, dirt and seeds." Stockton grinned. "You ever built a compost pile?"

"A what?"

Stockton started laughing. Here was the difference between the city boy and the country boy. "Compost. You know, manure. Best reefer in the world is grown in cow shit and dirt. But I got to have a container big enough to grow it in."

"How big?"

"Least five gallons."

Linwood thought a minute. "Let me see what I can do."

It was the beginning of a beautiful friendship. Over the next few days, Linwood came over to chat, pulling up his chair on one side of the food slot while Stockton upended a trash can on the other. They talked about the cases that sent them here and how they figured their chances in appeals. Linwood insisted he didn't kill the DJ but was home changing a flat when Meekins drove up in Gallaher's car and sold him the jewelry. His execution date was already set for August 1984. Yet he didn't seem worried, adding that he didn't plan on sitting around until then.

If the execution proceeded as scheduled, Linwood would be the second man to die in the state's electric chair since 1962. The honor of being the first had gone to Frank Coppola, a former policeman who abandoned his appeals and got the hot squat at 11:25 P.M. on August 10, 1982. On the street outside The Wall's A-Basement, where executions then took place, protestors sang "Amazing Grace." Across the street from them, death-penalty supporters yelled, "Throw the switch." Newspapers reported that Coppola said, "Fire it up," but not everyone agreed with that account. According to Joseph Ingle, one of Coppola's ministers and co-founder of the Southern Coalition on Jails and Prisons, a Nashville-based foundation devoted to prison reform, the words were spoken by a prison administrator to Coppola's right as he walked through the door to the death chamber. Ingle, who was a step behind Coppola, said he was so filled with revulsion at that moment that he asked the guards to let him out of the chamber. Thus, he did not witness the final act. Just the same, the executioner obliged whoever said it, sending two fifty-five-second charges of

2,500 volts coursing from the electrode-studded cap on Coppola's head to the metal band clamped to his ankle.

Coppola's was the fifth execution in the nation since the death penalty's reinstitution in 1976. Executions had actually stopped as far back as 1962 due to issues of legal fairness, the thorniest being the discriminatory use of capital punishment against blacks. The landmark *Furman* v. *Georgia* case made the halt official when the Supreme Court abolished the death penalty in 1972. When the justices reversed themselves in 1976, it was with the proviso that states would impose rigid legal standards before allowing someone to die. These standards were similar from state to state: the condemned must be found guilty of specific capital offenses, such as murder for hire or murder during another violent crime like rape or robbery; the courts must also comply with "guided discretion" statutes providing jurors with specific sentencing guidelines. On the surface, the formula seemed to even the racial mix somewhat. Of the fifteen other inmates on The Row when Stockton arrived, nine were black, five white and one Asian. Coppola was white and in time more whites would arrive until the ratio was nearly fifty-fifty. But other patterns still existed: most of the condemned were in their twenties, most had killed white victims and most were poor. Foes said one form of discrimination had simply been replaced with another.

Coppola's race had a political significance that was not lost on Linwood. Although the new standards may have altered The Row's racial composition, they didn't abolish racial politics. Governor Charles Robb was a young, white, moderate Democrat married to President Lyndon Johnson's daughter Lynda Bird. He'd campaigned and won with a get-tough-on-crime platform. It was assumed he had national aspirations—a correct assumption, since he successfully ran for U.S. senator after his governor's term expired. Linwood had originally been scheduled to die before Coppola, and the racial card would have been a strong draw in his clemency plea: it could have been politically inconvenient for Robb if the state's first inmate to be executed against his will in twenty years was black. When Coppola butted ahead, everything changed.

Linwood resented Coppola's choice, but like most inmates held the man in awe. A former altar boy, class president, basketball star, seminarian and policeman convicted of the 1978 murder and robbery of an elderly Newport News woman, Coppola shaved his head in prison and sported a Fu Manchu mustache. He turned defiance into a political statement and personal style, a stance admired by other prisoners, and was one of the seven inmates who participated in the ACLU's class-action suit against Mecklenburg officials. Friends told of his eating live spiders, dead birds and razors, and he did nothing to dispel the tales. For four years, Coppola did as most Death Row inmates did and appealed his sentence, receiving five stays. But then he grew tired of the unending process, fired his lawyers and "volunteered" for execution, notifying the courts that he no longer wished to fight.

He preferred death to life in prison. The choice was the only way he could maintain his dignity, he said. "I'm not asking them to kill me, I'm *telling* them to kill me," he told a reporter. "I've taken control of my own destiny." He added that death was also in his family's best interest, and asked the courts to set a summer date so his two sons would not have to face other children at school. The judges honored his request and set the execution for August 10, 1982. Five days before it happened, he joked about the electric chair, saying he would throw the switch himself if the state could not find a volunteer. He was thirty-eight, The Row's oldest inmate until Stockton arrived.

Linwood thought Coppola was a bigot, but he recognized his significance for Death Row at the same time as he disliked the man. In fact, Coppola's death transformed him into The Row's own privately held legend. His execution sobered them all, forced many for the first time to seriously consider their fates. How would they face the executioner? Conversely, how could they get away? Long after his execution, inmates framed events as something "Frank would have done." Others who dropped their appeals used Coppola as precedent. Apocryphal tales grew around him: one concerned an alleged strip search of his mother when she came to visit. Inmates accepted it as gospel and swore it pushed Coppola over the edge. There was a story that Coppola hung up when the governor phoned and offered him life without parole; there were tales that Coppola was involved in early plans for a breakout, that he had hidden somewhere a .45 automatic. Like a phoenix, rumors of this gun kept rising long after Coppola died.

Stockton sometimes glimpsed Linwood's younger brother watching as he and Linwood talked, and he wondered if JB would come and introduce himself now that the ice had been broken. But it was not to be. It soon became apparent that JB expected people to first come to him, not the other way around. In many ways, JB was Linwood's polar opposite. He was heavier than his older brother, taller by half a foot. He too wore a mustache and goatee, but grew his hair longer, wearing it in dreadlocks or a large Afro. News reports said Linwood remained stoic when the jury read his death sentence. JB cussed. Linwood had adapted to his surroundings and could sit tight, but JB was always on the prowl, bullshitting with guards, pacing the four corners of The Row as if probing for any weakness in prison security. He was the one in 1981 who masterminded the failed attempt to smuggle in guns and ammo. He was the one whose thoughts showed on his face. The other inmates respected Linwood. They feared JB.

Linwood and JB were also the only inmates to own "punks," prison slang for prisoners who traded sex for protection. Yet even the punks were as different as the brothers.

Linwood's punk was John Joseph LeVasseur. Small and frail-looking, he was quiet like his master until threatened, then he used Linwood's name as a shield. This was typical punk behavior, but in every other way LeVasseur was unique. Born Tran Quang Vu Tuan, in December 1966 he became the first orphan caused by the Vietnam War to be adopted by a Virginia family. Sixteen years later, he was convicted of one of the most violent crimes his new home, Prince William County, had ever seen.

Kenneth LeVasseur of Norfolk was on a navy tour in Saigon in 1964 to 1965 when he spotted the two-and-a-half-year-old boy in a Catholic home for malnourished children. The Vietnamese government frowned on adoptions by couples with children, and the LeVasseurs already had three, but the adoption was eventually approved by special decree from Premier Nguyen Cao Ky. Yet even with that auspicious beginning, LeVasseur's life was one of turmoil. Prison psychiatrists said he had a history of antisocial behavior, drug and alcohol abuse and low self-esteem. On February 25, 1982, he killed Pamela Benner, a nineteen-year-old friend from high school. The back of her head was crushed; she bore more than forty wounds and had been doused with bleach. A cooking fork and ice pick protruded from her back. LeVasseur turned himself in to police, claiming he was tripping on LSD when the murder occurred. He also confessed to stealing $3 from the girl.

LeVasseur arrived on Death Row on November 5, 1982. At age twenty-one, he was the youngest man there; at five feet seven inches and 130 pounds, he was also the smallest. He was raped two weeks after arriving, in a laundry room just a few yards away from where a guard watched football on the dayroom's TV. Soon afterward, the rapist "sold" him to Linwood for two cartons of cigarettes. He later told a reporter: "One of the inmates said that I had to get it on with him, because if I didn't, then everybody else would think that I'm open season. He said we could go through it three ways: either minimal force; or he could just beat me up, knock me out and do it; or he could beat me up, knock me out and *everybody* do it. There's no compromise or leaving me alone. Besides my size, I ain't that strong. So I didn't fight. I figured this guy was going to overtake me anyhow, so that's not going to accomplish a damn thing." LeVasseur reported the rape and others that followed but never pressed charges, he said, because "I don't want to die."

But there was another side to the story. During his brief stay, Stockton had already heard the little man running his mouth, flaunting Linwood's protection. He brought a lot of his grief on himself, Stockton thought. He would have been smarter to keep quiet.

JB's punk was far different. Like his master, Timothy Dale Bunch was more in-your-face. Stockton decided he was also the strangest man on Death Row. He had already seen Bunch slip into JB's cell for an hour or so—the guards, on the other hand, acted like they didn't see a thing. A white guy with short brown hair, mustache, wire-rim glasses and lantern jaw, Bunch was a sergeant in the Marine Corps on January 31, 1982, the day he shot his lover, forty-year-old Su Cha Thomas. He tried to disguise the death as a suicide by hanging her in her Prince William County home. After the murder, he returned to his unit, stationed in Iwakuni, Japan, but police located him the next month by tracing the victim's Rolex, which Bunch had pawned.

Bunch told police he killed Thomas because "she was a slut" and because she reminded him of his estranged wife. He said he "felt real good" during the murder, so good that he "actually had sexual orgasm." He listened to his lover's stereo as she lay dying, but couldn't remember what played. He just remembered euphoria, like he "was up in the air."

Bunch grew up in rural Indiana, the son of an alcoholic father. He was long considered a loner, but had no criminal record prior to the murder. His career goal was to be a marine "cross-country chaser," the military equivalent of a bounty hunter assigned to bring back

AWOL marines. Before that, he'd dreamed of becoming a psychiatrist or writer, but was discouraged by his 1.5 grade average and normal IQ. He said he started out smarter but his intelligence plummeted when he began smoking marijuana at fourteen. He told a newspaper that he was worried he wouldn't get the death sentence during his trial: "If I got life, then I'd just be a regular person. What I've got now, the Big D, makes me more of an individual." He arrived on Death Row on November 12, 1982, at age twenty-three. He had purchased his own gray flannel burial suit in Japan before his arrest and kept it in storage for his execution.

Bunch had no self-confidence, so he bragged about the strangest things to compensate. As a result, he could be downright creepy. Most creepy was a sexual attraction for death: sometimes his neighbors thought he should be in Central State mental hospital, while other times they wondered if it wasn't just an act for his appeals. They couldn't tell. A wanted poster with Bunch's likeness hung on his cell wall, right next to the soft-core centerfolds. He said he tripped out at night, and at those times his hero, Gary Gilmore, would materialize through the ceiling. They would talk of love and death. Bunch's execution should be the apotheosis of his violent life, the holy Gilmore said. It was what gave his life distinction, and he should play the role well. He liked to quote Gilmore's words before the Utah firing squad on January 17, 1977: "Let's do it!" Bunch only hoped his final statement would be so well remembered. He bragged how a Catholic nun visited him monthly and he told her of his sexual fantasies. She tried to stay tranquil, but he could tell he was testing her faith. At night, he liked to replay Su Cha's killing, but now she had the nun's face. The other prisoners moved on when he got into one of these jags. Raping and slaughtering a nun was too much, even for them.

But other times, Bunch could talk intelligently about the marines, Japan, Eastern religions. And he could be generous: if he had a dollar and someone asked him for it, he'd hand it over. He was just that way, real free-hearted—if impossible to understand.

Stockton watched these things from his door when not talking to Linwood or replaying his own trial in his mind. After Linwood dropped by, he thought others might come and get acquainted. Most did glance up, but on the whole they stayed away. Still, two others did introduce themselves: Willie Lloyd Turner and his crony, Morris Odell Mason.

Mason, a short, gnomelike man from Virginia's rural Eastern Shore, arrived on Death Row on October 11, 1978, and was scheduled to die soon after Linwood. He'd been paroled from prison exactly one month when, by his own admission, he set out to rape and kill. On the night of May 13, 1978, he entered the home of a seventy-one-year-old Northampton County woman and ordered her to draw the curtains. When she cried out for help, Mason knocked her across the room, raped her, hit her with an ax and shoved the handle up her rectum. He then placed her in a chair, drove a nail through her left forearm and set the seat on fire. The blaze consumed the house.

Yet she wasn't Mason's first murder. Eleven days earlier, he had broken into the home of another elderly woman, killed her and set that house ablaze. The day after killing his second victim, he broke into a third house and torched it, then entered a fourth home, maimed a thirteen-year-old girl and sodomized and abducted her twelve-year-old sister. When the police asked what drove him to run amok, Mason answered: "I really don't know. Like I was on that dope, you know. Like it told me, you know, just to do something, so I went on and killed 'em, you know." He giggled when he received the death sentence and boasted: "I'm the killer for the Eastern Shore. I'm the only killer they ever had around here. I made the Eastern Shore popular."

Stockton could tell the guy was nuts, even if the courts said he was legally sane. In fact, Stockton sometimes wondered if this ruling was merely a legal fiction. It later came out that Mason had an IQ of 66 and as a teenager had been diagnosed as mentally retarded. In January 1974, he complained of hearing voices and was admitted for six weeks to the Veterans Administration Hospital in Coatesville, Pennsylvania, where he was diagnosed a paranoid schizophrenic. Mason seemed friendly enough to Stockton, and was certainly lucid whenever he talked about sports (which seemed like all the time), but he apparently had no concept of death and his condemned neighbors compared him to a "hyperactive eight-year-old." If anything, he got on Stockton's nerves: Mason's voice was the last thing he heard at night and the first thing he heard in the morning. "Shut the fuck *up!*" other inmates yelled from their cells, but Morris just giggled in his high, weird way.

Willie Lloyd Turner was a different breed. His journey to Mecklenburg started on July 12, 1978, when he fatally shot the fifty-four-year-old owner of a Franklin jewelry store during a robbery attempt. Just paroled from prison for the fatal stabbing in 1974 of a fellow inmate at Powhatan Correctional Center, north of Mecklenburg, Turner now found himself back in jail. A year and a half later, he was sentenced to die.

Turner never finished fifth grade and only learned to read and write in prison. But the death sentence brought out an odd genius in this complex little man. After the trial, Turner sawed through steel casings for several days to free a locking mechanism on his cell door. A month after the jury's sentence of death, he cut through steel bars, then he and a cellmate made dummies from newspapers and old bags, left them behind in their bunks and escaped from the Southampton County Jail through a ground-floor window. The guards didn't discover the ruse until early morning, throwing the rural area into panic. Yet for all his ingenuity, his actual freedom was ill-planned and short-lived. He hitched a ride to an aunt's, just a few miles away, where he was found sleeping. It was as if his real purpose was to fool the guards. After that he didn't know what to do, or care.

By the time Stockton arrived, Turner was The Row's inmate grievance clerk, collecting and recording grievances from his neighbors to pass to prison officials. This made him the only inmate in C-Pod to draw a monthly paycheck. He was a master tinkerer and could fix almost anything. He'd invented a piece of barber equipment while in prison and obtained a patent. He was also a licensed barber, but prison officials would not give barber tools to a Death Row inmate, assigning the job instead to an inmate from a nearby road camp. Monday was haircut day, and the inmates were let out of their cells one at a time. But the guy didn't know a thing about barbering and everyone screamed so much about their lousy haircuts that the poor guy finally refused to visit without an escort. In time, Stockton and Turner became friends and Willie would give him an excellent haircut using the disposable razors one could buy through the commissary. As they talked, Stockton learned that Willie was also a decent jailhouse lawyer. When Stockton mentioned that a few years back he'd filed a civil suit alleging inhumane conditions in the old and overcrowded Patrick County Jail in Stuart, Virginia, Turner produced some manuals on civil litigation and gave him free advice.

Yet he also sensed that Turner could be dangerous. Willie was a schemer, though so far most of his scheming seemed directed at the Brileys. He wanted to be pod leader, but could find no other followers besides the crazy Morris Mason. He envied the brothers their power and this turned to hate. There was also a second motive: sexual envy. Turner wanted Bunch for his punk, but JB had him. He next turned his sights on LeVasseur, but had no luck there either. In addition to sex, owning a punk represented power. It was a status thing, like owning a Rolls on The Outside. It would even be a kind of revenge, since both punks were white and Turner was black. But Turner knew it was impossible to beat the Brileys. It was almost as if he wanted what he knew he'd never get.

Stockton guessed that on some level they were all like that here. The condemned wanted what they could never get, though most didn't know what that was. At best, it was a hunger barely sensed, a gnawing never satisfied. Some, like the Brileys, blamed society. Many—the zombies staring from their doors—tried dealing with the guilt of their murders and failed. These were the ones that Stockton rarely saw in the dayroom, residents so depressed that they'd stay in their cells for days. A few, like Bunch, saw the flaw in themselves and called it names: "the other me," "the monster inside." They hoped to understand it before Execution Day, pleading for illumination from the prison psychiatrists. The shrinks might have a name for it, but the act of naming didn't bring the truth. The doctors understood it little better, maybe less, for they had never known the parting of the curtain when for a clarifying instant an innocent was sacrificed and the killer released himself to blood and rage.

Stockton shook his head as though to rid himself of such thoughts. It scared him that he knew these things. It made him one of them. Even though he didn't kill Kenny Arnder, hadn't his life been leading in the same direction, toward death and self-destruction? Hadn't his family always told him, *Dennis, you keep up this kind of life, you're gonna get yourself killed?* He'd known they were right, but something always drove him on. He remembered from childhood the deep voice of his grandfather, a lay minister, and how his words would fill the small church in the pines: *For now we see through a glass, darkly; but then face to face. Now I know in part; but then shall I know even as also I am known.* He shook his head again, but memory was a traitor, a Judas silenced only by a rope and a tree.

Where's my goddamn sleeping pills? he thought. When the fuck they coming? He wished he was someplace else. He wished he was someone else. He wished he'd made different choices.

He wished he were dead.

• • • •

It was then that he started writing.

The decision came as the hours of orientation dragged to days and he found there was little to do but sleep or listen as his thoughts swirled. The thing that scared him most was not the men outside, not even the ones he'd spotted as most dangerous. That was part of prison life, something he could handle. It was not even the vision of his own death in the chair. That was so distant it didn't seem real. The thing that scared him most were those men who stood for hours behind their doors, looking out like caged animals—not angry, just lifeless, dead. They'd become trapped in their whirlpool of thoughts and couldn't fight free.

Yet he saw no escape from such a fate until it dawned on him to keep a diary of his life on Death Row. Had anybody ever done that? He didn't know. Someday he'd be free and could write a book. Maybe they'd make a movie. He'd be famous! Then he grinned and thought, *Fat chance.*

Still, it was a world few knew and he kept playing with the idea. If he did write a book, it would solve one problem that had eaten at him for too long: his awful dependence. He had no other source of income than his mother and closest brother; he depended on them for everything and it was humiliating, especially concerning his mom. She was sixty-four and living alone in Mount Airy with nothing but a monthly Social Security check. At this point in life, he should be doing things for her, not the other way around. She was the one who always stood by him and now when he called her up, she cried. "It'll be all right, Mom, I'll be okay," he tried consoling her, but what was it like, living in a town where all her neighbors thought her son was a killer? Where she'd hear the whispers when she went to the store and try to pretend she didn't care? This was his shame that was worse than all others. If he wrote a bestseller, he could make it up to her, at least partway. He could prove he wasn't worthless. He could make her proud.

That was how it started, a simple money-making plan. Yet writing is a subtle trap, baited by the promise that the more you delve and pick, the closer you'll come to the truth, whatever that is. And soon his reasons for writing changed. The prisoner has a different perception of reality: claustrophobic, hemmed in. Writing is a way *out,* if not in body, at least in mind. He was not the first prisoner to succumb to its song. Caryl Chessman was the most famous, sentenced to death thirty years earlier for kidnapping and attempted rape; he tried exorcizing his past in a series of Death Row books he penned in his cell just a few steps from California's gas chamber. "A condemned man's nights are long and often sleepless," he wrote in one. "It is during the deep silences of the prison night that his past returns to be relived. It is then that he examines his life and necessarily comes to know something of himself. How much he learns depends upon his nature and the nature of his quest." Part of that quest would be railing against dying for crimes that did not include murder, and though his writing brought greater public awareness of the death penalty, it did not save him. In 1960, the almond-ammonia-scented cyanide gas floated up from the tray beneath his chair like it had for the others who passed through his memoirs.

Stockton, like Chessman, was an intelligent if violent man. Like Chessman, he was forced back on himself in a solitary cell. He started with a simple diary, yet this eventually expanded to an attempt to understand a life of extremes. At first, he was hampered by his lack of education: many words were misspelled and he knew nothing of punctuation, so he forced himself to learn. He figured that if the entries made sense to him, perhaps they would to others. In time, writing became a ritual: he'd swing out his metal seat, pluck a pen from the holder made from an empty peanut butter tub and straighten the pad of lined notepaper in the center of his metal table. In time, he would pen an autobiography, several works of fiction and a monthly newsletter with a national, if small, mailing list.

The diary was the first step. Between June 20, 1983, and July 15, 1984, he made 179 entries, filling fifty-two pages of notepaper. NOTES FROM DEATH ROW, BY DENNIS W. STOCKTON, he started. THIS IS PRIVATE PROPERTY. He didn't know it would find its way into the hands of an editor for a state newspaper, never guessed that its publication would ruin careers, initiate reform, ensure revenge. He didn't know it would be the inside story of the only mass escape from a Death Row in U.S. history. He just wrote things as they happened.

Weather data, baseball scores, stock-car race results. The executions of men whose wait for death had finally ended, while his had just begun:

> **June 20, 1983** I have been here now for 5 days. I came here on 6/15/83. Here . . . is Mecklenburg Correctional Center, Boydton, Va., where Va. Death Row inmates are housed. . . . Only 3 or 4 inmates have spoke to me so far, Linwood Briley who is next door in 65, Morris Mason who is in 61 and Willie Turner in 68. There is 4 other blacks beside the above 3 that I don't know and 2 young white guys who haven't spoke. . . . Linwood gave me a joint of reefer my second day here. Don't know where it came from but it was good. Security is tight here. Some of these guys have been here since 1979.

• • • •

On June 22, Stockton was released from his cell. He quickly learned the ways of this new world.

The first lesson was easy: the Brileys ran Death Row. It didn't take long to see how. They were the main drug connection, working through two sources. The main source was the other inmates in Building One who drew the clean-up detail. Official policy stated that no inmates could have contact with Death Row, but in reality the clean-up guys essentially came and went as they pleased due to lax security. Their first stop was talking business with Linwood or JB.

The other source was less dependable, but more surprising: some of the guards. Stockton eventually learned the names of four who smuggled for the Brileys. The brothers collected money from the inmates and reefer arrived a week or two later. The price was steep: bags of marijuana that cost $40 to $45 on the street brought $150 on The Row. If you were tight with a Briley, you could sometimes deal directly with a guard.

By now, Stockton was tight with Linwood, a friendship based on admiration for each other's cunning and a mutual fondness for pot. Many nights, Stockton and Linwood sat in the latter's cell playing Scrabble and smoking a joint. The first thing that hit him when he walked into Linwood's cell were the dozens of photos of nude girls taped to the walls. These weren't magazine cutouts but cheap, grainy Polaroids, black girls and white, all in bad light and every position imaginable, inviting him to take them home. "Where'd you get all these?" he said, peering at a close-up of a red rose in a place that must've been agony to tattoo. "They send 'em to me," Linwood said, grinning. "You wouldn't *believe* some of these women. Remind me to show you their letters. They're like something out of *Penthouse.*"

Besides being a porn emporium, Linwood's cell was also a commissary, everything piled on the bed, sink, shelves. There was barely room to move. Linwood kept ice in a homemade cooler to cool his drinks; he stored an expensive typewriter, hardly ever touched, on one of the shelves. He sold packs of cigarettes and snacks, and if an inmate wanted to buy something but was short on cash, Linwood loaned him the difference. He never exacted interest, taking repayment instead in favors and obligation. Even the guards borrowed snacks and smokes from Linwood's "canteen."

Linwood also brewed mash in his cell, two trash cans full. The Brileys were The Row's main bootleggers, though some of the others did a little brewing, too. They all hoarded apples, peaches and fruit cocktail from their meal trays, but the Brileys were the only ones with an outside source for yeast and sugar, which meant they were the only ones to brew mash in any quantity. They mixed it all together in a trash can and let it ferment four weeks, then strained it and drank the stuff down. Stockton drank a cup, but it gave him the runs. He stuck with dope instead.

A couple of days after orientation ended, Linwood told Dennis it was rumored that he was an undercover agent for the FBI. "That true?"

"No, whatta you think?" Stockton answered, outraged. He realized Linwood was doing him a favor by confronting him directly, thus giving him a warning, yet he also knew the seriousness of the moment. There was nothing worse in prison than a snitch. If you got that reputation, even if undeserved, you were considered a rat. Sooner or later, rats died.

Linwood eyed him carefully, then seemed to relax. "Well, I never heard of no fed who knew so much about growing reefer," he said. Stockton asked where he'd heard the rumor, and Linwood nodded to one of the guards who brought in drugs. "Who knows where he heard it?" he said, shrugging it off. "Bullshit rumors pop up here all the time." When Stockton confronted the guard, the guy looked like he'd gobbled a fish—his eyes got wide, he denied saying a word.

Stockton never learned exactly what happened, but it was as if he'd passed a test. Soon afterward, Linwood brought him a green plastic trash bucket and Stockton was growing the weed in his cell. He carried a sock when he went to recreation and filled it with dirt, mixing in potato peelings and a small amount of shredded newspaper. A couple of times, he crapped in the bucket. He planted the seed and set it in the window. Four days later, a sprout poked through.

Linwood was amazed. Dennis swore him to secrecy. If all went well, he said, they could sell some and split the take. It was pure profit, no overhead from paying the middleman.

The plant grew bigger and bigger, but this created a problem. Once those telltale leaves sprouted, any idiot could tell what grew in that window. Stockton set the plant under the naked bulb at the head of his bed. He set his cabinet at its foot near the door so that no one could see the plant from outside. Then he spread his mattress on the floor and slept there until the plant was ready to cure. There was also a vent over the sink, a natural blind spot. The vent had small holes, so he ran a piece of cloth through two of them and hung the plant upside down in a plastic bag. Now the THC, the tetrahydrocannabinol determining the reefer's potency, would run down the roots and throughout the plant. Only then did Stockton replace his mattress and sleep normally.

The Row had strange standards of normalcy and the guards shrugged their shoulders at lots of things. They said the place was the same as a madhouse, just a little quieter. It wasn't long before Stockton agreed.

On the surface, things seemed easy. The reefer supply seemed endless, and the inmates buzzed on homebrew. They called one another nicknames, just like in some of Stockton's old neighborhoods. They showed each other respect, the most important element for keeping peace in prison. They watched TV, ate meals, played rough games of pickup basketball without referees. They kidded among themselves.

The Row's best basketball player was Derick Peterson. Maybe he wasn't brilliant, but he had uncanny accuracy with a jump shot and could outleap some of the tallest players. The games were rough, and "Baylock," as they called him, as the best shooter, was fouled often and hard. Yet, he rarely got mad. In fact, he was *so* easygoing, it was hard to believe he'd ended up here. Peterson himself couldn't say why. His robbery career began at age fifteen, and he served time in a juvenile home. But that was no warning for what gripped him on February 7, 1982, when, according to prosecutors, he barged into the office of a Hampton supermarket, pulled a gun and demanded money. The store manager, Howard Kaufmann, offered no resistance, but Peterson shot him anyway, then grabbed a sack containing $6,000 and ran. Sixteen hours later, he pointed a gun at two women in a five-and-dime. He was arrested several days later when two supermarket employees identified him from photos. He was sent to Death Row on November 4, 1982, and was now twenty-three.

Stockton and the other inmates liked Peterson, even if he didn't have much sense. Since Stockton was the oldest, the others called him Pop. That stopped when he started calling them Mama . . . all, that is, except Peterson, who said Dennis was old enough to be his dad. The comment could have caused problems since Peterson was black and Stockton white. You didn't make racial jokes in prison. But Stockton just gave it back: "Maybe I am your daddy," he answered. "I did get around Eastern Virginia a lot a few years ago." The others hooted with laughter. "Baylock, he's talkin' about your mama!" Peterson just grinned.

There were racial tensions on The Row, but not as bad as in general population. There, inmates segregated themselves and racial hatred was often the norm. Stockton's side of C-Pod was mostly black and the other side white. Inmates could request a transfer if they couldn't get along, but most did. Death was what brought them all together. Those racial politics didn't seem to matter anymore.

Still, there were tensions—the strangest little tensions. They sneaked up from nowhere. Like Earl Clanton and his chair.

Clanton was imprisoned for robbing and killing a Petersburg, Virginia, woman just months after being paroled for the 1972 murder of an elderly New Jersey woman. In April 1980, he escaped from Petersburg deputies while awaiting trial on an unrelated charge. He hid out for seven months. Then, on the night of November 16, neighbors reported screams at the home of Wilhelmina Smith, a thirty-nine-year-old librarian at a local elementary school. When police arrived they found Smith murdered, and Clanton cowering under her bed. He said he was passing outside when he heard Smith scream, so he ran in to help and was attacked by an unidentified man. He defended himself with karate and jujitsu, but the man escaped just before the cops arrived. He hid under Smith's bed because he was a fugitive and didn't want to go back to jail, he said. But police said Clanton subdued his victim by tightening a belt around her neck, then stabbed her repeatedly to make her give him money. They found on him a five-dollar bill and three ones, all covered in blood. Clanton arrived on The Row on March 13, 1981.

Of all the inmates, the thirty-year-old Clanton had the quickest temper. Stockton and the others saw him as a bomb waiting to go off and were careful what they said to him. It was like he had something to prove. The guy was in constant motion, almost hyperactive: he worked out daily and was in excellent physical shape. He didn't like whites, yet tolerated Stockton because of Linwood. In fact, his devotion to the Brileys almost seemed religious. It was "Goldie," as they called him, who aided JB in his aborted escape attempt. He was as jealous of the Brileys' attentions as a child. He didn't like it when Linwood spent time with Stockton during their nightly Scrabble games; he'd find a hundred reasons to interrupt. "Goldie's my little dog," Linwood said quietly after one such interruption. "All I have to do is whistle and he comes."

One day, Stockton almost got mauled. One of the rules of the dayroom was that the men had their own chairs. They marked them with their names, always sat at the same places when they ate. Stockton ate with Turner and Mason, Clanton with Linwood and JB. One day, Stockton came to eat and found the wrong chair in his place. He was switching it back when Clanton yelled, "Leave the fucking chairs alone! Don't be messing with them!"

Stockton didn't want any trouble, so he put his food tray on the table and sat down. But Clanton was in a rage. He stormed to his cell, grabbed a crayon, stormed back out and scrawled "Goldie" all over the back of his chair. "I just want to see someone fuck with my chair," he yelled.

The pod grew quiet. Even the guards froze. Clanton glared about, then stomped away.

Yet Clanton was merely an extreme reflection of them all. Violence always lay waiting. At first, Stockton reveled in how laid back it seemed, but soon he wrote in his diary: "It's got to the point where nothing I see or hear surprises me. Some of these people are really fucked in the head."

Court documents showed they were indeed "fucked in the head," but not in ways society understood. They were not ruled insane;

otherwise, they would be in Central State, not here. The thread that bound them all was a violence that arose suddenly from nowhere. All had violent histories, even those who might be innocent—all had records stretching back to their teens. Many had histories of physical or sexual abuse. Stockton and Bunch were beaten, while Turner was choked unconscious by his mom. Their lives had made them different. Their punishment defined them as outside the pale.

But most dangerous of all was JB.

He prowled the dayroom, radiating menace, a steady wave upon wave, like something atomic. He reminded Stockton of a boxer, how he came right at a person, his black eyes boring in. When he talked, he always wanted something, crowding in on a person's space, bearing in. He wanted allegiance, and if not that, submission. His body was a field of scars: one over his right eye lifted his eyebrow in a scowl, a second on his left arm, a third on his chest from an old bullet wound. The threat always lay underneath with the others, but JB wore his like a suit. Even the guards seemed cowed.

JB was probably the prison's biggest wheeler-dealer. Where Linwood seemed content with drug sales on The Row, JB sold to inmates in all five buildings through a network of convicts and corrupt guards. One of JB's most reliable sources for drug money was through a contact in Greensboro, North Carolina. Somewhere between Mecklenburg and Route 58, an envelope stuffed with bills would be dropped off, then retrieved by an officer. The envelope would eventually make it to JB's cell.

JB played in the nightly poker game around a table in the dayroom. One night Stockton watched, wondering if he could afford the stakes. Somehow JB seemed to come out ahead, even if he wasn't a regular winner. A pile of chips grew in the middle and as Stockton watched, JB splashed his chips on the pile while raising, making it hard to count without slowing the game. Stockton had seen this kind of cheating before, but maybe it was just a mistake. When Clanton saw JB's quarter and raised him another, JB called, throwing in more white chips. But he tossed four instead of five! He was deliberately shorting the pot. He'd occasionally "forget" to ante up unless someone reminded him, then he'd laugh and toss in, or he'd rake off a chip with his palm while pushing the pot across the table to the winner.

Stockton soon saw that gambling was like life for JB. Leave nothing to chance, whether it meant leaving no witnesses or cheating at cards. Then he saw something he absolutely could not believe. Peterson was dealing five-card draw. They made their bets and JB discarded one card. Then he called for two. It was so brazen, yet no one else had seen it. He watched as JB nudged the cards together in a neat stack, then spread them delicately in his palm. His face was impassive. Some ashes dropped from his cigarette and landed on the table. He swept them onto the floor. When the players started betting, he fanned the cards on the table. Stockton only counted five. JB had palmed the sixth card and dropped it in his lap while sweeping away the ashes.

Stockton studied the other players. Their eyes were glued to their cards. They had no idea what had happened. But some sixth sense told JB he'd been spotted. He looked around and found Stockton. His eyes widened, then narrowed, daring Stockton to say a word.

"Fifty cents," Turner said, starting the bet, but JB's eyes didn't budge. It was the stare of someone who could do anything to anyone, and wait as long as it took. Stockton looked away. For the first time in a long time, he was afraid.

JB saw the bet and raised. "Too much for me," Peterson said, and folded. Clanton called, as did another. Turner called and raised again. Everyone held.

JB splayed his hand. A straight, Jack high. Turner grinned and showed: full boat, sevens and threes. He reached for the pot. JB's eyes snapped back to Stockton like it was his fault he'd lost. "You playing or rubbernecking?" JB asked.

"Ain't got the money for this game," Stockton answered.

"Okay, then."

Stockton lingered in the dayroom a little longer, then went back to his cell, the door clicking behind him. For the first time, he was glad the doors locked automatically when shut.

True, he couldn't get out.

But JB couldn't get in.

3

Stockton measured the summer's passage by the progress of his reefer crop. His modest cannabis, starting from a tiny sprout, yielded two and three-quarter ounces of good homegrown. He and Linwood kept some for their own use and Linwood sold the rest for $1.50 a joint. They made $80, a handsome profit off one plant. They split the take and Stockton planted another seed.

It was a little variety in what proved their common enemy: time. New faces arrived, guard shifts changed, seasons dissolved into one another, yet they never escaped the crushing sameness that hung over them all. It was not unusual for a diary entry to start: "Nothing much happened around here since I wrote last." He might struggle with the day and date, but he never forgot that today was a duplicate of yesterday and the day before and tomorrow would probably resemble them too.

Stockton wondered how to fight a clock that always seemed stuck. He watched his neighbors and saw that some found religion while others got into sports or raising hell. Some read, others masturbated or schemed for homosexual conquests, a few tried learning The Law in the dim hope of saving themselves. Memory was a constant companion, and your life and trial seemed to replay like a video. Many simply drifted into nothingness and spent their time asleep. That was the easiest way to shut off the video and stave off despair. But sooner or later the despair caught up. You either struggled out of it like a swimmer or sank forever into the permanent half-sleep of hopelessness, letting time pass until that day it finally ended for good.

Then in mid-October 1983 something happened to give him hope again.

A guard came to his cell and said he had a visitor, then led him to a small interview room. There, across the nicked brown table, sat Bob Day, a Patrick County sheriff's investigator who was part of the same detectives' bureau that charged him with killing Kenny Arnder. Day watched him sit, a quizzical look on his face. "I won't beat around the bush," Day said. "I've got evidence Kenny's murder didn't occur in Virginia. That means the trial should never've taken place in Stuart, if at all."

Stockton stared at him, stunned. Cops didn't question their department's convictions, at least not openly. *Especially* not in front of the guy they sent to Death Row. The detective said he thought the evidence pointed to another man as the real killer. Stockton's breathing grew quick; he tried pumping Day for details. But the detective smiled and played it close, switching on the tape recorder by his elbow and asking Stockton to go over his tale.

For what seemed the one hundredth time since his arrest, Stockton told how in late July 1978 he'd walked in his door and the phone rang. It was Kenny, scared he'd get arrested for stealing some tires, begging Stockton for a ride to nearby Kibler Valley to hide out with some girls. If only he'd walked in that door five minutes later, Stockton always said. But he agreed, picking the boy up at his mom's, waiting while Kenny told her not to worry, he'd be back in a couple of days. Five days later Kenny's body was found near a stream in Mount Airy, hands hacked off at the wrists, a bullet between the eyes. After his burial, the hands of the stone angel on his gravestone were knocked off at the wrists. A message from his killers, even after death: *Don't fuck with us!*

Four years passed and no one was charged. Then, in 1982, a thief named Randy Bowman told investigators that in 1978 he was trying to sell a stolen gun to a notorious local fence and drug dealer, Tommy McBride. He walked in his house and McBride was ranting and raving; he suddenly turned to Bowman and said he'd pay him $1,500 to kill Arnder. But before he had a chance to answer, Bowman told detectives, Stockton interrupted. "I'll do it," he allegedly said.

Stockton told investigators, his lawyers, jurors—anyone who would listen—that until the day Bowman told this story in court he'd never laid eyes on the man. Still, he knew the type too well. They seemed to spring up like weeds around Mount Airy. Bowman was a big man, all barrel chest and belly like a villain on *Saturday Night Wrestling*. His head was shaved cue-ball smooth, his right bicep tattooed with a knife-pierced heart. The word was he was a biker wannabe who never made the grade, considered too untrustworthy even by the west Carolina outlaw gangs. Instead, he lived off petty theft, hawking his stolen goods to fences like McBride. A man who preyed on the weak—perfect prey for cops offering deals. And though Stockton had no proof, he felt sure he was the sacrifice when the big man made a secret deal to save his own skin.

Bob Day nodded, clicked off the tape and dropped the other shoe. The November elections were coming and Jay Gregory was running for sheriff against his longtime boss, Jesse Williams. Gregory had been lead investigator in Arnder's murder and was the one who charged Stockton with capital murder and murder for hire. Now he used Stockton's conviction as centerpiece of his campaign. "Jesse'll win, sure, but if he doesn't you know what'll happen to this investigation," Day commented. Better to be safe than sorry, he added, then asked Stockton if he knew any dirt on the man who sent him to Death Row.

That's what this is about, Stockton realized. Patrick County politics as usual. In his civil suit over Patrick County Jail conditions, Stockton claimed Gregory and other deputies gave inmates drugs and booze in reward for crime tips, but Jesse Williams wouldn't touch that because he too was named as a defendant. That was all he had, Stockton said, thinking this was the last he'd ever see of the man.

The detective shrugged and rose. Then, to Stockton's surprise, Day reached across the table and shook his hand. "Dennis," he said, "I don't think the murder happened in Virginia, and if it didn't, you shouldn't be here."

• • • •

There is a fable Stockton once stumbled upon in his reading, one set in mankind's first age. People were virtuous then and the gods liked to visit, but as evil spread on earth the visits became less frequent. In time, Justice was the only god still willing to make the trip, yet even he grew reluctant as mortal life got uglier. He compromised by visiting only occasionally and at random. But that created a problem. His followers could not predict the whens and wheres of his appearance. They trained experts who developed rites to get his attention. This was soon called The Law. Yet The Law was fickle, changing from land to land. The experts bickered over whose Law was correct until everyone threw up their hands in frustration and admitted they could never predict where to find Justice. Even if they could, lifetimes might pass before he visited again.

Stockton remembered the tale after the detective left. What was the nature of justice, he wondered, as the long prison hours returned. Why did it differ from state to state? In North Carolina, where Kenny Arnder's body was found in a shallow grave, authorities never felt they had solid evidence to charge *anyone* with murder. In Virginia, based on the word of a felon and the assurance of authorities, jurors sentenced a man to death. Was there some formula he'd missed? Some hidden key?

The mystery had as much to do with tradition and history as with crime and punishment. North Carolina had more people on its Death Row than Virginia, but far fewer executions. A 1996 study of violence in the South suggested why. Although 70 percent of Americans said they supported capital punishment, it was overwhelmingly in the South that executions occurred. Of the 157 American executions from the death penalty's reinstatement from 1976 to 1991, 140 of these, or 89 percent, occurred in Southern states. Yet even here there was a split, and this along historical lines. An execution, "which can be regarded as an extreme form of violence for the purposes of control," was far more likely to be allowed by the appellate courts of states that had a history of slavery, wrote Richard E. Nisbett and Dov Cohen, authors of a 1996 study on violence in the South. They said that, like capital punishment, slavery was a system that "legitimized violence for the purpose of discipline, control and punishment," and found that from 1977 to 1991, states of the slave South were three times more likely to have executed someone than states of the non-slave South. Nisbett and Cohen theorized: "It is possible that the practical demands on southerners of forcibly maintaining a slave and caste system created the institutions, procedures and actors capable of carrying out real violence." Virginia was a state of large tobacco and cotton plantations dependent on slave labor; North Carolina, though it too had plantations, was primarily composed of small holdings worked by the farmers and their families, not slaves.

A close look reveals how cultural differences can breed vast differences in each state's approach to The Law. North Carolina courts were tough on crime but allowed hearings on new evidence, partly accounting for a slower execution rate. Virginia's supreme court rarely granted retrials, even when evidence seemed overwhelming. The court stuck religiously to procedure, loathe to admit error in the belief that doing so would undermine public confidence in the quality of justice.

Stockton's case was a tale of how two cultures used power, how each defined The Law. To the north lay Stuart, Virginia, municipal seat of Patrick County, where Stockton was tried for Arnder's murder. Immediately south and west across the border lay Mount Airy, North Carolina, largest town in Surry County, where Arnder's body was found. Stuart officials have said bluntly that many of their felons come from Surry County, while Mount Airy residents speak of byzantine Patrick County politics sacrificing justice for the sake of careers. Stockton was Stuart's first death penalty conviction in the twentieth century, and its local newspaper reported that citizens cheered when his jurors pronounced death. The Mount Airy paper said that justice was thwarted and Stockton did not deserve to die. Not surprisingly, no love was lost between the uneasy neighbors. Yet the roots of this conflict went beyond local politics into how the past shapes lives. If mental habits "indirectly determine our institutions," as Judge Learned Hand asserted, these neighbors were good examples.

Patrick County marks the western limit of Virginia's "Southside," a broad political swath running along the North Carolina border from the Dismal Swamp on the east to the mountains on the west and north as far as Richmond. This was the state's Old South, where the plantation psychology was most pervasive, and drowsy county seats all seemed identical with their huge magnolias and Confederate monuments. It's the Virginia of Smithfield hams, peanuts, tobacco, soybeans and wood pulp, and also of the state's grittiest cities and most of its low-income blacks. This was the Old Dominion that, until recently, was ruled by a wealthy few—a hierarchical tradition as old as Virginia itself, imported from England with the colonists and supported by their government and church as "the natural order of things."

One result of this rigid social order was that criminal disruption was punished instantly, often quite severely. The death penalty was as common in Virginia as in the mother country, and scores of felonies were classed as capital offenses. The method of execution was a trip to the gallows. A sample of forty-seven court sessions from 1737 to

1772 showed that 164 people were convicted of felonies. Of them, 125 were hanged. Punishments also varied greatly based on social rank. Literate criminals could escape the noose by pleading "benefit of clergy" and reading aloud a biblical passage dubbed "the neck verse." Members of the lower classes who were not to be executed were branded on the ball of the thumb with a hot iron; gentlemen were sometimes branded with a "cold iron," leaving no mark on their flesh or honor. The poor and illiterate went to the gallows. This helps explain why Virginia has the greatest number of documented executions of any state in the Union. From 1608 until December 1994, Virginia executed 2,048 people, and the advent of the twentieth century merely changed the state's preferred method. When the electric chair replaced the gallows in 1908, the old patterns of justice remained.

The first to be electrocuted was Henry Smith in 1908, a black man accused of raping a seventy-six-year-old white woman in Portsmouth. From 1908 to 1962, 235 men and one woman would follow Smith, over 85 percent of them black. Fifty-one of these black defendants would be executed, like Smith, after being convicted of rape or attempted rape, not murder; the alleged rape victims were always white. The most notorious case was an alleged gang rape by seven black men who came to be known as the Martinsville Seven. Each man was convicted by all-white juries of raping a white woman who said she was attacked when she went after dark to the "colored" section of Martinsville, a Southside town about fifteen miles east of Stuart. Although the case galvanized civil rights activists around the world, the publicity did not save the condemned men. On February 2, 1951, four of them were executed at fifteen-minute intervals. Three days later, the other three met the same fate.

Whites who were executed were always convicted of murder, but justice could be swift if they too assaulted the established order. On February 28, 1913, this fate caught up with Floyd and Claude Allen, a father and son described by newspapers as "lawless products of the Virginia mountains." The Allens were found guilty of killing four people in a courtroom in Hillsville, a small town about twenty-five miles west of Stuart. It started when a judge sentenced Floyd Allen to a year's incarceration for helping some relatives escape from jail. "Gentlemen," Allen said, "I don't aim to go." At that, the Allens opened fire, killing the judge, the prosecutor, a deputy sheriff and a spectator. During the melee, Floyd Allen was shot in the leg: he still limped when he passed his son a year later on his final walk to the chair. A few minutes later, Claude Allen followed.

The differences in Virginia and North Carolina can be seen in the two towns that formed the stage for Stockton's arrest and trial. Stuart, municipal seat of Patrick County, Virginia, is a small town of colonial and Greek Revival architecture and dogwood-lined streets that prides itself on tradition and Virginia gentility. A future governor and state attorney general would hail from there after Stockton's death sentence in 1983. That same year, it was also home to two political hopefuls for local office: Jay Gregory, lead investigator in the Arnder murder whom the detective told Dennis was now running for his boss's job, and assistant prosecutor Anthony Giorno, who represented the state at Stockton's trial. Both men won their political races—Gregory beat the incumbent to become Patrick County sheriff, and Giorno was elected prosecutor. Both men admitted that Stockton's death sentence helped their victories, but said they just merely sought the truth. Some in Mount Airy disagreed.

"Stuart is a different world than Mount Airy," said Tom Joyce, managing editor of *The Mount Airy News*. "People there don't question authority. . . . If [officials] say something's true, it must be." The little paper, which called itself pro–capital punishment, repeatedly went on the record against Stockton's sentence, saying their local son had been unfairly tried. One Mount Airy journalist privately told colleagues of receiving anonymous death threats after such editorials appeared.

Although separated from Stuart by just forty miles of farmland and corrugated foothills, Mount Airy, North Carolina, could be on the other side of the moon. The little town, with a population in the 1980s of about 6,800, was home to Stockton and his alleged teenage victim. It was the hometown of Andy Griffith, but the Surry County mill town was a far cry from TV's gentle Mayberry. Dubbed "Little Chicago" for its criminal element, Mount Airy had a mean streak, a culture of outlawry living on its margins. Part of the blame was placed on chronic unemployment, as many of the mills shrank operations or simply shut down. Moonshining was big business in the hills and hollows surrounding the town. Weekend reports of gunfights between pistol-packing white trash were common reading in *The Mount Airy News*.

Since colonial times, North Carolina has been called a "vale of humility between two mountains of conceit," meaning its haughty neighbors, Virginia and South Carolina. Here is a state known for three large industries—tobacco, furniture and textiles—not presidents, big cities or historic acts. While Virginia was producing George Washington and Thomas Jefferson, and South Carolina was firing the first shots in the Civil War, North Carolina was producing fiercely independent small farmers who owned few slaves. Unlike in Virginia, these were not gentlemen farmers who traced their lineage to kings with a vested interest in maintaining the "natural order." Instead, they were poor when they left the British Isles in the mid-eighteenth century and they remained poor in North America. Predominantly Scotch-Irish, they were also a proud and quarrelsome people who demanded to be treated as equals, a trait of the lower ranks that was not appreciated by their betters. They were encouraged to settle the "backcountry," a vast land of deciduous forests and folded mountains extending south from Pennsylvania along the Appalachian ridge. Since the backcountry was also inhabited by Indian nations that still considered it theirs, savage fighting started that would stretch into the early nineteenth century.

Yet centuries of war with England along the Scottish Borders had prepared them for such hardship, creating a completely different set of mental habits from those of their patrician neighbors to the north. There was no "natural order" in such a dangerous world. Generations of strife had shaped them into warrior clans where leadership was not a "natural right" but an honor bestowed for strength and cunning—an honor that could just as easily be taken away. Other forms of authority—local lords, the church or state—were distrusted. From this rose the ideal of "natural liberty" that would spur them to cross the Cumberland Gap and explore the widening frontier, an ideal opposed to the "natural order" of the Virginia planters. And although the ideal helped shape the new nation, one unintended result was the creation of "a society of autonomous individuals who were unable to endure external control and incapable of restraining their rage against anyone who stood in their way."

Thus a new culture developed across the border from the old. North Carolina politics would be more contentious than Virginia's, and though there was more room for dissent, there was also a greater tolerance for violence. Prosperity might have calmed matters, but throughout the twentieth century, North Carolina's industrial workers' earnings were near the bottom compared with those of workers in the other forty-nine states. Textiles were the chief culprit: the mills paid the lowest wages of all major U.S. industries, and were the least unionized. In 1980, the textile industry's low wage scale sank North Carolina's per capita income to forty-first in the nation. By 1984, only 6.5 percent of North Carolina's workforce belonged to unions, the lowest rate in the country—when workers had a job. For this period also saw the textile industry relocate mills to Central America or the Caribbean, wooed by solicitous governments, cheap labor and no corporate taxes.

The effects could be seen around Mount Airy. Like much of the state, Mount Airy industrialized without really urbanizing, the best indicator of this being the number of mobile homes. After Florida and California, North Carolina had the highest number of mobile home sales of any state. These were not the homes of retirees or itinerants, but of workers in low-paying jobs unable to afford "site-built" homes. There was less of a feeling of permanence than in Stuart, as if, like their quarrelsome ancestors, residents of Mount Airy were always ready to pick up and move on.

It takes no great imaginative leap to see how the outlaw becomes a hero in such a culture. "We should be men first, and subjects afterward," Henry David Thoreau declared as America moved West. His words mark an early hint of a cultural schizophrenia that remains today: though one must obey the law, manhood means freedom from constraint. The true individual is subject to justice, yet lives outside man's law. Instead, the law is internalized: he abides by a code of honor and expects the same from others. When that doesn't happen, the rule is *lex talionis,* an eye for an eye, and violence, his tool, equalizes all men, highborn or low. He lives and dies alone, subject to no order but his own, as American as Wyatt Earp. Or Jesse James.

• • • •

Stockton entered this world late but embraced it with a convert's zeal. He was born in Shelby, North Carolina, on October 26, 1940, "exactly fifty-nine years to the day of Wyatt Earp and Doc Holliday shooting themselves into the history books at The Gunfight at the O.K. Corral," he would write in the opening of his unpublished autobiography. Frontier imagery figured high in his makeup: his first memories include watching the Durango Kid at the movies; he dreamed of becoming a cowboy and wrote several letters to Santa asking for a horse. His favorite author was Western writer Louis L'Amour. His career was a thief's, not a gunman's, but the potential for violence grew in him like cancer.

Perched near the South Carolina border, Shelby, at the time of Stockton's birth, was a small town. Made by cotton mills, it was packed with mill workers who rented their homes. Stockton's parents, Yates and Ailene Stockton, were part of this class. The second of four children, the young Dennis lived with his family in a white house on a quiet street. His grandfather, a lay minister, preached in a deep voice each Sunday about the wages of sin. During the week, Dennis earned high grades and fell in love with baseball. The sport dominates his earliest memories: how he played till waning light, then ran home to a late supper and his mother's smile. How he tuned the family radio to Mutual Broadcasting's "Game of the Week" and listened as announcer Al Helfer said the magic words "Mickey Mantle." He dreamt of one day playing with the Yankees and the Mick, and began the long process of becoming a left-handed pitcher. He set posts in the ground beside home plate, and a rope running between the posts held an old tire two feet off the ground. The goal was to gun a ball through the tire every time.

Baseball, Mom, a small white house in a small country town. To Stockton, life in Shelby was a happy adventure where folks weren't rich but were content. Friends who knew him then called him an "all-American boy."

But everything was not perfect in Shelby. Death could come quickly. Fathers, sons and brothers died in the war. Yates was a sailor in the Pacific, and Ailene could not hide her fear when she heard of deaths in other families. As poor as they were, they lived at the edge of Shelby's black section where "bad things"—beatings and shootings—were said to occur. Sometimes death was closer to home. There was the day Dennis played with a friend and his new red wagon, an American Flyer. The friend pulled the wagon up the steep driveway to his house then flew, laughing, downhill. Dennis watched as he zipped across the street into the path of a cab. There was a sickening crunch and the boy went flying, his body smacking the pavement then rolling limply to a stop. There was silence; people started to scream. Dennis ran into the woods, hiding there till night, when his mom and granddad found him in a spot where the neighborhood kids played fort. They told him his friend was dead, but he already knew.

Around this time, his father returned from the war. Yates Stockton didn't figure often into his son's early memories, but when he did there was trouble. One memory involved Christmas and his first meeting with his dad. Yates came home on leave: he was in uniform and carried a large duffel bag of gifts. His mother seemed glad to see him, so Dennis figured the tall man must be good. That night after supper the family gathered together while the stranger unpacked the duffel and handed out gifts to his mother, brother and sister. But there wasn't a gift for him and Dennis cried. Yates threatened to whip him if he didn't act like a man. The next day, the stranger returned to war. Dennis was glad to see him go, but Mom was on the bus, kissing him and crying. She stayed on as the bus started and Dennis knew he'd never see her again. When she did step off the bus, he grabbed her hand tightly as if he'd never let go.

Yates returned from war an easily angered man. Conditions in Shelby didn't help. Money was tight and jobs few. He and Ailene started a diner, but it failed. There were fewer happy memories now. Ailene, always so cheerful, became prone to nervous breakdowns. Yates gave Dennis a baseball glove, but he was not aware that his son was left-handed and the glove was for the wrong hand. There were many beatings, Yates exploding at the least infraction. Dennis did not write of this, but one of his brothers recalled the times Yates took a leather strap to Dennis and his arms, legs and back were covered with blood. He punched him with his fists. "He threw a hammer at him one time, missed him and hit my dog and killed him," the brother said.

In 1952, Yates Stockton took a job across state as a salesman for a hardware company. This meant moving his family nearly 150 miles northeast to White Plains, a little town outside Mount Airy. They rented a tidy brick house near the town's small school. The first sign one saw upon arriving announced, "White Plains, Unincorporated." Beyond it lay a second noting the town's claim to fame: White Plains was the home of Eng and Chang, history's most famous Siamese twins, who settled there as farmers after retiring from life in a circus sideshow. They died in 1874, their grave designated a historical landmark. Dennis was twelve, going into the seventh grade when his family moved. Four years later, police would take him from his tenth-grade class and book him for forging checks; the court sent him to prison to teach him a hard lesson. It had the opposite effect—the bulk of his life from sixteen until his death sentence at forty-two would be spent in prison or jail.

What happened to the all-American boy in four short years? Law officers said he just had a mean streak, but no one seems to have seen it in Shelby. One of many lawmen with whom Stockton faced off—a detective who was himself booted from the force for assault—called Stockton "the most dangerous man in Surry County." His father believed he ran with the wrong people. Stockton believed his life would have been so different if he'd never moved to White Plains.

One theme that keeps arising in his and others' memories is that of culture shock. Stockton often compared Shelby to Walnut Grove, site of his favorite TV program, *Little House on the Prairie.* It was a simple place, a land of double-feature movies charging nine cents' admission, nickel candy bars, an ice man stopping by your house with ice and milk, fireflies blinking as boys ran home from late-evening baseball. Life in Surry County was much different. Soon after entering school in White Plains, Dennis learned that one of his classmates' fathers was a bootlegger. He wrote in his autobiography that baseball took a backseat to "cussing, smoking, talking about sex and taking a sip of moonshine." Bootleggers were heroes. He wrote: "Junior Johnson, a legendary bootlegger from nearby Wilkes County, was just beginning a racing career and Curtis Turner, my first racing hero, was known as the wildest of the wild and bootlegging racing crowd. At school, too, I learned that it wasn't very manly to make good grades. School was something that was to be endured until one was old enough for the real business at hand, that being quitting school, getting drunk, raising tobacco and making babies."

Life suddenly seemed more hardscrabble in his new home. Shortly after Dennis's family arrived, school let out for tobacco season. To help pay the rent, Dennis, his sister and brother worked in their landlord's tobacco fields. They made 40 cents an hour, 20 cents less than the adults. It was hot, dirty work in a hot, dirty life. At the end of the day, the hired hands gathered around the smokehouses or curing barns and talked of moonshine and sex. At least half the hands were women, who joined in as freely as the men.

One of Stockton's first memories of Mount Airy in the 1950s makes the place sound like Dogpatch from "Li'l Abner." He and his brother would accompany their mother to the main part of town. While she shopped at the Piggly Wiggly, they headed for the Blue Ridge Hotel at the town's main intersection. "There would be people sitting there that had long beards and they'd be whittling and there'd be shavings all over the sidewalk," he wrote. "And they would have these jars, pint jars, half-gallon jars of white liquor, and they'd be sipping out of it." He'd never seen anything like it in his life.

Ten days before his seventeenth birthday, Stockton was charged with two counts of forging his father's name on checks and sent into the prison system's waiting arms. But it was not his first brush with The Law. A year earlier he had been picked up for passing bad checks in Mount Airy and thrown in the city jail. When his dad came to bail him out, the chief said, "Mr. Stockton, why not leave him in there awhile and teach him a lesson so's to keep him from getting in more trouble?" The idea appealed to Yates, and they left him in for the weekend.

Dennis stayed alone in the drunk tank, a dingy cell smelling of vomit and booze. On the second day, the turnkey brought back a soda and candy bar. He said Dennis would soon be out on bond. He wanted to believe this: it was inconceivable that his mom and dad would leave him here. A few hours later, the turnkey returned with more soda and candy. He reached through the bars and fondled Dennis's penis. Dennis got hard—excited and ashamed at the same time. "Take it out," the turnkey said thickly. "Let me see it." But in the distance a door creaked and someone walked their way. The turnkey left. He never touched him again but kept bringing back treats. When his father took him home, the turnkey looked up and said, "Come see me sometime."

Now, convicted of forgery, he went to prison for the very first time. He was sent to the state penitentiary in Raleigh, where he met his first mentor in crime, an escape artist and safecracker named Bill Broadwell, who ran an illegal poker game in front of his cell. Stockton was posted as lookout and proved so efficient that Broadwell taught him how to survive. "Don't back down from a threat," Broadwell instructed, "but don't go looking for a fight neither." Never become a "dog boy," a prisoner who helped train bloodhounds to track escapees. Never snitch on a fellow inmate. And no matter what you see or hear, always hold your tongue.

One other thing kept him going that first term in prison, and that was baseball. Back then, each prison fielded a team. Competition was stiff—better teams were even scouted by the pros. Stockton wrote about the day former Yankees pitcher Tommy Byrne watched him pitch for the Butner Prison team in North Carolina:

> It was the most nervous day of my life. It was the spring of 1959 and we were playing the Goldsboro Youth Center, which was a youth center for blacks in those days. I walked the very first two batters to come up. The coach came out to the mound and told me to take it easy and try not to think about Byrne being there. But that was easier said than done because I couldn't help but see Byrne's big Cadillac parked across the road behind the back stop. Every time I looked to the catcher for a signal I couldn't help but see that car.
>
> Anyway, I remember the guy on second was staying close to the bag but the one on first kept dancing way off so I picked him off and got out of the inning easy after that. I'll NEVER forget that final score. It was 17–0. I got three hits too, one a triple. After the game Byrne came over and spoke to me. He had a World Series ring on his finger. I asked him about Mickey Mantle, Yogi Berra, Billy Martin, Whitey Ford and Hank Bauer and let him know right quick that I knew a lot about the Yankees. Byrne paid me what I thought was the supreme compliment by saying that he thought I could play ball professionally. He said I had a lot of "potential."

Byrne would later recall visiting the prison camp to scout a prospect, though he didn't recall the kid's name. But he did remember the game and the car he drove was a Cadillac. A big one, he said, the color of gold.

Yet baseball couldn't save Stockton and when he returned home in 1960 after three years in prison, now a young man of twenty, people saw a change. He seemed bitter, distant, cold. They asked what happened, but how could he say that old cons like Bill Broadwell taught him more about life than his own father? How could he make them understand that weekend on Carolina's Death Row, the darkness, fear and anger which he barely understood himself? There was a feeling like he'd slipped his moorings and couldn't trust anyone, at least not in the straight world. So he entered the outlaw culture like there was no tomorrow, running moonshine, worshiping NASCAR drivers who got their starts the same way. Drugs hit the prison culture long before the counterculture, so when pills and reefer blossomed in the late 1960s and 1970s he was there as an advance man. His own personal addiction was "crank," crystal methamphetamine, injected into his veins. He sold stolen goods, with a weakness for chain saws, eventually graduating from petty theft to contract arson and safecracking, skills he learned in the pen.

Soon after his return, his dad took him on a hunting party in the mountains. By now Yates was a prominent businessman: many of Surry County's respected citizens were customers of his hardware company and they invited him to their "hunt club," a log cabin in the woods. They drove up an old logging road that ended at the cabin's front porch. The view was beautiful, overlooking a clearing that dropped into a green valley. At dawn and dusk, deer grazed at the forest's edge. Inside the cabin, the mayor of a small town near Mount Airy had donned an apron and was cooking stew. He stirred a large pot on the woodstove with a long-handled spoon, throwing in whatever canned goods were handy: pork and beans, apple sauce, corn, stewed tomatoes, fruit cocktail and beef stew. Beside him stood the turnkey from the Mount Airy jail.

The mayor and the turnkey stared at Stockton as he walked in. Several times over the next hour, the mayor brushed against the crotch of Stockton's jeans. The turnkey smiled. Every time Stockton turned around, the mayor had drawn near. Finally, Stockton went out on the porch to escape. He watched as a farmer from nearby Beaulah drove up with twenty-four gallons of moonshine in his flatbed. It was the worst liquor he ever tasted, but just the same, he and all the others were soon drunk. They ate the mayor's stew as the sun went down.

Stockton sat on the porch, watching the fire-red sky fade into purple and black. Above that were the stars, dazzling as diamonds, yet distant and cold. A store owner came out with the mayor in tow. He made introductions, mentioning that the mayor was also a magistrate and had the power to issue warrants, set bail, preside at probable cause hearings. An anger flared in Stockton as red as the sky's. He knew what they were saying: *He'll do you right if you just play along. Just like that time in jail.* The mayor stood drunk and happy, waiting for the understanding to be sealed with a handshake. He grabbed the mayor's tie and tightened; the little man's eyes bugged as Dennis screamed, "I'm gonna fuck this little bastard!" Others rushed out and pulled him off. His dad came up and slapped him in front of the others. He balled his fists and stared at his father, then walked off down the dark road. He didn't get far before passing out drunk.

Yates came and got him. His father was shaking him awake, the car idling above him, lights on. He crawled into the backseat, where he slept through the night. The next morning he grabbed his rifle as the others still cleaned theirs and walked off into the woods.

He found a quiet glade and sat under a tree. Two deer crept within thirty feet. He watched till they walked off, then fell asleep again. When he woke, it was afternoon. His dad sat by him. Yates's hand lay on his shoulder, but he drew it away as his son stirred. There was silence as each waited for the other to mention the outburst. But neither did. "I saw some deer but didn't shoot 'em," he finally mentioned. "Sometimes I don't neither," Yates said.

Dennis listened to the breeze moving through the treetops. "D'you ever wish we never left Shelby?" he finally asked.

His father looked at him in surprise. "Yeah, I miss it. But I couldn't make a living there, you know that."

"I know it," he answered, poking with a stick by his feet. "I miss it, though. I miss Granddad, and our house, and my friends. I never had friends like the ones I had in Shelby."

Yates sighed. "Son, you make do with what life hands you. You got to try to get along."

"It don't work that way," Dennis answered softly, still staring at the ground. He paused and looked around. He felt an immense sadness like nothing he'd felt before. It included his father and him, and this quiet spot in the woods. It was as though it spread in green ripples from this spot to the future and the past. There were things he could say that might somehow heal it, but they were always beyond his reach. He could never find the right words.

"Dad," he finally said, "can we just go home?"

• • • •

He was twenty-four and the anger lurking underneath crawled to the surface. It radiated from him, terrifying his family and friends. One night he turned a corner. "There used to be a café in Mount Airy called the B and B," he wrote. "I was all messed up on redbirds and I went in there and two policemen had come in to get their free meals and drink their free coffee." One was part of the duo who had dragged him from school in 1957, two men he'd never forgiven. "I stuck a cigarette in his coffee. . . . I challenged him to a shootout, one of these old cowboy things. Drugs'll cause you to do a lot of things. Nothing really happened except I just made a fool of myself . . . and I embarrassed him real bad. But that is something that police don't never forget."

Now he was the outlaw in the eyes of the police as well as his own. He started carrying a gun. Loyal and funny around friends and associates, he played the junior badass in public, deliberately provoking The Law. The results were expected. During the late 1960s and early 1970s, "Dennis was a suspect in everything," one officer said. Although he was charged only with property crimes, the police began saying he was a suspect in some unsolved murders, sometimes with no more evidence than his attitude. He was questioned in the disappearance of two men in 1971; although they were never found, the two were believed killed and their bodies thrown over a bridge. The Surry County sheriff called him a suspect in the April 1978 killing of a fifteen-year-old girl whose body was found floating in the river; records showed Stockton was in prison at the time and couldn't have been involved. In 1979, he was questioned in the murder of a man shot through his living room window; Stockton proved he was working at a textile mill the night the man was killed. As he proved his innocence, his hatred for The Man grew by leaps and bounds.

There were other reasons to hate. At this time, police corruption had reached a high mark in Surry County. As one thief said, "The cops were crookeder than the crooks." In 1977 or 1978, Stockton had broken into a drugstore in the middle of the night when a police car pulled up outside. He fled out back and up a hill where he could watch the cops. He thought they were after him but now saw another car in the parking lot with the cruiser. A man and a woman were inside. The man stepped from his car and Stockton recognized him as a member of a prominent Mount Airy family. There were sharp words, but too far away to be heard clearly. As Stockton watched, the man made a sudden move. The police stepped back. There were shots. The man fell.

The killing was a scandal, one never fully explained in the press. Soon authorities learned that Stockton had witnessed the shooting. Now he was even more of a threat than before.

He was vulnerable, yet did little to cool matters. Instead he acted meaner, more desperate, as if daring police to take him on. Friends warned him that the most likely outcome would be death. He shrugged them off. If anything, he seemed like a man with a death wish, seeing how far he could go before the Reaper caught up.

One story of this time tells volumes. It was the late spring of 1980; Stockton had escaped from jail and had been hiding out in New Jersey for seven months. By now he was a serious addict: his mind never felt sharper than when he was high; he never had more energy. It was like there was nothing he couldn't do when high and he liked to prove it. So when a dealer friend asked him to run twenty ounces of pure crank to North Carolina, he agreed. Before leaving Jersey, he shot up forty units of crystal meth; he loaded the same amount in three diabetic syringes and stuck them in his shirt pocket. He stuffed his loaded 9mm Browning into his shoulder holster, popped Lynyrd Skynyrd into the tape player, hit I-81 in his rebuilt Merc and floored it, making the 1,100-mile round-trip in less than a day. He had all the ingredients needed to get himself killed.

During the night he stopped at a twenty-four-hour Shell for gas and to empty a syringe into his veins. He was doing so in the bathroom when he heard what sounded like a shotgun blast. He snatched out his pistol and peeked out the door, wondering if the station was being robbed. Instead, his right rear tire had blown out from the heat generated by his hell-bent speed. A frightened attendant who'd been pumping gas was now spraying it straight in the air. Stockton laughed and closed the door. Only later did he realize his stupidity— the speed, the drugs, the gun. What if a cop had pulled him over? What then?

He was no longer himself, willingly embracing a darker Dennis that scared old friends and family. His siblings, those who still talked to him, warned him he was destined for an early grave. His mom would sit at the table and cry. *Why, Dennis?* she pleaded. *You had so much going. You're smart. The baseball. This wasn't you in Shelby. What went wrong?*

He couldn't explain, though he wished he could. It was around this time that the first whispers of homosexuality started around him. He would find it hard to defend himself against the rumors. In this part of the country, in his cops-and-robbers crowd, the brand of homosexuality was the same as social death: you became an outsider among outsiders. He had plenty of girlfriends, yet was also surrounded by young men ages seventeen to twenty. The evidence suggests they were drawn more by the glamour of the badass than anything sexual, yet the rumors persisted. Soon they crept into court. In Stockton's civil suit alleging inhumane conditions in the Patrick County Jail, two witnesses quoted Randy Bowman as saying he "lied on" Stockton during the Arnder murder trial because he "hated queers." Denials only made things worse. It was one more shadow Dennis carried with him, another mask that made him harder to see.

Yet sometimes he lifted the mask and let others peek in. At those times people responded, even cops. They discovered there was something about him they couldn't help but like. To their surprise, he was challenging, polite and smart. Details he supplied about crimes almost always turned out true. He was developing the habit of truth-telling that would turn so self-destructive, and it only deepened the mystery. Was Stockton as cold-blooded as they called him? What had happened to this boy?

From the 1960s to mid-1970s, David Beal was a North Carolina State Police investigator before being elected Surry County clerk of court. He remembered one encounter that made him question the cold-blooded hype. "I went to the prison on a hot, hot summer afternoon to interview Dennis about a dozen things," he told *The Mount Airy News*. "Dennis had been placed in solitary confinement in a cinder-block building that sat by itself in the prison yard. This building had real tightly closed windows with heavy steel mesh over them. They only cracked so far. I went in and interviewed him for an hour or more. Both of us were just drenched. When I was ready to leave the building, on the ground outside the window were half a dozen biscuits. I stuck my head back in the door and asked why those biscuits were there. Dennis said the other inmates tried to throw them to him to eat. Some would make it under the little crack in the window and some would bounce. I had always heard of bread and water in solitary confinement. It made me realize it was probably true. I left that building with compassion for him."

It was a troubling moment. "I formed the opinion that Dennis would someday end up in the gas chamber," Beal said. But he didn't know why he thought this, and the premonition only made him sad.

• • • •

The best Stockton could figure, he was a man at war with himself, bent on self-destruction yet refusing to turn aside from the whirl-wind. It was a theme as old as his first memories of family, one that always centered around the men. His grandfather in church quoting from Romans: *But I see another law in my members, warring against the law of my mind,* he said. *O wretched man that I am! Who shall deliver me from the body of this death?* His father raising his hand to beat him, the beatings growing more bloody as Yates's eyes grew sadder.

Many in the modern world are uncomfortable with the concept of evil. It is cast as a quality, not a substance, a description rather than a thing. Satan and his minions are a myth expressing man's capacity to perform acts his reason or conscience should condemn. It is the theme from Romans: the man at war with himself, doing wrong when he wishes to do good. Yet parallel streams exist in popular thought just as in the Bible, and Stockton remembered the teachings of his child-hood and the depiction of evil in the Book of Mark. According to the story, Jesus came to Gadara, where he was led to a man possessed by demons. "Come out of the man, thou unclean spirit," Jesus ordered. "What is thy name?"

"My name is Legion, for we are so many," replied the demon, beg-ging Jesus not to cast him bodiless into the world. Instead he sug-gested a herd of pigs, two thousand strong, and Jesus complied. He dealt with the devil, and the pigs promptly plunged to their death in the sea.

It would be nice to personify evil in that way, Stockton sometimes thought. As though evil were a growth that could be cut away as eas-ily as a putrefaction; as if it recognized itself and even assisted in its excision. Framing it this way could be so consoling—evil was a blight that visited randomly, yet stayed apart from the soul. He watched as others on The Row took that route. It aided their conscience, lessened the blame.

But Stockton could not follow. This was not the real nature of evil, he said in his darkest moments when he had to be honest. Evil was a cancer twining about the heart, a response to the anger and evil you'd already endured. It was a conscious choice. He didn't kill Kenny Arnder, but he'd surely been heading in a direction where someone would die. To a place where he would hate and rage until finally breaking the last taboo. They were all like that on The Row, the guilty and the innocent alike, the damned and the saved. When you hated the world, you wanted revenge. When you lived for revenge, you embraced evil. You wanted to tear everything down.

It was a sobering thought. Was this why he could put himself in the mind of Timothy Bunch or become best friends with a serial murderer like Linwood? They shared a common anger. They warred against the world. The reasons might be legion, but The Row was their reward.

All of the condemned were seduced by evil. Some, like the Brileys, were in control when they decided to kill: they willingly crossed the line to eliminate witnesses. For others, like Bunch or Morris Mason, the act controlled them. They were in its grip and couldn't break away. They reveled in the will to lay waste, to fiddle joyfully as everything burned down. It was a seduction more exciting than the arms of any woman, for there was the added spice of revenge.

One didn't have to be a criminal to see it. This motive, not material gain, was the true heart of crime, said sociologist Jack Katz in *Seductions of Crime: Moral and Sensual Attractions of Doing Evil.* "The closer one looks at crime . . . the more vividly relevant become the moral emotions," he said:

> Follow vandals and amateur shoplifters as they duck into alleys and dressing rooms and you will be moved by their delight in deviance; observe them under arrest and you may be stunned by their shame. Watch their strutting street display and you will be struck by the awesome fascination that symbols of evil hold for the young men who are linked in the groups we often call gangs. . . . The careers of persistent robbers show us, not the increasingly precise calculations and hedged risks of "professionals," but men . . . who take pride in a defiant reputation as "bad." And if we examine the lived sensuality behind events of cold-blooded "senseless" murder, we are compelled to acknowledge the power that may still be created in the modern world through the sensualities of defilement, spiritual chaos, and the apprehension of violence.
>
> Running across these experiences . . . is a process juxtaposed . . . against humiliation. In committing a righteous slaughter, the impassioned assailant takes humiliation and turns it into rage.

Stockton never denied the excitement of crime. His blood raced. His senses grew increasingly focused. The danger rushed at him, yet his hand stayed firm on the wheel. He had *absolute* control. It was what he'd always sought: it came to him on the pitcher's mound; it came again on his drug run. It came so infrequently in anyone's life, you simply hung on when it did. There was a strange sense of being *apart* and watching from a separate height. It almost seemed absurd. One such moment happened in 1970 or 1971 during his first attempt at safecracking. He was the youngest of a trio that had gone to western Carolina to rob a safe in a department store. The leader, once known as one of the best safecrackers in the Southeast, was still willing but getting old and in his dotage. Stockton watched as he drilled holes in the safe, cut dynamite into small pieces, then packed each hole with a "cap." He attached a wire to each, spliced the wires together and ran the long wire to a bathroom in the back. Stockton's job was to stay behind and touch two wires to the battery posts, setting off the charge. He wrote:

> I was the youngster and didn't have much choice in the deal. . . . I went to the bathroom and touched one wire to the positive post and one to the negative. It sounded like World War III had started. The whole building shook. I ran to the front to get the money but when I got there, the safe was gone. So was the window.
>
> I looked outside and the safe was laying on its side on top of a parking meter it had flattened. I went through the hole and grabbed the safe door. It came right open. There I was standing on the sidewalk, putting all the money in the sack, feeling like a fool.

He got back to the car and told his partners what had happened. The second man, the lookout, looked at the leader and asked, "Use a little too much dynamite?" The old man grinned and answered, "I guess I did."

This was criminal, but not evil, Stockton believed. He regaled friends with such tales and was the life of the party. Such acts were devoid of cruelty, no cold-blooded reduction of life as something easy to extinguish, no drive to power by making others beg. Yet the fiasco with the safe also marked a change in direction. The explosion scared him to death, but he acquired a taste for excitement and apocalypse that satisfied something inside.

He was more reckless now. Soon, in addition to running moonshine and burglary, he began a career in contract arson, torching buildings for owners who wanted the insurance claims. This led to people hiring him to torch the businesses of their competitors. He made sure no one was inside before striking the match, and once abandoned a job when he heard voices. But it was easy money, and he was surprised how many businessmen sought his services:

> I recall a period when I'd been on escape for nearly a year when I happened to go by the business of an acquaintance to learn he was in dire straits. A rival business had gone up directly across the highway and it offered a much larger selection of goods and a larger parking area. When my friend asked how much it'd take to torch the other place, I said $500. He said he'd give me $1,000. I quickly accepted.
>
> Now among the other goods that other store carried were at least a hundred country hams. I borrowed a pickup from a friend and parked behind the business of the man who hired me an hour before the rival business closed. I waited till all the employees were gone before walking over, prying open the door and checking the place out. I carried along a 5-gallon can of kerosene. It was so easy. I returned and got the pickup, loaded it with ham and cigarettes and then went down the aisles with that kerosene. Back outside, I flicked my Bic before climbing under the wheel and driving away.
>
> The next morning when I drove up, I found the ashes still smoking from the fire. The entire roof had collapsed. A mile before getting there I smelled ham and once I got out and parked learned I'd missed a storeroom filled with still other hams. The friend that hired me was pleased with the results. So much so that he bought the stuff I'd loaded from across the road.

He had become the agent of another's cruelty. He knew he had edged over a moral line.

In March 1978, he returned to The World from prison for the last time and things had changed. Mount Airy had expanded, annexing surrounding towns. Prices seemed ten times higher than before his imprisonment. His first job paid minimum wage and he soon was in debt. He would never be a baseball player. He would never be a race car driver. He knew he was smart, but would never use his intelligence in the conventional sense, going to college, getting a degree. He was a failure in everything but crime.

Then a different type of contract crossed his door:

A friend who ran a carlot in a neighboring town asked me to drop by his office. When I did, I found an envelope in my name containing $2,000. The bills, twenty of them, were crispy new and consecutively numbered. I walked out to the car to inspect the envelope while my friend waited on a customer. I was driving Mom's car that day, unable yet to afford my own. I stuck the bills under the floormat and went back to talk. My friend had received the envelope along with instructions to deliver it to me. I drove back home, put $500 in my pocket and hid the rest.

A few days later, a letter arrived with instructions what the money was for. It identified a person who had testified at a criminal trial a few years earlier. The person no longer lived in the area, and soon another letter arrived giving the address of where he now could be found. The author of the letter wanted this person killed. The $2,000 was a down payment. Another $3,000 would be paid when the killing was done.

I didn't tell anyone about the letter but took it down to the basement and hid it. I never killed the person. As far as I know, he is still alive. I never could find him. Perhaps if I had found him, I would have done it. It's hard to say. I just don't know.

Now he was intrigued by taking that last step over the moral line. He toyed with the idea, dandled it in his fingers, allured by an awesome fascination with destruction. There was a story from this time, yet another rumor both paradoxical and impossible to prove. When police searched his house, they allegedly found a severed penis preserved in formaldehyde. They used this to buttress their rumors that he was responsible for other murders, the same rumors that were subsequently disproved. Yet Stockton had never kept the sideshow curio hidden. He'd shown it around at drunken parties, relishing the looks of horror, the badass points that accrued. He reportedly bought it from an outlaw biker gang, the apex of meanness in that part of the country. He was "bad" by association. Ironically, the letter writer probably used Stockton for the same purpose.

Stockton took the blood money but was never confronted with the pivotal moment when he would have had to choose to kill or not. Yet instead of returning the money or alerting police, he kept the letters. Soon another arrived, naming someone else to be killed. He kept getting calls from the car lot; when he'd drop by, another $1,000 waited.

It became a joke. The temptation passed and he saw the letters as they were: absurd testaments to the writer's ego. The man kept sending money even when it became obvious Stockton would not kill for him. He told the man he had no intention of fulfilling his wishes, but the letters still came. The writer, a prominent citizen, had been seduced like Stockton by the idea of evil. It was playacting and dress-up; the man gloried in seeing himself as a gangster, dropping Stockton's name as his "underworld connection." He was "bad" by association, just like Stockton with the outlaw gang. Stockton shrugged, thought about a fool and his money, and spent it all.

On July 20, 1978, Kenny Arnder called Stockton at home, begging for a ride to Kibler Valley, a remote, wooded picnic spot in Virginia between Mount Airy and Stuart. Kenny was scared and said a man spotted him and their mutual friend Ronnie Tate stealing tires off a car. Stockton considered Arnder a basically good kid: a little short on brains, without direction, but easygoing and without that mean streak he saw so much of nowadays. He'd met him only a month or so earlier at a party where everyone was drinking and popping pills. His parents were separated and his mother, Wilma, tried to hold the family together. But it was hard with six children and the starvation wages she made at the nearby poultry plant. Kenny was the oldest of two boys; his younger brother was already serving time for forgery and breaking into a car. But all families have their troubles, and most who knew Kenny called him an average teenage boy.

Stockton picked Kenny up at about 6 P.M. and let him off at Kibler Valley. He returned at dusk. A campfire was burning and a tent was up under the trees. Ronnie Tate was there, as well as others Stockton knew by sight or name. He told Kenny he was on a drug run and must hurry to Winston-Salem, nearly sixty miles southeast, but promised he'd come back later that night to see if he wanted a ride back home. He returned around midnight and a party was in full swing. Kenny saw the headlights and walked up to the car. He told Stockton he'd decided to stay for the weekend. Stockton nodded and drove away.

Five days later, Kenny's body was found in a gully off a dirt road in Surry County, North Carolina, so badly decomposed that at first identification was difficult. The body was partially covered by a six-foot pine sapling; Kenny's arms were stretched out as if he'd been crucified. His hands were chopped off at the wrists and he'd been shot between the eyes. He wore blue jeans, a long-sleeved work shirt, a light blue T-shirt with the words HOW DO YOU SPELL RELIEF— COLOMBIAN GOLD, and a teardrop necklace with a white stone. Stockton felt sick. This was how Kenny was dressed the last time he saw him alive.

Soon the police arrived. Stockton had been expecting them. He knew he'd be a suspect. After all, he drove the boy to Kibler Valley; he was with him the last time Wilma Arnder ever saw her son alive. He couldn't blame her for talking. Two detectives came to his door and he invited them inside. They asked questions about the ride to Kibler Valley, then, to his surprise, veered off into questions about the murder of a fifteen-year-old girl and a man shot through his window. What's going on, he wondered, but the questions just as quickly veered back to Kenny. Stockton showed them his guns and offered to let them go out back and fire them into boards, then take the bullets in for tests. The guns were a Colt Airweight .38 and a .30-caliber carbine rifle. The detectives said it wasn't necessary—these were not the calibers of the murder weapon. They went on their way, apparently satisfied.

But now various rumors began to float of "contract killings"; rumors that Kenny cheated Tommy McBride on a Valium deal and McBride wanted him killed as a warning to others; rumors that Kenny crossed a New Jersey dealer in a matter involving a girl; rumors that McBride and a Patrick County deputy plotted to kill that county's prosecutor, and Kenny and Stockton were somehow involved. The rumors took on lives of their own, disappearing for a while then springing up somewhere totally unexpected. Yet something soon became clear to Stockton. The businessman who'd wanted him to kill others must have talked. The cops had heard something from someone.

The frightening events continued. One of the people present at Kenny's murder confessed to Stockton. "I beat the hell outta Kenny," said the man whose identity Stockton never divulged; this witness then told how, after the beating, Ronnie Tate shot Arnder between the eyes. Tate later as much as confirmed the tale. There were still unanswered questions, things that didn't quite make sense. Stockton heard rumors that Kenny was actually brought back to Carolina, tied to a tree and tortured before he died. Tales that the boy's hands were buried "on the grounds next to the long driveway by the old Smith place." But suddenly a feeling hit him like drowning. He was sinking into a blackness so deep he would never break surface again.

Why did he still refuse to go to the police? He stayed tight-lipped. The silence made him look guilty to many who investigated the case then and later, but he never spoke up. Innumerable people would ask him about this over the years. His lawyers. His pastor. Reporters. If he knew the truth, why not say it? But he shook his head and never said, mystifying them all.

Conscious evil ran like jet-black ink throughout the investigation. A sinister feel attached to the case: mention the killing of Kenny Arnder and you felt the chill. The hunt became an obsession for local lawmen, but there were no charges. Then something strange happened that reverberated long after Stockton was tucked into Death Row.

It was 1980, two years after Arnder's killing. Stockton was in the Patrick County Jail, serving time for shooting into the building of a man he claimed owed him money but who refused to pay. The charge had nothing to do with the Arnder murder, just one more hotheaded stunt that, when the anger passed, seemed more and more stupid to him the older he grew. He was in his cell when he heard rumors from other inmates that the Arnder investigation was again swinging his way. He recognized the source, the old rumors of contract killings, so he decided to show police where the rumors began. He took Jay Gregory, the Patrick County investigator, and Bill Hall, the Surry County sheriff, to his house. His brother was there and made the men cold drinks. Stockton went down to the basement and brought back the tattered bundle of letters from the prominent citizen wishing death to his rivals. He gave them to the lawmen, who said they would look into things.

Instead, the letters were somehow lost. Hall said Gregory had them. Gregory said the opposite. Reporters asked questions, political opponents made allegations, but the "contracts" were never investigated, the letter writer was never charged.

Before his trial, prosecutors offered Stockton a chance to save his skin. If he would testify against McBride, say, "Yes, Tommy offered me fifteen hundred dollars to kill the boy," they promised to recommend life imprisonment instead of death. It's a lie, Stockton replied. There never was a murder contract. There never was a party where he accepted $1,500 to kill the boy. He was no great friend of

Tommy's, but he refused to play along. The prosecutors just smiled and said, "Think about it." They returned twice more with the offer. Each time, Stockton refused.

And so he went to Death Row. His lawyers hammered at him to save himself. If he claimed he was innocent and knew the real killer or killers, they argued, what was the point of keeping mum? But there were hints that anyone who ratted would pay. Maybe Stockton was beyond reach on Death Row, but things began to happen to his family, especially as more people started talking about his innocence, speculating that maybe he'd been framed. His sister was woken repeatedly by late-night calls: part death threat, part obscene, then a click and dead air. His baby brother—a Vietnam combat veteran with the 101st Airborne—returned from two tours of duty to harassment by authorities in both counties.

His closest brother was hounded the worst: the nearest to him in age, only three years younger, whom he called his best friend. Several new tires were slashed as he made his rounds as an accountant. There were death threats in the middle of the night. A county deputy drove a felon to the brother's house and dropped him off. The ex-con raised the hood of his pickup and threw an oil-soaked rag atop the engine block so it would ignite when the engine grew hot. The next day, the truck caught fire and burned. The attacks got worse after Ronnie Tate's brother Mike got out of prison. Mike ran into Stockton's brother on the job and said he'd been in prison with Randy Bowman. The big man had laughed and bragged how he'd lied in Stockton's trial. How he'd even made money out of it. In time, Dennis's brother was forced to move out of state to protect his family.

Then more sinister things occurred. Others linked to the killing began to die. The deaths stretched into the mid- and late 1980s, long after Stockton went to The Row. There was Mike Tate, reportedly killed in a traffic accident after his allegations about Bowman were published in the Mount Airy newspaper. There was a man named Junior Danley, shot to death in a domestic incident. Danley told his girlfriend, Linnie Davis, that Arnder was killed in Kibler Valley and that four to six people were present but that Stockton was not among them. He said this in front of Davis's two daughters, who detailed Danley's story in sworn statements. The two said Danley was covered with blood and admitted stuffing Arnder's body in the trunk of their mother's white Olds. He also said he was the one who cut off the hands. There was a man named Robert Hershberger, pumped full of lead in suspicious circumstances in the Midwest, though police called it suicide. Finally, there was Dianne McBride, Tommy McBride's wife, who committed suicide. Like many suicides, her reasons were never clear. Some said she killed herself to escape drug addiction, others that it was only made to look self-inflicted. A third group said she was wracked by a guilt that came with Kenny's death—a guilt that never went away.

And as he heard of these deaths, Stockton discovered a truth of evil, one of its many shades. It was nothing like the dark wind he imagined on his night ride from Jersey. It sank deep, layer on layer, even through the foundations of the institutions formed to fight it. Few paid to the same extent as Stockton, but it drew everyone in: good and bad, innocent and guilty, lawful and lawless. There were so many: Bill Hall, the Surry County sheriff, investigated for alleged corruption and criticized by political opponents for "losing" the letters; Jay Gregory and Tony Giorno, both accused of hiding evidence to further their careers; Tommy McBride, dogged by questions of guilt and watching his own wife commit suicide; Wilma Arnder and her children, watching the legal battles continue, believing less and less in justice; Randy Bowman, waiting in the wings for Act Two. And finally others who over the years said they knew the truth of the killing but never went public for fear of their lives.

Something rotten grew in Mayberry. Its truth was simple: there's no escape once the evil takes hold.

4

It was late October when Linwood first mentioned a breakout.

They were playing Scrabble in Briley's cell, the pornographic babes smiling archly from the walls. The summer heat had passed, the prison green was quiet. It was Stockton's turn—he stared at the smooth wooden tiles. All vowels.

"You ever think of leaving here?"

Stockton looked up. The remark seemed offhand, but he knew by now that Linwood did and said nothing unplanned. In just one more year they would tie the leather mask around Linwood's face and pull the switch. Stockton recalled his friend's remark that he didn't plan to wait around for that to happen. He wondered how many other inmates Linwood had approached like this, so casually, feeling them out for determination or ideas.

"Not in a box, you mean?"

Linwood grinned. "I'm just thinking, is all." The way he had it figured, there were three ways to break out of Mecklenburg. One was to get someone on the outside to smuggle in guns, but JB's foiled attempt two years earlier put the guards on the lookout for that. Body searches of all visitors were now common. A second method was to take hostages, but that rarely worked and people just got killed. The third way was to outsmart the guards. This had possibilities, but Linwood admitted he hadn't figured out a scam.

"If it was me, I'd make do with what was available," Stockton said. "I sure wouldn't depend on others Outside. All they hear out there is how this place is escape-proof. They hear it enough, they start to believe it."

Linwood nodded, his eyes bright. "Yeah, but so do the guards."

Stockton asked what Linwood knew of Mecklenburg's layout and was surprised how little he did know. The others were the same, locked up so long in C-Pod that the prison's changes had completely passed them by. Unlike the others, Stockton had been in and out repeatedly, taken west to Danville for his appeal, east to South Hill to see a urologist about recurring kidney problems. He had the local roads memorized, could even draw a map if required.

The problem was, he didn't want to escape. Not yet. Not now. He was excited by the detective's speculations. The man's parting words kept coming back: *You shouldn't be here.* On top of that, his lawyers thought his appeals stood a chance. They were outraged that all charges against Tommy McBride had been dropped for allegedly paying Stockton $1,500 to kill Arnder. McBride's case had been sent to North Carolina, where prosecutors took one look at the evidence and threw it in the circular file. How could you send one man to Death Row for murder for hire, they asked, yet drop charges against the man who supposedly footed the bill?

Yet Stockton didn't tell this to Linwood. It somehow seemed cruel, what with his own execution right around the corner. Plus, it might not be smart. On some things you were either with Linwood or against him. There were no in-betweens.

Yet even considering the long odds against escaping Death Row, he couldn't drive the thought away once he returned to his own cell. He lay in bed, a joint dangling from his lips, listening to his personal anthem, Lynyrd Skynyrd's "Free Bird," playing on the radio: *If I leave here tomorrow, would you still remember me?* He chuckled. Once you break out, honey, they *never* forget. You're always on the run.

Still, Stockton had to admit that being on escape could be the sweetest times in a con's life—especially the first few days. Food tasted better, clothes felt more expensive, sex never seemed so good. There was this feeling of possession, like the world belonged to you. True, you always waited for the knock at night or the nervous cop's voice from behind telling you to kiss the street, because they always caught you. *Always!* But that just increased the high of being alive.

The greatest high was the escape itself. In moments of extreme peril, time itself slowed down. You got tunnel vision. You were scared shitless, it was so intense. Those inmates who'd gotten a stay within minutes of Old Sparky said the same: how every color was brighter, every smell stronger. The high came from the absolute terror of knowing that any second you might die.

He remembered the last time he'd escaped, March of 1973. He'd been picked up in Virginia on burglary charges and was assigned to a road camp at Chatham near the Carolina line. Each morning, he and forty-nine others were driven out to cut a right-of-way through some woods. One evening he decided he wouldn't be returning and made his preparations. He stuffed a couple packs of cigarettes and two packs of peanuts in his pockets so he wouldn't go smokeless and hungry, then wrapped two books of matches, a tiny mirror, comb, clean pair of socks, $40 in cash and $2 in change for phone calls in a large bandanna and wrapped the entire "survival kit" in plastic to keep it dry. The next morning he picked his spot and worked in that direction. The gun boss was at the other end of the crew when Stockton tossed down his ax and rabbited for the woods. He'd just reached the trees when one of his cigarette packs hopped from his shirt pocket; he bent low and sideways to nab it when he heard the shotgun blast and watched a path clear where his body had just been. The air cracked as the shot passed: he remembered the slow-motion splinters as it tore through the trees and high weeds.

Every escape taught you something new if you only paid attention. Toward evening a soft rain started falling, covering his tracks. He overnighted in a barn, exchanging his brown prison jacket for a blue one he found hanging from a hook. The next morning he headed south on a backwoods road when he heard a car crunch up behind him. He turned around. It was a 1959 Chevy with a big-boned black man sitting behind the wheel. Stockton hadn't been around many blacks except the ones he'd met in prison and he distrusted them. But this guy asked where he was headed and told of a manhunt for a prison escapee not far away. He didn't ask questions, just offered a ride. Stockton got in and they drove south through Danville. The black guy bought him two sandwiches, took him to the state line and turned around. Before he left, he pulled a pint jar of moonshine from under the seat. They shared a drink. "Good luck," the man called as Stockton ran into the woods.

That night, he thought about the black man's kindness. He had to have known Stockton was the fugitive, yet he wasn't the least afraid.

Maybe he'd been on a road crew himself. It was all pretty confusing. There was no reason in the world for this guy to help a white man, yet he had. In later years, when a white person would ask why some of his best friends on Death Row were black, he would recall this ride.

But not every escape attempt ended so well. Most ended in capture, or worse. You were fair game during an escape: your keepers no longer kept their own terror under a lid. He'd learned this in the summer of 1961, his second stint in prison. He was assigned to a road crew near Boone, North Carolina, paired with a boy named Paul McIntosh, to clean and shovel out drainage ditches clogged by mountain rains. They'd just quit for lunch near a stand of trees. Beyond that grew a field of knee-high corn. Stockton sat by the roadside when he heard a quick movement to his left and, in the same instant, a shot. He looked back and saw the guard standing with his rifle raised to his shoulder. His eyes followed the line of fire to where McIntosh lay in the grass about thirty feet away. He'd been running for the trees when the bullet entered his neck and left by his face, tearing a hole where his forehead had been.

There was stunned, sick silence as the crew boss drew his pistol and ran to the boy's body. Seconds later, he ran back, pale and grim. He ordered the entire gang to stand in the ditch on the other side of the road. Other guards drew their pistols and screamed for quiet when the prisoners started cussing. The hacks were plain terrified: Stockton realized in that instant how easy it would be for another of them to get shot down. No questions would ever be asked. Life was cheap, and you could die as quick as a kid squashes a bug. A silence filled the ditch, broken only by the whir of locusts and croak of a blackbird. He felt dizzy but dared not move. One minute you were alive and eating lunch, the next you were dead, and except for the queasiness of spectators, no one cared. It was a sobering moment, as defining as that weekend on Carolina's Row.

Blood and death—this was the probable outcome of any Death Row escape attempt, he thought. About a half dozen of them had few appeals left and their executions neared. Stockton had no doubt that the Brileys were up to staging a breakout. But could they convince the others?

It wouldn't be hard, he thought. After all, they had little left to lose.

• • • •

They were eating breakfast in the dayroom when a shakedown came, the first since he'd arrived. As they watched, the riot guards stormed into the pod; some inmates rushed to their cells but were blocked by the guards. A white shirt announced they would be called out from the dayroom to watch as their cells were searched, but that was as far as they'd get. Linwood and JB were called first, as if the guards already knew what they'd find. The tub of mash was carried from Linwood's cell. In JB's, they found seventy-five joints of Colombian weed. "JB, you don't learn," the white shirt gloated. The younger Briley looked away in disgust and didn't answer.

Then it was Stockton's turn. The white shirt called his name and he stood outside the door. Twenty joints of homegrown reefer, hidden inside the vent, were overlooked. But there was no missing the green tub sitting in the window with the tiny plant poking from the soil.

"What's this?" the guard asked, scowling at the second money-maker.

"A shade tree to cool off under." Stockton plucked the four-inch plant from the dirt, popped it in his mouth and smiled.

The white shirt scowled and told the guard to take the tub.

Was this merely random, or had someone snitched? It was impossible to tell. Within a week, inmates from the maintenance department built a wall between Death Row and B-Pod, their neighbor on the second floor. A door was set in its center, always kept locked. The cleanup guys could enter, but not as freely as before. The idea was to end JB's dope trade. The effort slowed sales, but didn't shut them down.

To take up the shortfall in reefer, mash production bloomed. On a warm day Stockton could smell the brewing yeast throughout the pod, but the guards still didn't seem to care. Some days, especially weekends, it seemed as if all the inmates got falling-down drunk. One afternoon, Turner and Mason got so smashed their speech was slurred. They hung on to each other as they staggered around the dayroom. Two white shirts passed in the hall outside and stared at them, amazed.

Stockton filled the hours in another way. He learned The Law, grabbing on to it like a lifeline. His capital appeal was scheduled for January 1984 and his lawyers seemed confident that he would be granted a retrial. When not wading through that, he tinkered with his civil suit alleging inhumane conditions in the Patrick County Jail. He arrived at the county lockup in 1980, charged with shooting into the building of the man who owed him money, and didn't leave until 1983, after his capital murder trial. Sheriffs nationwide complained about frivolous suits by inmates and Stockton's, seeking $5 million in damages, was nothing more than revenge for these years behind bars. He claimed that the jail was a bug-infested firetrap where he was harassed by guards, denied proper medical attention and denied contact with his attorney. Not surprisingly, the judge threw it out.

Yet his depositions accidentally hit pay dirt. Two inmates swore in affidavits that Randy Bowman boasted to them about lying during Stockton's trial. Bowman "said he would . . . say anything for anybody if the money was right," one said. The judge preserved this testimony for Stockton's appeals and his lawyers planned to use it as proof that Stockton was denied a fair trial.

He'd discovered by accident what law students took three years to discover: the truth was revealed by misdirection, if at all. In a land of laws, The Law itself was so hard to understand. It wasn't just the language, though that was bad enough, twisting and doubling back like a maze; it was more the feeling that he'd entered a completely different world where normal logic had changed. A world where the truth didn't matter so much as the means to reach it; where what you said was less important than how you phrased it . . . the correct incantations used. Where the thing that mattered most was the rules of the game.

The Law was a religion, the leather-bound tomes with gold-lettered titles like *Federal Rules for Criminal Procedure* as holy as the Bible, the black-robed judge both lawgiver and priest who interpreted The Word. *In the beginning was the Word, and the Word was with God, and the Word was God,* he could still hear his grandfather say. But sometimes, this Word didn't make sense. The Law's assumptions didn't jibe with the real world.

Take, for instance, "due process." This was the belief that truth would be revealed if the rules were followed. If so, how did you explain the twenty-one-day rule that prohibited the introduction of new evidence even if the rules were broken in the original trial? Take, for instance, the "adversarial system," the faith that justice would become manifest if both sides fought it out fair and square. It was trial by combat, God siding with the victor. But Stockton knew from experience that street fights rarely ended that way.

Sometimes he had to laugh at himself. His whole adult life had been pitted against The Law. Now that he knocked at its door, did he really expect entrance? He'd been so naive. In some ways, Willie and Morris Mason were the wiser. It was easier to stay high.

October became November . . . his possessions arrived from Richmond . . . his cell felt more like "home." He painted the walls, floor and ceiling robin's egg blue with a strip of ivory ten inches from the ceiling. There were three coats on the floor, which he scrubbed daily. Anyone entering had to take off his shoes. Linwood gave him two *Playboy* centerfolds, which he hung over his door. Pictures of Dale Earnhardt and his race car were taped to the walls. Next to these hung photos of his mother and ninety-six-year-old grandmother (who wasn't aware he was on The Row), a calendar and a bumper sticker that said WE HAVE IT MADE IN VIRGINIA. He placed old issues of *The Sporting News* and *Grand National Scene* under his thin mattress to make it softer. Linwood's unused electric typewriter became a permanent fixture, stored in the cabinet. His books, radio and peanut butter jar containing pens and pencils were lined like soldiers in the window. By day, his radio was tuned to a station playing Lynyrd Skynyrd and Bob Seger; by night, he picked up WABC from New York City, the station of the Yankees. He rubbed shoe polish on the door's glass strip to keep out the dayroom's twenty-four-hour lights and at the bottom stuck a card that said "Lynyrd Skynyrd." At the top he stuck another proclaiming, "Reality is for people who can't handle their dope."

The others started to see him as a hermit. That was fine with him. Not that he was completely antisocial. He got along with the others, even observed a schedule as regular as the old nine-to-five. On weekdays, he and the others were allowed out of their cells for meals and at night. On weekends, they were allowed out from lunch till 11 P.M. They watched TV, played cards and Scrabble, talked. Their trips outdoors for recreation were seasonal. From October 1 to May 15, they went outside for one hour daily, five days a week. From May 15 to October 1, rec was 6 to 8 P.M. on Tuesday, Thursday and Saturday. Most everyone played basketball. Stockton shot some hoops when the games weren't going, but he preferred to lift weights and jog. Yet his favorite activity was to go out during the summer and hold the water hose over his head. He'd pretend he was at the beach, or maybe up at Kibler Valley having a swim.

On Sundays they shopped, which meant filling out commissary orders. The prices were inflated, about a third or double the prices of The World, but that was normal for prison. Also normal was the way your account disappeared even when you didn't touch it. Graft was a part of prison life, a constant source of complaint and impossible to prove. Other than drug sales, one of the few ways to counter the graft was to get a job, but the only one available on Death Row was to sign up for cleanup detail. One man worked the eight-to-four shift, another the four to twelve. You signed up for a month, the pay 90 cents per day. Stockton added his name to the list, figuring his turn wouldn't come until February or March. By then his appeal should be decided. He hoped he'd be long gone and someone else would take his turn.

All predictable, even peaceful in a limited kind of way. Yet the violence always had a way of breaking through the veneer. Both sides, inmates and keepers, participated in the dance, unwilling partners. One afternoon in early November, he glimpsed how far it could go.

He lay in bed reading Louis L'Amour when he heard a disturbance and looked outside. Joe Giarratano, an inmate on the left side, was at the bars talking to Assistant Warden Harold Catron, the chief of prison security. Giarratano, stocky and wild-eyed, held a mop handle like a club. Catron held a tear gas gun. At Catron's side, a guard videotaped the confrontation. Several years earlier, the DOC ordered that guards videotape all incidents with inmates in which force might become necessary. When the ACLU filed its class-action suit against Mecklenburg, its lawyers used more than a dozen of these tapes to show that inmates were habitually beaten. Along with Frank Coppola, Giarratano was one of the original seven plaintiffs. The other prisoners called him "Joey G.," a beefy, soft-spoken man with long hair. On his right arm, he'd tattooed a Bowie knife with the inscription CONTRA MUNDUM, Latin for "Against the world."

In time, Giarratano would become one of Mecklenburg's most famous prisoners, supported by conservative columnist James Kilpatrick, interviewed by Caroline Kennedy, filmed by *First Tuesday,* the European equivalent of *60 Minutes.* He would publish several articles on constitutional law, be called one of the nation's best constitutional litigators, pen a landmark case guaranteeing legal representation to Death Row inmates throughout their appeals instead of only through the first round. He would be one of the few inmates granted conditional clemency by a Virginia governor, his execution changed to life imprisonment at the eleventh hour due to doubts about his guilt. But now, he was just beginning this metamorphosis. Right now, he was still the drug-dazed, suicidal misfit demanding death to escape the voices in his head.

By all accounts, Giarratano was jobless, homeless and constantly strung out when forty-four-year-old Barbara Kline and her daughter Michelle invited him to stay with them in their Norfolk beach apartment. At twenty-two, he already had a long history of mental problems and had tried to commit suicide at least six times. He was abused by his mother, started his drug use at age eleven, made his first suicide attempt at thirteen. He was almost always in a drug or alcoholic haze and soon had liver problems. He was sent to reform school, escaped, was recaptured and at sixteen sent to Florida's infamous Raiford Prison, where for the first time he met his natural father, a fellow prisoner.

All this is documented. What happened on the evening of February 4, 1979, remains a mystery. When police received a call from the Klines' landlord and entered their apartment, they found Barbara Kline on the bathroom floor in a pool of blood, her throat sliced and her chest a sieve from stab wounds. In another room, officers found the nude body of her daughter, strangled and sexually assaulted. Neighbors remembered that the Klines had taken Giarratano into their apartment: he had a terrible temper, they said, and hadn't been seen for the last two days. Norfolk police took out a warrant for his arrest.

At 4 A.M. the next morning, Giarratano walked into a Greyhound station in downtown Jacksonville, Florida, after an all-night bus ride. He approached a state trooper eating breakfast and said he had killed two people in Norfolk. He wanted to turn himself in.

So began the first of five statements in which Giarratano confessed to murdering the Klines. The details were different each time, yet in the one finally heard in court, Giarratano said he raped Michelle, then strangled her when she wouldn't stop screaming. Afraid that the mother would implicate him, he waited for her to come home from her clerk's job at a nearby 7-Eleven and stabbed her three times with a butcher knife as she walked through the door. He said he was high on cocaine and Dilaudid, a drug prescribed for cancer patients that is often called "the poor man's heroin." He rejected a plea agreement that would have resulted in life imprisonment and, over his attorney's objections, pled not guilty by reason of insanity. He said he looked forward to execution as a way to escape "George," the voice reminding him of the killings. In May 1979, a judge granted his wish and sent him to die.

Yet Giarratano had no independent memory of the murder. That day, after injecting the coke and Dilaudid, he'd gone to the Klines' to sleep off the high. When he awoke there was carnage around him, so he panicked and boarded a bus for Florida. During the long ride, he thought about what he'd seen. He decided that the only explanation was that he'd killed his two friends. He grew convinced he was evil and had to pay for his sins.

When Norfolk detectives arrived, Giarratano's confessions slowly began to fit the facts with each succeeding interrogation. When he was thrown in a Norfolk jail cell, he noticed blood spots on one of his shoes. He decided this was final proof of his guilt and tried to aid the executioner by attempting suicide twice before the trial.

Yet the investigation suffered from a serious fault, one endemic to modern police work when detectives get a confession that finally fits the facts and other murders demand their immediate attention. Forensic evidence that did not support Giarratano's confession was not followed through on. Someone else's driver's license was found in the apartment; in fact, police had secured an arrest warrant for another man but dropped it when Giarratano turned himself in. Several pubic hairs that didn't match Giarratano's were found near Michelle Kline's body but were never tested. Photos of the crime scene showed a trail of bloody bootprints leading from Barbara Kline's body, yet the boots did not match Giarratano's and a state expert who tested the shoes knew there were no traces of blood on his soles. Yet none of this evidence made it into trial.

Giarratano arrived on Death Row on August 17, 1979, and from the very start refused to pursue his appeals. One of the first inmates he met was Frank Coppola. The ex-policeman saw something in the kid and took him under his wing. He prodded him to fight back. When Giarratano sank into depressions, Coppola smacked him on the head and told him to never give up and never give in. He became the lost father, introducing Joey to his own wife and two boys. For once, someone cared whether Giarratano lived or died, even if it was another guy on The Row. It worked. On June 12, 1980, Giarratano was thirty-seven hours away from execution when he decided to pursue his appeals.

Two years later, Coppola chose the route he'd convinced Giarratano to abandon. But there was another side to this decision, one that few people knew. Frank told Joey G. he was already dying. His kidneys were a mess. He suffered continually from stones. Prison doctors wouldn't prescribe narcotics and he suffered excruciating pain. He was told that within a year he'd probably be hooked to a dialysis machine.

Death would be a relief, he told Joey G.

So Coppola was executed, and his death brought to Virginia another player in Giarratano's transformation. Marie Deans, project director for the Virginia Coalition on Jails and Prisons, had been asked by Amnesty International and the Southern Coalition on Jails and Prisons to investigate conditions in Mecklenburg. What she found appalled her, yet Deans was no stereotypical bleeding heart. In 1972, her mother-in-law had been murdered by an escaped convict. She knew all the convict games, could look a con in the face and tell him to stop the bullshit or she'd walk away and he could fry. She had founded on a shoestring budget the Virginia Coalition, devoted to helping condemned inmates with their appeals. Through this, she met Joey G.

By now, Giarratano was at a crossroads. With Coppola's passing, he again wanted to die. But he was also coming off drugs for the first time since age eleven. He quit taking his daily 900 milligrams of Thorazine to convince psychologists that he was competent to seek execution. With the sedative cloud lifted, Deans started getting through. Her own history as a murder survivor surprised him: he couldn't conceive of a person like her giving a damn about a murderer like him. She encouraged him to research capital punishment and gave him books to read during the long hours of isolation: Joseph Campbell's works on mythology; the philosophy of Søren Kierkegaard; the writings of Christian thinker Dietrich Bonhoeffer, the noted theologian and prisoner of conscience who died during the Nazi regime. Campbell's work on death struck closest to home. Giarratano later told a newspaper: "Death is there for all of us. We try to run from it. But when we start walking with it . . . when death becomes a reality, then you realize that you're responsible for every action you make in your life."

This was the new Joey G., whose transformation Stockton and the others discussed in the dayroom, fascinated by the change. Yet sometimes the old, wild-eyed Joey G. returned, like now. Stockton watched through the food slot for half an hour as Catron and Giarratano talked, Joe's voice rising and echoing through the pod while Catron's stayed a deeper, steady mumble. "Joe, calm down," Catron said again and again. Then something happened: the guy with the camera stepped back, Catron leveled the tear gas gun and fired a canister through the bars. Gas spurted in white trails from the canister. The sally port opened and six guards piled through dressed in full riot gear. Giarratano doubled over coughing, but lunged forward as they entered. They beat him with their clubs and he fell over screaming; the inmates pounded on their doors and screamed louder, their screams amplifying in the sealed prison warehouse, the din ricocheting from cell to cell. It really is a madhouse, Stockton thought as the guards tied Giarratano's hands and dragged him from Death Row and the air vents spread the gas throughout the building. Stockton wet a towel and covered his face. A guard opened the pod windows, but nothing helped. The gas was everywhere, burning throats, turning eyes to fire.

The incident merely solidified Catron's reputation among the prisoners as the most hated man at Mecklenburg. To them, he was the man in charge, the warden a mere figurehead. He was so hated that he rarely talked to inmates unless separated by fences or bars. The condemned blamed him for rules prohibiting personal fans in the sweltering heat and TV in the cells. He became the focus of all anger, the devil incarnate, the center of their seven levels of hell.

What they failed to take into account was that if anything went wrong, Catron's head landed on the plate. Since Mecklenburg was the state's showpiece, it was understood that nothing better go wrong. So far he'd succeeded: no escapes since the prison opened, no full-scale riots that seemed a normal part of life in other places, like The Wall in Richmond. Yet he always worried. Something was brewing in Mecklenburg besides fruit wine. He begged for more money for guards and security yet was turned down. He guessed that smuggling was rampant and worried that his guards were involved. Higher pay might curtail this, but the state wasn't interested. He could set up a bureau of in-house investigators, but that would be seen as a Gestapo move and lower morale even further. The whole setup was a catch-22. Whatever you did dug you in deeper.

And Giarratano? He was thrown into isolation. In the sameness of that small cell, he wrote his first legal brief, charging that guards still used excessive force in violation of the federal court order that settled the old ACLU suit. He showed it to Deans, and she talked him into expanding it into a lawsuit seeking better access to the legal system for condemned prisoners. A year later, he forced the state into a settlement giving Death Row inmates more legal rights. It would be the first of several attacks on Death Row conditions, arguments that finally reached the U.S. Supreme Court. He got inside The Law's logic, arguing that the condemned were entitled to court-appointed attorneys through all stages of their appeals under the First Amendment's guarantee of meaningful access to the courts. Countless high-priced attorneys had lost the same fight using the Sixth Amendment—right to counsel—as a weapon. When Giarratano came from another angle, the justices agreed with the con.

In a way few would realize until years later, the most hated man in Mecklenburg had done Giarratano the greatest favor of his life by locking him in solitude.

• • • •

"Umm umm, Roger, that sweet ass is *mine!*"

The violence could be psychological as well as physical, and maybe solitude was best. The place was a pit for everyone, the snares custom-made for each man's particular fears.

Today's victim was Roger Coleman, a baby-faced Buchanan County coal miner charged with raping and slitting the throat of his eighteen-year-old sister-in-law. For a guy like Roger—meek looking and easily intimidated—the place could be worse than hell, Stockton thought. It was like those TV nature shows where the wolf or hyena pack sensed weakness and attacked. Coleman had been harassed by other inmates, each wanting him for his punk, but none worse than Morris Mason. It was Mason who yelled now across the dayroom, his catcall followed by the weird laugh. It would give anyone chills. Coleman tried to ignore him, but they were all boxed together like rats in an experiment. Since he couldn't avoid him, the next best thing was to face him down.

Of all his fellow inmates, Stockton felt sorriest for Coleman, a quiet, bespectacled twenty-six-year-old. Coleman's main expression was one of bewilderment, as if he woke each morning amazed to find himself here. "You know that show *The Twilight Zone* where the characters wake and don't know what's happening?" he once confided to Stockton. "That's how I feel every day." Stockton felt he had the most in common with Coleman's situation. Both men were convicted in small towns of killing people close to them. Both maintained their innocence, in time producing evidence casting doubt upon their guilt. Both kept to themselves. The main difference was that Coleman didn't stand up for himself, the equivalent of suicide here. Stockton simply *looked* too mean to mess with: once when Mason made a crack, Dennis asked loudly if he wanted his face rearranged. That stopped that. But Coleman looked like a victim with his thick-lensed glasses and adolescent fuzz. Instead of fighting, or even giving in like LeVasseur, he tried to flee, walking to his cell, closing the door and calling for a guard. The next day, he was moved to the right side of C-Pod, separated from Mason by the bars.

Yet his escape was only temporary. With Coleman's transfer, Mason became obsessed with the idea that he'd never get "pussy" before he died. That was all he talked about, a white piece of ass. "Shut up, man!" Turner finally snapped. "You think you're any different than the rest of us? Go buy yourself some, damn!" So he did just that, promising to pay JB $100 if he let him screw his punk. JB agreed. Mason couldn't get enough, Bunch later said. The man was an animal.

But then Mason reneged on his deal. He refused to pay JB. "Watch your back, you little fuck," JB said that night during the poker game and everyone knew what he meant, even the guards. Stockton figured the guards also knew about the sex between Bunch and Mason and looked the other way, though in here one could never be sure. Mason was put on lockup for three days, then moved to the other side. Turner watched quietly as his only disciple was led away.

The first thing Mason did was walk up to Roger Coleman and slap him on the back. "Hi, Roger," he said. "Just like old times."

The look on Coleman's face was heartbreaking, as if there was no escape from his demons. The others laughed, but Stockton had to look away.

November turned to December, and now it was nearly Christmas.

Stockton talked to his mom by phone. The tree was up, most of the presents bought. They planned to make turkey this year. "That was one of your favorites, Dennis," she said, then started to cry.

Christmas cards arrived. Out of one dropped a *Mount Airy News* clipping dated early November. Sheriff Jesse Williams had lost his re-election bid to Jay Gregory. Tony Giorno, the assistant prosecutor who'd gotten Stockton's conviction, was also elected the common-wealth's attorney. Both men admitted his death sentence helped them win.

There goes the investigation into my innocence, he thought. Merry Christmas.

But life went on. Linwood and JB ran off gallons of mash for a tra-ditional Christmas party. Reefer reappeared. Stockton won Pepsis off a guard three times with the same card trick. The guard laughed and paid up, dumb but decent, filled with Christmas cheer.

Christmas Eve. The Salvation Army passed out Christmas gifts: a bag with a comb and a toothbrush, shampoo, soap and lotion, as well as hard candy, an apple, an orange. Stockton gave a Pepsi to his neighbors. JB gave him two joints, Linwood gave him one, Bunch gave him one, Clanton gave him a candy bar. He called his brother and learned no one would visit from home. He smoked a joint and listened as "Free Bird" played twice on the radio.

Then it was Christmas. The doors were unlocked for breakfast but he didn't come out. He stayed inside and smoked reefer, working on motions in his civil suit. Fuck them all, he thought. You were alone on this earth. No one could save you . . . no fairy tales of Jesus, no fairy tales spun by detectives or politicians or lawyers. You had to save yourself.

Outside everyone fell down stoned and dead drunk, singing Christ-mas carols as they slumped to the floor. The guards turned their heads: a happy bunch, no trouble. A squad of inmates came to Stock-ton's door and started pounding. "C'mon, Dennis, join the party!"

"Leave me be, I'm busy!"

"C'mon, Dennis, it's Christmas!"

He threw down his pencil, wanting like hell to be angry but unable to keep from laughing. What a fucked-up bunch of cons. He wished he had a movie camera to show them later what a bunch of drunken bums they were. He walked outside, laughing. "Hell, it *is* Christ-mas," he said.

Late that night he turned on his radio, but flipped it off with all the Christmas music playing. The carols made him sad. It was quiet now, even in the other buildings. Tomorrow he'd have an awful hangover and would probably sleep till lunch. He wrote:

> With all the doings on Death Row, one would think the men here didn't have time to stop and think or reflect on the reality of their situation. But that is simply not true. Reflection, or any other way of facing reality, is the one thing condemned men hate doing. Still, regardless of how one tries to stay occupied, there are many hours alone in a cell with thoughts of the inevitable specter facing you. Perhaps that is why some are so anxious to see the guards as they enter to let us out for meals and other out-of-cell activities. Perhaps that is why, if one awakens in the early morning hours, he can hear sounds that he hears at no other time. An anguished sob that leaves one wondering just which cell it came from. A nightmarish cry. The sound of someone praying. Or, on other nights, the intense quiet—a rare occurrence—that is so welcome it is viewed as a blessing.
>
> Finally, other times one can hear loud snores of someone in contented sleep and looking out learns that, no, it's not coming from one of his neighbors' cells. Instead, it's the third-shift guard, sitting in the pod, with his head and arms resting on the table.

He put away his pencil, restacked the pages of his diary, swiveled his seat back under the table. He lit one of his Christmas reefers and lay on the bed. He hoped that 1984 would be no worse than 1983. It didn't look promising. Several executions were already scheduled. The death chamber was no longer a vague possibility, an intellectual game argued in the courts. It was real for them all.

What kind of Christmas prayers do you make on Death Row? he wondered. If you make them, do they even get heard?

He doubted it, but just the same prayed they were still alive by Christmas of next year.

5

Two weeks into the New Year, Stockton was moved to The Wall in Richmond while his lawyers argued his appeal before the state supreme court. Although it was his life, he wasn't allowed to attend. They treated him like a spectator. The rage caused a flare-up in his kidneys that sent him straight to the hospital, and he didn't return to Mecklenburg until month's end.

Right away he sensed a change. There was a feeling of excitement, anticipation, overriding The Row's deadening routine. The first hint came from Tim Bunch. The day after he returned, Bunch handed him a joint. "Welcome back," he said and added, "You wanna get it on?"

Stockton blinked, stunned with surprise. It was the first time Bunch ever propositioned him—a sudden shift in reality, as if a life-long neighbor asked for a quickie. "Leave me alone, Tim," he said. "You know I ain't interested in that shit." Bunch smiled again and walked on.

Stockton shook his head. If anyone else had made that kind of move on him, he probably would have punched him out. With Bunch, however, he was simply amazed. He didn't think the kid had the balls. He didn't belong here so much as in "Punk City," another part of prison where admitted homosexuals were held in protective custody. The guards said they dressed the part, very feminine, shirts tied at the midriff, tight jeans. It was like the old cowboy movies where the painted ladies lounged on the whorehouse balcony. *Come up and see me sometime!*

Excepting the Reaper, sex was *the* sore point on Death Row. There were the punks like Bunch and LeVasseur, and sexual predators like Mason. For many, rape and sexual assault were inextricably tied to their crimes: Bunch, Mason, Coleman, Giarratano and the Brileys, to name a few. Nude centerfolds from *Playboy* and *Gallery* adorned cell walls throughout the pod. Sex couldn't be ignored, yet it made them all uneasy. Notwithstanding the rape of LeVasseur, homosexual encounters on The Row were usually voluntary. The threat of rape existed, but more commonly the men drifted toward memory and abstinence over the years.

This was why Bunch's come-on took him by surprise, but no more than what happened next. Three days later, Linwood and Stockton spent the afternoon smoking reefer and painting their cells. Linwood had taken down the snapshots of his "Death Row groupies," as the women were called who wrote and sometimes fell for the condemned. Now he picked from the top of the pile a Polaroid of a dark-haired white girl, pretty smile on her face, naked as the day she was born. "I'll give you five joints to type a letter to this chick," he said. Linwood picked up more photos and handed them over: the girl-next-door in every pornographic pose. Linwood had been writing her and she apparently thought he was white; he showed Stockton some of her letters and all she talked about was sex, in every position, in all kinds of places, what heaven awaited once he was free. They laughed. "She'll be waiting a long time for salvation, won't she?" Stockton said.

Groupies were one of Death Row's great mysteries. This woman apparently knew little about Linwood, yet she knew he was a killer and acted like all she dreamed about was getting him in her arms. Many of the other women who wrote him were well aware of his crimes—including the rapes. It was as though his deadliness was part of the attraction, as if they wanted some of his power over life and death. How would they feel, he wondered, if Linwood escaped and appeared on their doorstep demanding action instead of words?

Murder groupies had been around since there were prisons, but psychologists paid more attention to the killers than to the women who loved them. They came from all economic classes and all ages, though most were in their thirties or forties. They usually made contact through personal ads, pen-pal clubs or letter-writing campaigns organized by prisoner advocacy groups. Letters streamed in to all kinds of lawbreakers, but it is the murderer—the most dangerous correspondent with the least chance of release—whose letters filled the mailbags. The more notorious the killer, the more letters that arrive. The mystery of the murder groupie became a public phenomenon during the trial of handsome serial killer Ted Bundy. The first row behind the defense table was reserved for "Ted groupies," pretty young women "who blushed and giggled with delight when [Bundy] turned to flash a blinding smile at them," wrote Ann Rule in *The Stranger Beside Me*. The Ted groupies knew their hero was accused of killing women just like them, yet that was evidently part of the attraction. There is a term for this excitement: *hybristophilia,* from the Greek root *hybridzein,* meaning to commit an outrage against someone. Coined by sexual researcher John Money, professor emeritus of medical psychology and pediatrics at the Johns Hopkins University Medical School, in his 1986 book *Lovemaps,* the term describes a state in which sexual arousal and even orgasm depend on being with someone known to have committed a violent crime. Others prefer a German term, more direct and chilling: *Liebestod.* The love of death.

Yet falling for a killer went far beyond the simple turn-on, said Sheila Isenberg, author of *Women Who Love Men Who Kill,* one of the few studies ever conducted. When Isenberg interviewed such women, she found they came from all professions—teachers, journalists, lawyers, prison officials, as well as welfare moms and biker chicks. Yet almost all came from loveless or abusive backgrounds. The women were drawn to the enormous amount of attention the prisoner gave them, the frequent letters and long collect calls. They became the inmate's lifeline to the outside. Suddenly, perhaps for the first time in their lives, they also controlled a relationship. The absence of sex could be a plus since many had been abused sexually. Isenberg tried to prove that the forced chastity added to the romantic purity, just as voluntary chastity theoretically glorified the medieval ideal of courtly love. Yet Linwood's many photos suggested that this was not always true. Instead, sex seemed another form of control, a vow of intimacy once the killer got free. In exchange, the inmate promised to be a one-groupie man.

On Death Row, the odds for freedom were very, very slim. Still, there were advantages for both parties. The woman received unparalleled attention and had a relationship she completely controlled. The man gained an advocate, someone fighting for retrial or release who believed unconditionally in his innocence. In at least one case, the woman even helped her adored killer escape. Tennessee attorney Mary Pentacost Evans fell in love with her client, convicted murderer William Timothy Kirk, and in March 1983 helped him escape during a trip from prison to a psychologist's office. She slipped a gun to Kirk and he disarmed the three guards serving as his escort; Evans and Kirk then ran to her car and drove away. They were on the lam for four months before finally being captured in a motel in Daytona Beach, Florida.

Evans was ruined—disbarred, convicted and sent to prison for two years. Her defense for kidnapping, robbery and escape was temporary insanity. If passion is like madness, she didn't lie.

Sometimes the help was even more bizarre. Veronica Lynn "Ver-Lynn" Compton, a successful and attractive West Coast model, fell in love with "Hillside Strangler" Kenneth Bianchi. She wrote letters, he responded, and soon they saw each other daily in the L.A. jail. When he returned to Bellingham, Washington, to stand trial for the murder of two coeds, VerLynn followed. "I want to help you," she told Bianchi. He answered that if she truly wanted to help, she should go out and kill someone in the Strangler style. After the body was discovered, he could tell detectives that he obviously wasn't the killer since the murders were still going on.

Instead of running the other way, VerLynn agreed. She would strangle a woman and mutilate the body; one problem, however, was that victims were always found anointed with semen after they were tortured and killed. Always resourceful, VerLynn visited a sperm bank and got some semen, then took a room in the Best Western of Bellingham. One night, she chatted with a woman who sat alone at the motel bar. VerLynn asked if she wanted to come back to her room for a drink, and the intended victim, a tall redhead, agreed. Once inside, VerLynn leapt on the woman and tried to strangle her, but the woman fought her off, escaped and called police from a nearby pay phone. VerLynn fled back to California, but detectives guessed her identity from the redhead's description and what they knew from her frequent jailhouse visits. She was arrested, convicted of attempted murder and sentenced to serve a life term in Bellingham.

Yet even then, the story didn't end. In the late 1980s, VerLynn escaped briefly with another woman; there was speculation that she heard through the prison grapevine that Bianchi was about to marry another groupie and escaped in an attempt to contact her old flame. She was recaptured and Bianchi married the other woman. Soon afterward, VerLynn fell in love with another serial killer, "Sunset Slayer" Douglas Clark, convicted of killing and decapitating prostitutes around L.A. He took home the head of one victim for oral sex while his live-in lover, a registered nurse, painted the face with makeup. In a letter to Clark, VerLynn wondered: "Our humor is unusual. I wonder why others don't see the necrophilic aspects of existence as we do."

Death Row romances more commonly ended in marriage than attempted murder. Stockton was aware of one such marriage in the works at Mecklenburg. For months, Alton Waye had petitioned prison authorities to let him marry his girlfriend. At six feet and 225 pounds, the twenty-eight-year-old Waye was one of The Row's biggest men. Yet instead of appearing threatening, he mooned around like a schoolboy in the throes of first love. He spent hours at the dayroom tables, smiling to himself and writing long letters to his love. He professed to be a Christian, the only condemned man then to do so, but like JB he shorted the pot in the poker games. Stockton liked Waye, but wondered if he was retarded. He was so slow, so easily led.

Waye's fiancée thought he was innocent, but the killing was one of Death Row's worst. On the night of October 14, 1977, he downed six pitchers of beer and some moonshine, then stopped his car outside the house of LaVergne Marshall at the end of an isolated country road in Lunenburg County. He asked to use the phone, and the sixty-one-year-old widow, dressed in her nightgown, escorted him upstairs to her bedroom. Suddenly Waye turned and raped her with such violence that he left bite marks on her buttocks and breasts. He beat her face beyond recognition, then grabbed a butcher knife and stabbed her forty-two times. Next he dragged the body to a bathtub, submerged it in water and doused it in bleach. Before leaving, he ransacked the house to make it look as if the murder occurred during a burglary. When Waye got home, he told his father what he had done. "Alton acted as if he were floating in a dream," his father said. Waye called deputies and later told them: "I did it just like they do on television. I wiped the knife and everything. Man, wait until my friends hear about this."

The rural jury took ten minutes to convict Waye, who was black, of raping and killing Marshall, who was white. They took another twenty-five minutes to sentence him to die. But all the evidence didn't make it into the trial. Waye was, in fact, borderline retarded and had brain damage. Prosecutors said that hairs found at the scene were Waye's, but lab tests actually showed nothing more than that they came from a black person. That raised the question of the part played by Waye's cousin, who allegedly sat outside in the car during the murder and was the state's main witness. Years later, the cousin would be jailed in Michigan for the similar rape of a white woman. He was also a suspect in several other rapes. After an interview with the cousin, a prosecutor–turned–defense attorney said in a sworn statement that he believed the cousin was present at Marshall's killing, not sitting out in the car as he said on the witness stand. He could have been the real killer, the lawyer said.

Married or not, the Death Row groupies were prisoners of a roller-coaster passion composed of pain and longing punctuated by brief, bittersweet reunions. It was a prison of their own making: a voluntary incarceration, a triumph of the imagination as they fed the imaginations of their men. Yet here a strange frisson occurred, for many of their men were guilty of sex crimes, the ritual mutilation of the female body, often accompanied by orgasm. This too was an act of imagination, of a darker kind. The sex crime, in all its ritual and pattern, was an expression of frenzy written not in ink, but blood. Although the Brileys' murders were accompanied by rape, the brothers were considered sociopathic career criminals who killed to protect their identities. Rape, like money, was one of the spoils. But Mason, Bunch and Waye were sex criminals—if not in a Bundyesque victim count, at least in style.

Death Row had entered the age of the sex crime. FBI statistics showed that in the twenty years preceding these men's convictions, serial murders increased over 600 percent, from 644 in 1966 to 4,118 in 1982, and many of these murders had a violent sexual component. Nearly one hundred years after Jack the Ripper announced what British author Colin Wilson called a "watershed between the century of Victorian values and the age of violence that was to come," the Death Row groupies danced on the edge with their murderous lovers, spared only by the walls they wanted to tear down.

Robert Ressler, the former FBI profiler who coined the term serial killer, explained the huge increase in terms of opportunity and killing style. The FBI divides such killers along two broad lines. "Organized" killers, who stalk their victims, are methodical in how they trap and kill them and are careful not to leave clues. "Disorganized" killers, people with full-blown mental illnesses, do not show the same control. Ressler estimated that two-thirds of modern serial killers were organized and felt the number was growing. "My guess is that there has always been a certain unchanging fraction of disorganized killers in society, from the earliest days until the present—men who are quite deranged and who now and again go on killing sprees that stop only when they are caught or killed," he wrote. He felt the number and percentage of organized killers was increasing, just as statistics indicated, and added: "As our society grows more mobile, and as the availability of weapons of mass destruction increases, the ability of the antisocial personality to realize his rapacious and murderous fantasies grows apace."

For those inmates beginning to see themselves as political prisoners either because of their professed innocence or because their poverty made them unable to afford the kind of defense that later saved O. J. Simpson, the age of the sex crime was bad news. If nothing else, they appeared guilty by association, making their own appeals less likely to find sympathetic ears. They were right. This was the age of Charles Manson, John Wayne Gacy, Jeffrey Dahmer, the Hillside Strangler, the Zodiac Killer, the Green River Killer, the Night Stalker. Even as authorities learned more about these killers, there was growing evidence that their actual numbers were overblown by police and the media. The condemned men at Mecklenburg, as well as in the nation's other death rows, found themselves in the middle of what Philip Jenkins of Pennsylvania State University called "the serial killer panic of 1983 to 1985." Jenkins's article in the *Criminal Justice Research Bulletin* (1988) cited many magazine and newspaper stories which pointed out that there were more unsolved murders in the United States than ever before and many of these were erroneously blamed on serial killers. Ressler, the FBI profiler, agreed with Jenkins, believing that at the same time that police learned more about serial crimes, there was a tendency to attribute unsolved murders to mobile killers. The Henry Lee Lucas fiasco was the best-known example. Lucas told police that he'd killed (and sometimes ate) hundreds of victims across the nation, either alone or with fellow drifter Ottis Toole. He was interrogated by scores of detectives, and during the interrogation would be given details of the unsolved crime. Using such sloppy techniques, police from thirty-five states cleaned the slate on 210 unsolved murders, often with no more evidence than Lucas's questionable confessions. The sham finally became obvious when Lucas confessed to killing the followers of Reverend Jim Jones, who died more than five years earlier in the Jonestown murder-suicides. When an FBI agent asked how he got to Guyana to commit the murders, Lucas said he drove. Eventually, Lucas admitted committing five to ten killings. "He had told all those lies in order to have fun, and to show up what he termed the stupidity of the police," Ressler said.

Still, from the viewpoint of Stockton and others on The Row who paid heed to public sentiment, the damage seemed done. They began to sense less tolerance for Death Row appeals. They began to hear the argument that it was better to kill the occasional innocent than let the guilty go free. One even heard Death Row inmates begin to state they believed in the death penalty "for some of those guys in here." The pace of executions jumped from five across the nation in 1983 to over twenty in 1984, and those numbers would never drop to 1983 levels again.

So, uneasy as he was about the subject, Stockton composed a letter to Linwood's groupie, a condemned Cyrano de Bergerac rhapsodizing on love, sex, drugs, the mountains, Lynyrd Skynyrd and Harley choppers, all to his unseen Roxane. Linwood signed the letter but was so impressed that he mentioned Stockton in a letter he wrote on his own. Soon the dark-haired groupie started writing Stockton, and true to form she emphasized sex. He began to think of her as the "sex freak," and tore up her mail. There was a lot of anger in this: it was hard enough being here without such vivid reminders of what you missed. After a couple of months he sent her pictures back and wrote that he wasn't what she sought. She never wrote again.

The letters also made him deeply uneasy in a way he didn't understand. His writing normally avoided sex, as if doing otherwise would link him with those for whom the act of love was also the act of death. An old girlfriend still wrote, but he faithfully protected her identity, destroying all letters except some chaste pink Valentine cards. He first spied her through a screen door, asleep on a sofa on a hot summer day. His description was a schoolboy idyll, woman-as-unattainable goddess.

I couldn't take my eyes off this girl. She had long hair the color of straw that has been stacked out under the sun to cure. . . . She had a beautifully chiseled face and her bra held a pair of pear-shaped breasts. She had a slender waist and long beautiful legs. Even her dainty feet were beautiful.

There was one other exception to this silence: his description of his first sexual encounter. Once again, he watched something from which he was separate, but this time by age and understanding. He was a little boy, still in grade school. "There was a girl some years older than me who lived" nearby, he wrote:

By going through our back yard you could arrive at hers. Whenever Mom could afford it she would buy me a comic book and after looking at it till I got tired, I'd do as the older kids and trade. One day I went to this girl's house to see if she wanted to trade. This was in the summertime. Her house had a screened-in back porch and someone had put up a hammock to lay in. She had a bunch of bananas and a jar of peanut butter. She took off her shorts and while I talked trade she laid down naked on the hammock. She appeared to be listening, but she did something I thought unusual. She would peel a banana, shove it into what I heard called her pussy, then pull it out and spread some peanut butter on the end. She'd eat that, then repeat the process. I had never seen this done before, so I watched while she went through several bananas. Finally she traded me a book and I went back home. Something told me it was dirty, so I didn't tell what had happened.

A few years later, the girl was sent away. "Something was wrong with her," he was told. "But when I asked what, no one would say." It was his first taste of what happens to those who aren't "good."

• • • •

By mid-February, Stockton strongly sensed that something was up. There was an air of anticipation. Of preparation. One day, he was jogging around the rec field when JB flagged him down. "Hold this while I shoot some hoops," he said, stuffing a roll of bills and some reefer in Stockton's hands. Ever since the shakedown, JB left nothing of value inside his cell. It was okay if another inmate got busted in his place, but not him. The roll was a fat one, drug money, and Stockton glimpsed a number of $50s and $100s. There must be $2,500 or $3,000 in that roll, he figured. Why did JB need all that cash?

Each day brought a fresh trampling of the rules. On February 2, his turn came for cleanup detail. He was making his rounds when JB called him to his door. Briley lifted the food slot and whispered: "Pick up a package for me. Down at the door to B-Pod." Just like he said, someone slid a manila envelope under the door in the new wall, the one built to kill this trade. Stockton squeezed the package between his fingers and felt the dry reefer crunch inside.

It was like JB was charmed. He could get away with anything. More proof came the next day when Bunch was caught in JB's cell. One of JB's guards came to the door and from the way the man reacted, JB and Bunch must have been having sex. Yet instead of alerting officials, the guard froze. Suddenly Clanton started yelling that he needed the laundry room unlocked so he could wash some clothes. The distraction was well timed. The guard walked off, mumbling. Bunch got out. Nothing more was said.

The next morning, Stockton rose early and smoked a joint. What was going on? One or two days of this might be coincidence, but not several in a row. There was a wired anticipation about the place, yet the guards didn't notice or didn't want to. Once their compromise grew too great, they were part of the problem. Like those packages, which came most every day—there was no way the guards couldn't notice. Their contents also changed: sometimes the envelope contained reefer, other times cash or a "shank," prison slang for a homemade knife. Sometimes the door between B-Pod and C-Pod was even left open, contrary to all regulations. The signs were so thick: the small groups of inmates in earnest conversation, with Linwood or JB doing the talking. The silences till he passed. The guard from another building who ran a package straight to JB's cell.

Finally, he couldn't take it any longer. Linwood sat alone at one of the tables, playing solitaire. Stockton plopped next to him, tapping a red-black combination he'd missed. "It's my damn game," Linwood said, waving him away.

"What's going on?"

"Not much. What's going on with you?"

"No, Linwood, I mean *what's going on?*"

Linwood snapped a card off the pile. "You think something's up?"

"I ain't stupid."

"Then why you here in this place?" he shot back, grinning. It was an old joke, a Death Row *gotcha.* Then he added, "Don't worry, I was getting to you."

He waited until the next morning to deliver. Stockton was working in his cell on his civil suit when he heard a tap. Linwood laid a joint in the food slot and asked, "We been making a plan while you were gone. You still want to leave?"

"You know it," Stockton blurted, his quick response surprising him. But he was so disgusted by the way the state supreme court had treated him that he might as well hedge his bets.

"Okay, we're thinking about taking over the building and walking out in guards' uniforms." Linwood looked proud.

That was the plan? Stockton nearly laughed, but knew better. Instead he said: "That's okay, but what you gonna do once you get out, if you do? That's when your problems begin." He told Linwood about the times he'd escaped, just to get picked up again. "If a bunch of us leave, they'll have the National Guard, state police and North Carolina troopers after us, close as we are to the border. Then there's helicopters, don't forget them. You gotta get far away from the prison."

"We thought of that," Linwood said. "What we're going to do is, once we get control of the building, we'll call that there's an explosive over here, for them to bring a van to the gates. We'll all be dressed in uniforms by then, riot helmets." They were putting together a list of all phone extensions and their locations, plus another of two-way-radio call numbers and codes. They already knew that 10-33 meant "disturbance in progress." If they heard that, they'd know their cover was blown. "If everything works out, we'll carry the 'bomb' on a stretcher to the gate, hold it open and drive away."

"What about the chains?"

"What chains?"

"The ones on the gates." They had to be unlocked before anyone could drive outside, Stockton said. During the wait, anyone in the sally port's gun tower might spot the ruse, though the last several times he'd gone out that tower hadn't been manned. There was also a shift commander's office nearby, though he didn't know where. This stuff couldn't be left to chance. These were the small details that could ruin everything.

"We're still planning, Dennis," Linwood said, smiling as if Stockton had reacted just as he'd predicted. "I just wanted to see what you thought."

"If we get the sally port open and a van to ride in, I think it'll work," he said.

Stockton was in, but not everyone was so quick to accept him. Later that day, JB slipped up to him and asked about the chains. "I never heard of them," he said.

Stockton repeated what he told Linwood. But JB just narrowed his eyes and studied his face. "I'll ask around," he said. Stockton suddenly realized the younger brother was possibly jealous of the trust Linwood showed in him. That might explain the way he ordered him around—if Stockton lost his cool and fired back, JB could use it as a wedge. *This is grade-school stuff, no better than Clanton's jealousies.* He'd laugh if the stakes weren't so high.

Later that day, another man confirmed the chains. JB grunted, but said nothing more.

It soon became clear that the Brileys were directing this play. Linwood said they needed a meeting to get organized. Until that happened, he and JB handed out informal assignments and approached other inmates. All were relieved that Morris Mason had moved to the other side of C-Pod: the guy couldn't keep his mouth shut and was too unhinged to be trusted. They began to look for things that could be turned into weapons and gathered as much information as possible. Their roles evolved according to ability. The guards liked the Brileys and Derick Peterson best, so these three chatted them up for phone extensions and radio codes. It wasn't hard: every guard had a radio hooked to his belt, and the static and chatter was part of the pod's background noise. They'd hear a code and innocently ask, "What's that mean?" The guards usually said.

Clanton did the same, but by intimidation. The guards were scared of his size and temper—one in particular, a white guy who seemed terrified of all the black killers. It was pathetic to watch. Clanton would stand in front of the guard, towering over him, and ask where another guard was posted. Then he stared. "He's working the tower," the guard finally said.

"The tower? They switch you guys to the tower?"

"It's rotation," he answered, shifting his weight nervously.

"How would you get in touch with him if you wanted?" Clanton asked, still staring.

"By phone. Or radio."

"What's the extension?" Clanton said, moving in even closer, crowding the man. The guard's eyes grew wide; his hand edged hesitantly to his radio. But Clanton just smiled. Stockton could see the guard's mind working. If he backed down and called for help, Clanton would just say he was making small talk. Sure, Clanton might be locked down for appearances, but it was the guard who would lose respect. The macho code was just as tough on guards as on inmates, maybe worse. It was a continual game of chicken, the winner always the last to back down.

The guard gave Clanton what he wanted. Clanton gave him room to breathe.

Stockton was impressed. As a convict, he celebrated any victory over the keepers. But he'd found this guard fairly likable. He felt a little sorry for him too.

Still, an inmate didn't have to come off as threatening to make the guards talk. It was surprising what they gave away, as if they were so sure of Mecklenburg's impregnability that any questions were beneath notice. It was another reality shift: Stockton had assumed the jailers had developed finely tuned early warning systems. Instead, they were so complacent that it never dawned on them that there were reasons for the questions. He tried it himself. During one of his kidney checkups, Stockton was escorted by two guards and a sergeant. As they drove through the sally port, he asked about the shift commander's office. The sergeant pointed it out: just to the right after entering the gates. Stockton passed the info on to Linwood, who got the shift commander's extension that night.

Meanwhile, he put his trips to Danville, South Hill and Richmond to good use. He drew a crude map, filled in Mecklenburg and the mileage from the prison to the other roads and the distance from each point to North Carolina. He gave the map to JB, who hid it where the guards wouldn't dare look for fear of legal hassles—among his court papers and mail.

On February 7, a new man arrived: Wilbert Lee Evans. This was a homecoming for Evans, also called Ed and "Slobber Jaws." His sentence had been overturned two months before Stockton's arrival when a federal judge learned prosecutors had used evidence in his trial improperly, but a new sentencing jury sent him right back to Death Row. He was thirty-eight, the second-oldest inmate after

Stockton, and big, standing six feet three inches and weighing 240. He loved to talk and seemed friendly, flattering Stockton by saying his cell was the cleanest he'd ever seen.

That friendliness seemed at odds with his crimes. Evans had been in and out of jail for nineteen years before fatally shooting Alexandria Deputy Sheriff William G. Truesdale during an escape attempt on January 27, 1981. Truesdale was returning Evans and two other prisoners to jail after a day in the courthouse; Evans was shackled to another man when he grabbed Truesdale's gun, shot him in the chest and blasted open the handcuffs. He ran as far as a nearby parking lot before being surrounded by police. He shot himself, but the wound was slight and he was taken back into custody. Evans, who was black, claimed he didn't mean to shoot Truesdale, who was white—he had grabbed the gun to blast open the cuffs and it went off as the two struggled. But a cellmate testified that Evans had planned the escape, lying awake the night before "like he was getting ready to go to war." The jury sent the cop killer to Death Row.

The Brileys immediately told Evans of the plan. Afterward, that was all he talked about. He lived for the breakout and was always recalling his escape from Truesdale. Stockton made the mistake of telling him about his guns back home, and soon regretted it. "You can get someone to drop 'em in the weeds along the road to prison," Evans badgered. "I seen 'em when they drove me in. They're high— no one could see 'em from the road."

Stockton patiently explained that the guns had been seized after his arrest and sent to the state police ballistics lab. A judge ruled their seizure illegal and the guns were returned. But he knew they'd been cataloged. "If they were found in the weeds, right away the heat would be on my family or friends," Stockton said.

But it did little good to explain. "We gotta get *firepower!*" Evans cried. His eyes got all spooky. *Firepower!* He couldn't leave it alone, like a dog worrying a bone.

Evans became Stockton's shadow. He couldn't even escape during his weekly trips to the law library located in the basement of Building Three, a three- or four-minute walk from Death Row. The two were the only ones to regularly make the trip—they were led across the oval in chains and locked in small cells equipped with a desk, chair and typewriter. Stockton would hole up with law books, struggling to understand the secrets in the leather-bound tomes. When he grew tired or discouraged, he looked up the cases of his neighbors in the abstracts of the Virginia supreme court. They made chilling reading, but he figured his would too if the record was the only thing one read. At times, he even found reasons for hope. On January 13, a North Carolina man facing imminent execution was granted a stay, but this proved temporary and he was fried. Of greater promise were cases like that of Lawyer Johnson, sentenced to death in 1971 but released eleven years later when a previously silent witness came forward and named the state's chief witness as the real killer. Still, Stockton thought, justice found Johnson way up north in Massachusetts. That might as well be part of another galaxy.

Evans always chose a cubicle near the back of the library, far from Stockton. He was regularly visited by two women who worked next door in the regular library. They flirted, keeping up a low mumble in the otherwise quiet room. Rumors of quick, groping sex between inmates and female employees ran rife in this place; most were bullshit, but hope sprang eternal. Evans never bragged of any conquests, and if he had scored, Stockton figured the news would be all over the pod. Instead, Stockton soon learned that Evans had a different goal. After one visit, Evans plucked a $100 bill from an envelope and showed it to Stockton. "Travelin' money," he said.

Now it was late February. The plotters had obtained two metal files, a major step in making weapons. When inmate workers visited the pod for repairs, the condemned men talked them out of metal strips for making shanks. They cut extra strips from the metal housing around cell doors. An arms race started: everyone wanted a shank but felt uneasy knowing others had them too. To Stockton, it was food for thought about what could happen on Breakout Day.

• • • •

The first meeting was held on March 5. Ten were in on the plot: Stockton, Linwood, JB, Clanton, Waye, Turner, Peterson, Bunch and Evans, as well as Giarratano on the pod's other side. Joey G. wasn't at the meeting, but was kept abreast through a vent near the downstairs showers where messages were passed between sections. The meeting was held in the dayroom; they shoved two tables together, pulled up chairs and piled law books so it looked like they were discussing their appeals. We're a regular board of directors, Stockton thought; all we need are suits and ties. He felt sure they'd be discovered—a guard sat thirty feet away, watching TV. But the sound was turned up and his eyes never strayed toward them. The only time he looked up was when someone needed into the laundry room, locked now after LeVasseur's rape. The guard in the control booth watched, but just out of boredom. Stockton remembered the old saying about hiding in plain sight. How true.

"This meeting is to sketch out the plan and get everyone talking," Linwood began. He sat at one end and immediately took charge. JB sat to his right. He went over basics just like he had with Stockton, walking through some of the plots already discarded. The first had been to go through the administration building, but that would be one of the most heavily guarded points and to get there they'd have to cross the oval. A bomb hoax seemed most promising: none of them could remember a bomb threat as long as they'd been there and the guards never practiced their drills. They wouldn't know how to respond. From here on out, they'd all have to be model prisoners: security was already lax, and this would further lull their keepers. JB scribbled something on a yellow legal pad as his brother talked. It was like they were two halves of the same mind. After a while, JB passed around the pad. It was an assignment sheet, just to make sure everyone agreed:

Outline of Plan

1. *JB*—Help take hostages, monitor phone calls. Give instructions (has all phone numbers for different locations). Extension in pod area.
2. *Linwood*—Help take hostages, roam and do as needed.
3. *Goldie*—Hide out in bathroom and take control booth when door is open. Open pod doors, help take and control hostages.
4. *Dennis*—Keep lookout at windows downstairs, see that hostages don't get loose, drive getaway vehicle.
5. *Waye*—Help take hostages, roam and do as needed.
6. *Turner*—Make weapons and stash, help Joe secure those on left side.
7. *Joe*—Secure left side, take over control, answer telephone.
8. *Peterson*—Help with hostages, dress in uniform and take downstairs control.
9. *Bunch*—As needed.
10. *Evans*—Help with hostages, make sure all are securely locked up. Get all keys and keep separated to avoid confusion.

The plan looked flexible. Stockton thought his part was easy. He was to stand post at a downstairs window overlooking the yard. He'd have a radio and a list of codes, so his job was to spot whether their bluff was discovered. Until then, he was to continue gathering information during his trips, as well as figure out an escape route that got them as far as possible from Mecklenburg in the least amount of time. Finally, he was tapped as driver. With all the dangers they faced, the conspirators were most scared of dying in a wreck. Linwood had apparently repeated some of Dennis's tales of driving moonshine. He was astonished to learn that, with the exception of Linwood, none of the others had ever gotten driver's licenses and it had been so long since Linwood drove that the others felt safer with Stockton behind the wheel. Linwood would be backup if Stockton were unable to drive . . . if, say, he got shot. "Let's not put *that* in the plan," Stockton said.

It all boiled down to nothing more than a bluff backed by initial force. The odds were long against going undiscovered, meaning some of them would probably get killed. But death was on the horizon anyway, so what the hell? Of all of them, Clanton drew the most dangerous assignment. In fact, the whole plan revolved around him. He was supposed to hide in the guards' bathroom, then spring out once the duty officer was lured from the booth and open the pod doors. He was on his own from the moment he went into hiding until he took out the guard.

JB said he'd copy the assignment sheet for everyone, then the meeting broke up. As they walked off, two of the plotters told Stockton not to drive too fast. They didn't want to risk everything just to get killed in a wreck. Stockton remembered an incident from his early days when someone *had* been scared enough to try switching off the ignition, nearly causing Stockton to crash. He caught up with Clanton and said, "Goldie, if we get as far as the van, I want you to sit up front with me, okay?" He said he planned to drive the speed limit unless they were chased. Then he'd drive like the devil—if the van got in a "power slide" on a curve, not to worry. He knew what he was doing. "Just don't let anyone interfere."

Clanton's grin was nasty. "If anyone tries to touch the wheel, I'll break his fucking arm." Stockton didn't doubt he was good for his word.

A second meeting was called after supper that night and JB handed every man an assignment sheet. "Put this in your legal papers or destroy it," he said. Linwood went over the sheet to see if there were any questions. Evans jumped in. "What happens if you don't get all the phone extensions?" he demanded.

"Then we'll get them from our hostages," Linwood replied.

"What happens if Goldie's discovered missing before he can take control of the booth? What if they take a head count?"

"Then I'm in a shitload of trouble and we're all in lockdown," Clanton snarled. "What can they do, kill me?"

JB stared across the table at Evans. "You wanting out, Ed? Is that it?"

"Naw, but I think I got a better plan."

No one said a word. JB looked at Linwood, who shrugged. "Okay, let's hear it," he said.

"We need to get somebody to appropriate us some guns down here and throw 'em over the fence so we can go to war," Evans said. "Then we go out commando-style, blasting away."

Stockton couldn't believe what he heard: it was the same argument Evans had tried on him. Didn't he understand that after JB's failed attempt in 1981 this would be the very kind of breakout the guards expected? Didn't Evans see it was almost a carbon copy of his own failed attempt in Alexandria? But there was also a fantasy element, as if Evans saw himself starring in a Rambo movie. From the faces of the Brileys, Turner and Clanton, they were thinking the same thing.

Evans didn't notice. "I don't see why we don't talk to our people," he said. "Dennis, you said yourself you got them guns. Linwood, JB, if you can get dope, you know you can get guns. I've got connections of my own. If y'all get the guns brought down and throwed in the woods, I'll get them in."

But Evans's private movie didn't stop there. He had greater plans. "We should all stick together when we get out instead of splitting up," he said. "That way, we'll be harder to find." Then came the clincher. "Me and another guy robbed the North Carolina Employees Association back in 1980 of a lot of money. I can train y'all as guerrillas and we'll get rich robbing places across the country. We'll be like a combat unit. We'll go from place to place, always on the move." His eyes glittered with the glory of his vision.

The plotters were stunned. Stockton felt his jaw drop open and closed it. Linwood leaned back in his chair, staring at the ceiling. Bunch cleared his throat. Finally JB answered, his voice soft and slow: "Ed, if we could get guns, we'd get them. But me and Goldie tried that once and it failed. So we have to use the best we got—our brains! We can't wait around for someone else to come and break us out. Some of us don't have that long to wait."

There was silence, then Bunch said they were wasting time over things that weren't in the plan. The meeting split up, the men drifting into small groups or back to their cells.

But Evans wouldn't quit, grabbing Stockton's arm as he headed toward his cell. "Dennis, it'll work, I know it," he begged. "I got proof." He fished around in his pocket and held something out in his palm. Stockton looked closer: four .38-caliber bullets, copper-jacketed.

"Where'd you get these?" Stockton demanded.

"I can't tell you," Evans said, but he was proud and excited. "I got a gun too, but not here. Someone's holding it for me. All I got to do is give the word."

"It's those librarians? You think they'll come through on something like this? Ed, they'd run the other way."

"No, no, I ain't sayin' who it is." Evans nearly giggled with excitement. "But it can be done, I tell ya. Just think about it. That's all I ask. Just think about what I said." Then he rushed off to try convincing the others.

"Evans is gonna cause problems," Stockton said later that night to JB and Turner. "You wait and see."

Still, the meeting represented a watershed where the breakout evolved into more than a daydream. People came to life, like they had hope—something Stockton hadn't seen since his arrival. They talked about the future, once a taboo subject. Peterson stopped him and asked where he was headed once he escaped. The answer popped in his head: South America.

"South America?" Peterson laughed. "They speak a different language, don't they?"

"I'll learn." It was big and free and open, with people discovering gold and Indians attacking explorers. Just like the Wild West—like something out of Louis L'Amour.

Bunch walked up and caught the tail end. "Can I go with you, Dennis? At least at first? I don't know anything about surviving in the woods. I won't hold you up, I promise."

"I'm going on my own," Stockton replied. "I don't want to be responsible for no one but myself." He went back to his cell and smoked a joint. He fell asleep, thinking how this was foolishness, that they'd never make it. Still, he was happier than he'd been forever. It was one of the best night's sleep he'd had in a long time.

• • • •

Now the plot entered high gear. Stockton still held cleanup duty, so he would stop at different cells, relay messages, pass along the metal file, talk to inmates about the plan. Peterson and Clanton lived side by side and one day Stockton stopped and shared a joint with them. "You need any help taking over the control booth?" he asked Clanton.

"Naw," the big man answered, "just make sure you got that escape route right."

"I figure what I'll do is drive the van deep in the woods, then cover it with limbs and weeds before lightin' out," he said. According to the plan, Stockton was supposed to be the last one with the vehicle, doing all he could to make it disappear. "If they can't locate the van, they won't know where to start looking."

"You still thinking of South America?" Peterson asked.

"I think so," Stockton answered. "'Least, it sounds better than here."

"I don't know where I'm going," Peterson said. "Goldie and me figure we'll hang together. But that's as far as we've planned."

"Why don't we all three stick together?" Clanton asked. "That way we can watch each other's backs." The offer surprised Stockton since he figured Clanton would stick with the Brileys. But those two already said they planned to leave the country and wanted no taga-longs.

Stockton just smiled. "I appreciate it, but I figure I'll just go solo. You know how hard I am to get along with."

"Why you such a loner, Dennis?" Clanton said. "It ain't good, *al-ways* bein' on your own."

"You can't help your nature, I guess." He shrugged and moved on. But Clanton's comment struck home. He *was* a loner. Death Row just made it more apparent, as if coming here stripped away everything but the essential person. He'd learned the hard way that there was no one he could trust but himself; doing otherwise left him open for the knife in the back, the pistol pulled when his guard was down. It was better to disappear to some godforsaken jungle where the only one he was responsible for was Dennis Stockton.

At least one other person didn't waste his time dreaming, and that was Willie Turner. The little man made knives by night and slept by day, a Death Row elf from a dark fairy tale. There were fewer guards on the night shift, meaning fewer spot checks, plus the midnight-to-eight guards often slept the night through. Like Stockton, Willie didn't have a need for people, except to admire his works. He too had an isolated core.

One night, Clanton and Peterson stood in front of Turner's cell and called Stockton over. Turner had a proud look on his face as he showed off his first shank. It looked wicked—about eighteen inches long and sharp enough to shave the hair off his arm. It looked more like a short samurai sword than a jailhouse shank and gave Stockton goose bumps just thinking about it pointed at his belly. Once the guards saw that, there'd be no resistance. Turner said he'd tried making shanks from typewriter keys, and though the metal held stiff it was hard to hide the gap in the machine if anyone looked. Plus, it ruined a good typewriter. The best source he'd found was the metal around the cell door. He showed them how he'd cut the metal from the frame, then filled in the gap with a paste made of powdered coffee creamer and a few drops of water. It hardened like cement, then he painted over the paste and hung posters to conceal where the molding was stripped away. Since prisoners were always painting their cells, the guards never suspected a thing.

Turner was obsessed with hidey-holes. He told Stockton that he cut a hole in the hollow pipe connecting his table to the floor, stashed his shanks, then taped the hole and painted it. But one hiding place wasn't enough. He needed three or four. He was terrified that a snitch lay among them. If not now, soon, when people got scared and started thinking about deals. Word would get out that he was the weapons maker and the shakedown squad would troop straight to his cell. They'd keep looking till they found something. If he could plant a red herring, sprinkle his cell with bogus stashes, maybe the pigs would be satisfied once they found the first and not think to look for more.

Perhaps he was a prophet. The first shakedown rumor came two days after the first meeting in the dayroom. They'd heard that morning on the radio how a fugitive from a Tennessee prison got shot to death by cops in Carolina. Stockton was on cleanup and the others in their cells. Only Evans was gone, announcing at breakfast that he'd be off to court that day. The rumor came midmorning through one of

JB's guards. It spread from neighbor to neighbor, and through the vents between the upper and lower tiers. Everyone began erasing evidence of weapons or drugs. Turner looked like a trapped rat, his eyes skirting frantically from one stash to another as if each was topped with neon arrows. "I told you!" he said. "There's a snitch. This just came too fast. Let me know the minute the squad comes down the hall."

The most paranoid was JB. If a shakedown unit burst in, he was sure he'd be their first target. He had good reason to worry after the discovery of the seventy-five joints last fall. He kept his shank stashed over the cell-locking device in the lower laundry room, but his hideaway was known to others. Drugs were one thing, a shank much worse. The warden would throw him in isolation for years.

"Dennis, come here," he whispered. "Go get me my shank." He was panicking, the first time Stockton had seen him scared. It gave Stockton a feeling of satisfaction as he ambled over and tried to reach the shank. But the top of the metal box housing the locking device was too high. He walked back and told JB he'd have to get a chair.

"Naw, that'll give it away."

"You got it too high up, JB. I can't reach it."

"You're just scared of getting caught. Go get my fucking shank!"

"I need a chair, goddammit. You're just taller'n me."

About then, one of JB's guards walked into the pod. "Forget it," JB snapped. "I'll get him to do it." Stockton moved on and watched as he called the man over. The guard listened for a second, his eyes closed, then with a quick look at the control booth strolled into the dayroom, grabbed a chair and took it to the washroom. He pocketed the shank and took it to JB, but JB didn't want it in the cell with him. He asked the guard to put it down his sock and pull his pants leg over it. Stockton was stunned when the guard agreed.

This was the most amazing thing Stockton had ever seen in his entire prison career. Everything he'd previously learned and assumed about prison life was turned upside down, as if the moment upset the natural order, that age-old relationship of power between prisoners and guards. He almost felt light-headed, it all seemed so unreal. What kind of control did the younger Briley have over people? How could the guard be so corrupted by JB? Stockton watched the guard closely as the man circulated through the pod, half expecting, maybe even hoping, that he'd take the shank to the control booth and bust JB. Instead, when the shakedown failed to materialize, the guard returned it to where JB said.

The rumor of a shakedown was just the first of many that failed to come true. But more than that, the incident with the guard left Stockton shaken. JB thought nothing of sacrificing others to save himself. Throwing in with this man was like dealing with the devil. Stockton grew more convinced than ever that someone would get killed.

But soon he learned he had no choice. On March 9, his lawyer called and said the state supreme court had rejected his appeal. The attorney general asked for an execution date and a hearing was set for March 28.

Disbelief washed over him. The judges hadn't cared a bit about the evidence that Randy Bowman lied in his trial. It hadn't been raised "in a timely matter," the same old twenty-one-day rule. There were still the federal courts, generally more reasonable than Virginia's, the lawyer added. Don't give up yet, he said.

Stockton called his mother and brother and told them not to get too excited about anything they heard on the news. He still had a good shot at freedom, he said, wondering if they could tell he lied through his teeth. The truth was, he was going to die. His hopes had been raised too many times, only to be smashed. He cradled the phone and stared blankly at the guard in the control booth, who almost certainly monitored his call. He was going to die. The guard knew it. The court knew it. They were all laughing. Who was he trying to fool?

Later that night, Linwood passed his cell and slipped a joint through the slot. He'd been through it. He knew. Stockton reached for the joint and promptly got stoned.

There was no backing down now. You were in or out, no in between. He exercised daily to get in shape. They discussed the plans at night around the poker game: everyone was welcome now, and there wasn't even much cheating, just a "forgotten" ante or two. No more big meetings that could raise red flags. Things looked normal on The Row.

Maybe too normal. Some of the guys were returning to their old ways. One night Nurse Ethel Barksdale, the duty nurse, passed out the meds, each man getting his prescriptions in a marked envelope and water in a little Dixie cup. She was a looker, big eyes, cute ass swinging under the white dress. Peterson and Linwood stood together as she passed. "I hope she's here on the night we get out," Peterson said.

"I read you," Linwood said. "I plan to get some too."

Turner overheard. "The whole thing'll fall apart if we waste time on pussy," he snapped. No rape or unnecessary violence, the weapons maker preached.

"Shit, Willie, it's been so long, I won't take long," Peterson said.

"Baylock," said Linwood, "you probably forgot how."

The wolves were scratching at the door, Stockton thought. He watched them in their cells as he made his cleanup rounds. They stared out their vertical glass strips, watching the guards, learning their moves. They grinned and gave a thumbs-up as he passed.

One night he woke to scratching. It took a second for him to realize it was Linwood filing a piece of metal into a shank. Stockton tapped lightly on the air vent and whispered that he could hear. There was a pause, then Linwood's radio rose in volume. The scratching started again.

We're the wolves, he thought. But we want out, not in.

Through it all walked Bunch, reminding Stockton of a lost child. One night Bunch called him to his cell and proudly showed his knife. "I worked on it a week," he said.

"It's good, Tim. Nobody'll talk back with that. Instant respect." But he knew that wasn't why he called him here.

Bunch paused, then got to the point. "Did you think about me going with you? I don't think JB wants me along. It looks like I'll be on my own."

Once again Stockton said no, but this time felt bad doing it. The kook wouldn't last two minutes Outside. This was the only place he fit in. Partly out of sympathy, partly out of courtesy, largely out of caution, he told JB about his punk's request.

"He ain't going with me," JB said. "If you want him, fine. Where me and Linwood are going, a white boy would bring heat for sure."

Bunch just sighed when he heard of his master's comment.

"You got a plan?" Stockton asked. "Anywhere you can go and hide?"

"Who'd take me?" Bunch replied. "My family?" He started laughing. "I'll probably get caught, but I'll make it last as long as possible. As soon as I get out, I figure I'll break into a beauty shop. I'll shave off my mustache and dress like a woman. Take off the glasses. Add some eyeliner. If I drive down the highway and run into a roadblock, the troopers'll let me through 'cause they're looking for a man."

"While you're at it, you'd better shave your legs."

They looked at each other, then laughed so hard their faces turned red.

On March 13, the threatened shakedown finally came true. But by then, they'd had plenty of time to prepare. The searches came up with zip. A few days before the search, JB had stashed the knives in a downstairs maintenance room to which he'd somehow obtained a key. The room was blocked from view by the stairs to the second tier. When JB opened the door, the plotters stood before the TV as if something big were playing, further blocking the view of the control-room guard.

The shakedowns continued. There was an urgency they'd never seen, like The Man was really worried but didn't know where to begin. It further convinced them that a rat lived in their midst. One day Harold Catron watched as the shakedown turned up nothing bigger than a couple of joints. The inmates smiled back at his stares. His face grew dark. "He's gonna have a stroke," Peterson whispered, but Stockton nudged him to stay quiet. They couldn't gloat, not yet. Time was still with the keepers as executions sped up across the nation. There was one on March 14 in Texas, March 16 in North Carolina, March 31 in Texas again. On April 5, a doubleheader: the first in Louisiana, the second in sunny Florida. But it wasn't just them. It was almost like the whole prison sensed something and was on edge. He wrote in his diary:

> **April 9, 1984** Riot last night in No. 5 bldg. Bldg. literally destroyed. Several guards seriously beaten. Several inmates stabbed. Whole bldg. on lock up. Saturday nite riot in No. 3 & 4. . . .

They all felt they couldn't wait much longer and agreed on a date—April 15, a present for all the taxpayers who'd subsidized their stay on Death Row. But with this final step, they also caught a case of nerves. Some talked of dropping out. Newcomers to their side of C-Pod weren't interested. Waye got approval to marry and worried that it would screw up his wedding plans. "What if someone gets killed?" he asked. "I don't want to hurt no one." He dropped out, followed four days later by Evans, who said he had his own plan.

Then two new men arrived. They were immediately brought into the plot. The first was Willie Leroy Jones, housed on the left side with Giarratano. He could help Joe when the escape came down. The twenty-six-year-old Jones drew two death sentences for the murder and robbery on May 13, 1983, of an elderly Charles City County couple who had befriended him when he lost his job. Jones shot seventy-seven-year-old Graham Adkins in the head, then asked seventy-nine-year-old Myra to pray for him before shooting her too. He stuffed her body in a closet, took $30,000 from a bedroom safe and set the house afire. Myra Adkins survived the shooting—the autopsy concluded she died of smoke inhalation.

Lem Davis Tuggle, Jr., arrived soon after Jones and was put in the cell next to Stockton. The two immediately hit it off. Tuggle was a jovial, thirty-four-year-old country boy built like a bear. True, he killed two women, but in here murder was a given. The Brileys asked Stockton to see if this new man was interested. Tuggle whooped in joy when he got the invitation. He definitely seemed interested, Stockton said.

In a way, Tuggle's arrival gave the conspirators a boost. He was like a good-luck charm due to his prior history of successful escapes. While awaiting his first murder trial, he fled Smyth County Jail by sticking a spoon in a jailer's back and telling him it was a knife. Later, he escaped from prison with a butcher knife lifted from the kitchen. Prior to this, he served a brief stint in the military but left with an undesirable discharge for going AWOL too many times.

Tuggle was arrested in 1983 for the rape and murder of fifty-two-year-old Jessie Havens, this occurring only 104 days after his parole for the 1971 rape and murder of seventeen-year-old Shirley Brickey. Both slayings took place in almost exactly the same spot and under nearly identical circumstances. Both victims were dancing with Tuggle at the American Legion Club in Marion shortly before they died. During his trial for the 1971 murder, he claimed that he blacked out from booze and drugs; when he woke, he was in a deserted house with Brickey. She lay beside him, choked to death. He took a bus to Baltimore, where he was arrested, then given twenty years for second-degree murder. The prosecutor argued for life. Twelve years later, on May 28, 1983, Tuggle met Jessie Havens and offered to drive her home at the end of the dance. Her body was found four days later, a half mile from where Brickey died. She was shot once through the heart, bitten and sodomized.

After the murder, Tuggle robbed a nearby gas station. Police pulled him over on suspicion and asked him about the holdup. "Yes, I robbed it," he said. "The money's in my pocket and the gun's in the trunk." He'd barely finished when word of Havens's disappearance came over the radio. "I'm tired of running," Tuggle told the officers and directed them to the body.

Like Stockton, Tuggle considered himself a good ole boy who liked NASCAR racing. His father, a tenant farmer, said his son was raised in church and picked up his evil somewhere other than home. He also picked up a macabre sense of humor. The words BORN TO DIE were tattooed on his right forearm. When he was sentenced to death in the electric chair, he told reporters, "I guess you can call me 'Sparky' now."

By now, even a newcomer like Tuggle could tell that the whole prison was in a state of heightened tension. During the riots of April 8, Stockton looked out his window and saw guards posted on the lawn, cradling shotguns. The spotlights whirled around the perimeter. Guards paced the gun towers in deadly silence.

"That'll be us soon." Evans laughed. "You're still not going with the others, are you? I got a gun, but it's stashed. That's the way to do it, Dennis. Come with me. Come up with the money and I can get you one too."

On April 10, Stockton's execution date arrived with the morning mail. They meant to kill him on July 27, in three and a half months.

He stuck the notice with all his other legal papers. Innocence and guilt had no meaning here, he thought. There was absolutely no reason for him to stick around.

That afternoon, a guard brought a package to JB. Evans and Stockton stood nearby. Stockton saw the telltale envelope tucked under the guard's arm, saw JB reach through the slot and Evans start to turn his head. Stockton spoke up, diverting his attention so he missed the handoff. But he was still curious. "What was that officer doing by JB's cell?" he asked.

"Beats me," Stockton said.

"Why are they always running to JB's cell?"

"I don't know, Ed. Why don't you ask them? Or JB?"

Evans looked at him, then walked away. Stockton was positive now that Evans was the snitch. But he didn't have proof, and to publicly brand him as one without hard evidence was the same as signing his death warrant. The state might play that game. Not him.

Just the same, he warned JB to be discreet with his packages. The walls had eyes, he said.

Then it was April 14, their last full day. A calm descended on Stockton: no more worrying and fretting, just do it and let the chips fall. He shaved carefully, letting the blade run smoothly over the curve of his chin. No nicks or blood, a good omen. He was surprised his hand was so steady, but wasn't that always the way? Hours of worry, then calm. He showered and put on the clothes he planned to wear to either flight or death. He packed a Trac II razor, two packs of matches, a toothbrush, comb, pair of socks and two packs of peanuts into a plastic bag and wrapped it all with rubber bands—his old survival kit, just like before. The ritual gave him confidence. He'd escaped before and never once was wounded. Maybe it would happen again.

And now he felt something else. Something new. He felt this would be a team effort—that they would have to help one another if they wanted a chance to succeed. He didn't have to be a loner. He would have to trust them, and the decision wasn't so hard. He showed his survival kit to Turner, Clanton and Peterson. They were amazed that so much could be crammed into so small a package, and went off to prepare their own. He gave Turner an extra pair of socks. Turner was short a pair, so why not? He'd just be leaving them behind. He put two packs of cigarettes in his shirt pocket and his little New Testament, provided by the Gideons, into his back pocket. A list of phone numbers and addresses was folded between the testament's grainy covers. He looked out the window and the sun was setting. He was at peace, as ready as he'd ever be.

But when he went to show his kit to Linwood, something in the eyes of his friend told him it was not meant to be.

"We're delaying it for thirty days, Dennis," Linwood said quietly. "Until after May fifteenth."

"What's wrong with now? Who's we? I don't remember being told."

Linwood looked hurt and uncomfortable, and Stockton knew the change came from JB. Linwood, always the loyal brother, wouldn't say it. "We don't have enough weapons," he answered instead. "After May fifteenth, we go back to after-supper recreation instead of day-time rec. That's the best time for Goldie to slip in the bathroom, when we're coming back from the rec yard. It'll be dark, and that'll help. You see that, don't ya? Besides, there's fewer guards working nights than during the day."

"Where'd you hear that?"

Linwood hesitated, but not for long. "My brother. His sources are good."

Just like he'd suspected. "We'll still do it, Dennis," Linwood said, almost begging. "This just gives us more advantage."

"Yeah, you're right, forget it," Stockton said, rising from Linwood's bunk. "I just had my hopes up, is all."

"We'll still have a chance to use your survival kits," Linwood tried joking. "And everything still depends on your driving."

Stockton nodded as he walked from the cell. He smiled but felt empty. Another smashed hope. Another missed opportunity.

Linwood was wrong, he thought. Next time could never be the same.

6

April is when the yardmen come out. The long spring rains sweep over the Piedmont from the Appalachians, blanketing the prison with a leaden sky, soaking the trampled yard, stirring the dull roots underneath. It is the season when gloom settles over the prison population and the men lie for long periods in their bunks, shrouded in their thoughts, listening to the steady *drip drip* outside their windows, a metronome of memory and desire. The cinder-block walls soak up the moisture; at night, when the mercury dips, the buildings themselves radiate cold. Flu charges through the cell blocks then, cutting down the keepers and the kept. But there are good days too, when the sun warms the cells and beneath their small windows the inmates can hear the yardmen working in the oval lawn.

Yard work is "make work," a job to keep an inmate busy, but a yard is also a prison's hub. To the jailers it is a symbol: order forced from chaos, the one spot of green where everything else seems gray. As the rain fed the yard and green shot through the winter brown, the inmates heard the mowers beneath their windows and smelled the fresh-cut grass. For many, it was the most pleasant thing they'd experienced in a long time.

That year, the prisoners would have seen something strange if they had watched the piles of clippings left beneath the windows of The Row. A pile would shift, then collapse. Something thin and shiny would separate from the clippings and scoot toward the wall . . . a shank, tied to a very thin wire, this tied to a string dangling from one of the windows above. The shank crept over the grass until hitting the wall with a *click;* it jerked up at an angle, then scraped slowly up the wall until disappearing through a window. This happened only at night. During the day, the yardmen cleaned the grounds beneath the windows; as they stooped to pull weeds, they tied the shanks to the wires, then covered both with clippings. Some of the yardmen lived in Building One's segregation unit and could have walked the shanks to The Row. But the guards were nervous these days and anyone entering there was subject to search. The wire was safer.

A prison arms race is a perverse testament to ingenuity where the resources for toolmaking are scarce. In truth, raw materials are everywhere. Nails are taken from light fixtures and honed to a stiletto sharpness on cement floors. Plastic spoons can be sharpened to an edge capable of removing morning stubble. The most common weapon is the Trac II razor, broken apart for its thin blade. A match is held to the plastic and the razor blade placed into the melted handle. During this arms race, much of The Row's imported weaponry came from the prison shop, where small pieces of discarded metal were easy to palm and sharpen when the guard's back was turned. The workers were always searched when leaving, but it was nothing to drop a shank out a window for a yardman, the next link in the chain.

The escape from Death Row had become a communal effort, a prison revolution. Those who saw themselves as the oppressed conspired against their oppressors, destroying the state's shining edifice from within. It was organized as any guerrilla movement's "cell system," with few of the players knowing the entire plan. The shop worker knew he was getting paid to make more shanks, but he did not know their destination. The yardman knew the destination, but not their hiding place. Each player knew he was in on something unusual, something striking at the myth of Mecklenburg's perfect security, the holiest of holies. They lived in hope of seeing that arrogance destroyed, though they didn't know who among them might strike at The Man.

Yet nothing is kept secret in prison. The extra help fed the grapevine, the main form of communication within prison walls. "Grapevine telegraph" was the phrase coined during the Civil War for rumor circuits that beat official channels in carrying urgent information. The civil war between the inmates and their keepers was no different. Both sides had their grapevines. The prisoner grapevine is capable of miracles, carrying news between blocks, even prisons, almost as fast as it happens, with no visible means of transmission. It penetrates official records through harmless-looking inmates who work in administration offices, passes among former cellmates now in halfway houses, other prisons or out on parole. Inmates pass information through walls and down toilets, trade gossip with cops and reporters, bribe guards, threaten other inmates who refuse to participate. But it is a mistake to think the prisoner grapevine works better than the warden's. Prison administrators are as obsessed with reading their inmates' minds as are the inmates with reading their captors'. It is a matter of life and death. They read the prisoner's mail, listen to his phone calls, shake down his cage. They know the way he thinks through counselors and therapists not bound by any oath of silence. The guards watch him in every phase of activity—eating, sleeping, working, shitting, masturbating, crying out in dreams.

Essential for the grapevine and caught in the middle is the informer—the snitch, who learns all he can and passes it on. Some inform in hopes of receiving special privileges, even commutation. Some snitch only against specific groups: blacks against whites, punks against straights. Some do so under duress, through fear of other inmates or of jailers. There is no right or wrong, simply survival, and even that's uncertain. If the prisoner doesn't inform, he is threatened by his keepers. If he does, there is the prisoner code of death.

In the convict hierarchy, the snitch is even lower than the punk. He is a cocksucker of a different stripe, sucking off The Man. At least punks were honest about what they did to survive. Some cons interpreted survival as escape by any means, and if that meant snitching on a cellmate, too bad. But it was often a losing gamble. Sooner or later a snitch came back to prison and his past almost always caught up to him. Others found out. Stockton had watched it happen in a Carolina road camp. One new guy had the smell, but he was cagey and wouldn't let on. Finally he was turned over to a sly old-timer who said: "Back years ago, I turned state's evidence on a man and got him thirty years. But that was when I was on another sentence, so it don't count now to my release." Every new guy wants an ally and this fish was no exception. "I done something like that myself to get out of a charge," he confessed. "Had to testify against a friend down in South Carolina." The old-timer signaled the others and they took it from there, beating the man so badly he was hospitalized under guard, then placed in twenty-four-hour lockup for his own safety.

Now it was April 15, the original day of the escape. Stockton woke in a foul mood with a head cold. He took apart his survival kit, deciding Willie could keep the extra socks. He went down to breakfast, chewed a cold piece of toast, nostalgically remembering the little pats of butter you got in restaurants, the plastic-sealed squares of grape jam. He watched JB talk to one of his guards. Listened, really, since the guard did most of the talking. JB walked over to Linwood, who bent his head as he listened. Something was up. It didn't look good.

Stockton waited until JB stopped talking before pushing back his chair. "Somethin' up?" he asked. Linwood nodded: "One of the guards said they know everything about our plan."

"The only way they *could* know is through a snitch," JB said.

"That's what I've thought since the shakedowns started," Stockton agreed.

JB's eyes narrowed: "The rumor is that you're him."

"What!" He looked at the brothers and they were watching him carefully. "I done as much as anyone to get this plan together. More. I thought that all ended with the bullshit 'bout me bein' undercover FBI."

"People say your trips to the urologist are bogus, that you went to talk to the warden."

"Waye has a brother who works as a janitor over at South Hill. If you don't believe me, ask him." But even as he said it, he grew more enraged. "Do you believe the rumors?"

"That's what everybody says," JB said.

"How long've people been saying this?" he hissed.

"For a while. Since the shakedowns started."

"That means that while I've been pulling this stuff together, people have been distrustin' me behind my back?"

JB shrugged. Stockton's heart pounded with hatred—it was all he could do to keep from springing at the younger brother, even though he knew it would be suicide. But his fury must have shown, for JB took a step back and Linwood stepped between them. "Forget it, Dennis, it's just a rumor," Linwood said.

But Dennis was past conciliation. "I'll get to the bottom of this!" he said, stalking away.

There was no trusting criminals. He'd lived his entire adult life wanting to believe there was honor among thieves, as if the fraternity of such men as Bill Broadwell could somehow be regained. He saw the foolishness of this now. That kind of world was no more real than what he read in Louis L'Amour. For the briefest moment he'd felt a sense of community as they pulled together on the escape. If successful, it would enter the history books: they'd be remembered forever for sticking a knife in the arrogant heart of The Man. Now he saw it all as an illusion. All his past values were mistaken. It tore him up inside.

He decided to drop out of the conspiracy.

There were pragmatic considerations besides his hurt and rage. The way some plotters harped on violence, Stockton feared hostages would be hurt or killed. To hear them talk, murder would come easy if they didn't get their way. What if he did get out, only to be recaptured? No telling what charges would result from the breakout: abduction, even murder. What good would it be for him to win a reversal on his death sentence only to get two hundred years or more for the escape?

That night he talked about his worries with Joey G. Although Giarratano lived on C-Pod's left side, separated from Dennis by walls and bars, they could talk to each other through the connecting air vents of the shower rooms. Each floor of cells had a shower at the inside end of the tier; thus, four showers abutted each other, top and bottom, side by side, at nearly right angles, the air vents forming a primitive phone line. Giarratano had finally emerged from The Hole, and now he was even more changed than before. He'd written his first legal brief, the one that would eventually be revised and argued before the Supreme Court of the United States. He had resumed his appeals and showed an interest in proving his own guilt or innocence, no longer assuming he was damned. Giarratano said he worried about bloodshed too. When Stockton told him what happened with the Brileys, he answered: "I don't trust any of them one hundred percent. I think they'd sell out their own mothers if it benefited them."

Turner heard the conversation and walked into the shower room. Giarratano and Turner had become friends over the past few weeks, and when Willie asked what was up, Stockton repeated JB's words. Turner was incredulous, but Stockton saw JB and motioned him over. It was getting like a damn convention in here. "Here's JB, ask him yourself," he said. JB confirmed it all, but added they still planned to go through with the escape.

But by now, Stockton had made his decision. "I don't know, JB," he said. "There's a time to lead, a time to follow and a time to get the hell out of the way."

"What does that mean?" JB sneered.

"It means I'm out of the plan."

The sneer fell from JB's face. "You're kidding," he said. "You can't back out."

"Just watch me," Stockton said, and mimicking the sneer he hated so much, the arrogance that assumed power over life and death, he got up and walked away.

• • • •

The conspirators suddenly realized they had a problem. Their driver was deserting. True, others had bailed out earlier: Evans, for his own "plan"; Waye, for his romance; even Bunch, though his desertions and reenlistments seemed daily occurrences. Others were on the fence, especially Giarratano and Turner due to their fear of bloodshed. Yet except for Turner, Stockton was the only one whose loyalty seemed essential. They all feared dying in a high-speed chase. His defection would cause others to reconsider.

During the first meeting, the plotters agreed not to discuss the plan any further with those who pulled out. It provided a slim measure of security and protected the ones who left from being branded a snitch. Now Stockton upheld his end. When Tuggle mentioned the escape the day after his defection, Stockton interrupted: "It's better for both of us if you don't mention that anymore, Lem. I got out."

Tuggle stared like he hadn't heard right. "You mean *out*? When?"

"Yesterday. People were talkin' 'bout me being the snitch. If they couldn't trust me, I couldn't trust them. It wasn't safe to stay in anymore."

Stockton's decision sent shock waves through the pod. Suddenly people changed. Clanton wouldn't talk to him. Peterson steered clear. Giarratano told him to watch his back. Turner told him he'd heard JB, Clanton and Linwood talking like they'd have to threaten to kill people or others would pull out too. Turner confirmed the rumor: "First they talk of killing hostages, then of killing those of us who don't go along. This is bad. It's not how it started. I'd get out too, but they'd kill me for sure."

Stockton was worried, but refused to act scared. He kept the door to his cell open as usual, except when asleep. Later that night Linwood came in and sat on his bed.

"I can guess what you're here for," Stockton said.

"I don't think you're the snitch, Dennis," Linwood replied. "I don't know who is. If I did, we'd take care of it." His hands were folded together; he spoke slowly, as if this was hard to say. "My brother thinks so, though. I tried telling him, 'Why would Dennis ruin something he worked so hard at?' But JB . . . I've seen it all my life. Once something's in his head, he won't let go."

"He's your brother, Linwood, and I don't want to say nothing bad about him," Stockton answered. "But I can't trust that somethin' won't happen to me."

Linwood shifted uncomfortably. "I'll tell them not to touch you."

Stockton smiled. "Can you guarantee one hundred percent that nothing will happen? And if something does happen and him and me get into a fight, whose side will you take? He's your brother, Linwood. I don't blame you for that. But I got to watch my own back, understand?"

Linwood looked up from his hands. "Can you at least draw me a picture of the van's dashboard? You leaving makes me the driver. That makes everyone nervous."

Stockton laughed and drew a detailed picture, locating the ignition, lights and turn signals, emergency blinkers, emergency brake, and showing Linwood how to operate the scanner. He went over each, then made Linwood practice the location of the brake and gas pedal. It was like a leave-taking, though neither said good-bye.

"I'm sorry about this, Dennis," Linwood said as he got up. "I didn't want it to happen." Only later did Stockton realize how many times he'd turned his back during this conversation, how easy it would have been for his friend to slip a knife between his ribs.

Friendships. They always seemed doomed in this world. One such friendship helped send him here: the shooting of Ronnie Tate on July 2, 1979, nearly a year after Arnder died. Stockton called it self-defense—prosecutors called it proof of Stockton's "future dangerousness" to convince jurors to send him to the chair. In the end, people would believe what they wanted, but one thing was indisputable: Tate's death was fallout from the Arnder slaying, one more victim in the spreading black pool.

Ronnie Tate was twenty-two when he died, a friend to both Arnder and Stockton, part of their crowd. A photo in *The Mount Airy News* shows a small, wiry guy wearing a Harley T-shirt and smiling into the camera. He has long hair and a scruffy goatee; half his face is in shadows, and his brow shades his eyes. His younger sister described him as a "perfect brother," but like Arnder he drifted from house to house, job to job. He was known as Stockton's gofer, but until that final day, Stockton seemed unaware his friend nursed the escalating rage of an Iago, the festering envy of the second fiddle. Tate was repeatedly rumored to have participated in Arnder's killing; he said as much to Stockton, but was also half buzzed and short on detail when he did so and Stockton knew Ronnie was prone to lying to build himself up. After the killing, the names of would-be killers popped up like forest mushrooms. Who could be sure of anything?

Kibler Valley, alleged site of Arnder's death, is a wooded valley along the Mayo River near the state border dividing Surry and Patrick counties. The Mayo comes to life high in the mountains, then broadens and deepens as it descends. It follows a rocky gorge to the flatlands, then shallows into several swimming holes. These are dotted with campsites and picnic tables, the few signs of humanity. While the valley itself bursts with dogwood and mountain laurel in spring and early summer, the surrounding mountains frown down, rugged and gray.

It was in this peaceful yet lonely place that Stockton said he stared down the barrel of Ronnie Tate's gun. A third person was with them: Robert Gates, scrawny, nervous, also a biker wannabe, a friend of Tate's and, Stockton learned much later, of Randy Bowman as well. It was ninety degrees in the mountains that day in 1979; the three decided on a swim after watching the dirt track races in a nearby town. Ronnie and Gates were both wanted for some thefts and smoked reefer to calm their nerves. Stockton emptied his pockets and dove into the clear, cold river while the two sat at a picnic table, talking between themselves. He walked back to his car, dried off, put his stuff back in his pockets and stuck his pistol down the small of his back. He always carried it now—there was so much paranoia after Kenny's killing, it was good to be prepared.

When Stockton walked to where the two still talked, Ronnie turned, a gun pointed at his belly. "Be still, Dennis," he said. "Raise your hands."

Stockton did as told. "What's this, Ronnie?" he stuttered, caught completely off guard. He focused on the pistol, its hammer cocked. Gates watched without expression. Stockton figured he was a dead man, though unsure what had led to this.

Ronnie laughed. "I'm gonna take your money, dope and car and there's not a damn thing you can do about it," he said. "Everyone thinks you're so bad, I wish they could see you now. I'm gonna blow you away and it won't be the first time I've done it to someone right here."

He was confessing again to Arnder's murder, but it didn't matter since the listener would soon be dead. He blamed Stockton for his being on the suspect list, forgetting that most people in their crowd had been interrogated several times. "You're the one that put The Law on me, you ratting son of a bitch. Say it. You're a rat, ain't you?"

There was no doubting the look in Ronnie's eyes. Any argument and he was dead. "Yes," he said.

"Yes, what?" He waved the gun in Stockton's face. "Say you told The Law about me. *Say it!*"

"I—I told The Law about you."

"That ain't all I told you to say. Say you're a rat."

"I'm a rat."

"You ain't so mean now, are you?"

"No."

"Tell Robert who's the meanest man in town."

"You are."

Ronnie laughed. He was having the time of his life, making Dennis crawl, savoring his humiliation. It was the apex of his short career, the badass never bad enough, the little man nobody feared. Gates watched silently, not moving a muscle. Ronnie fished a cigarette from his pocket and, using his left hand, lit it with a red Bic lighter. He fumbled with the flame. It was the only chance Stockton would get. He fell sideways, grabbed the pistol from his waistband and pulled the trigger three times. Ronnie fired once, then crumpled to the clay.

The noise was deafening, followed by an intense quiet: breeze through the treetops, water rushing downstream. Gates babbled in fear. "Shit, Dennis, what got into him? I didn't know he was going to do something like that!" Stockton's pulse pounded in his ears. He felt like pistol-whipping Gates for just sitting there while he nearly got killed. But maybe he wasn't lying, maybe he *had* frozen in fear. He checked Ronnie's pulse. Nothing there.

Stockton's mind was in chaos. Should he tell The Law? If he did, they'd just bend it outta shape—the cops would finally have the wedge against him they wanted and turn it into something other than self-defense. If nothing else, carrying a pistol would violate his parole and land him back in prison, maybe for good. Gates was also on parole, for petty theft, and had the same fears. They babbled excitedly between themselves, wondering what to do. Maybe they should just bury him and say they had no idea where he disappeared to when friends started asking. Yet when they carried his body up the road and laid it down, a sigh escaped, the lungs' final release of trapped air. "What's this son of a bitch made of, steel?" Gates screamed. He grabbed his own gun from his waistband and shot him again.

"He's dead already!" Stockton yelled.

Gates shook as though palsied. This was bad, Stockton thought, then it just got worse. The ground was hard. They had no tools. If they covered him with leaves, rats and other varmints would carry off the pieces, God knew where. A corn crib down the valley. A farmer's back door.

They finally settled on stuffing Ronnie's body in the trunk and driving south over the state line. Gates ate Valium like candy. They grabbed some tools and buried the body in a condemned Boy Scout camp between Mount Airy and Winston-Salem. It later dawned on Stockton that the state's scenario for Kenny's killing fit Ronnie's exactly. Was some sort of cosmic justice, or simply more goof-ups like now?

Years passed and, as in Arnder's death, there were no arrests for Ronnie's demise. Fast forward to 1982. Stockton is in jail serving time for the 1980 charge of shooting into the building of a man who owed him money when he hears he is getting blamed again for Kenny's murder for hire. He tries handing over the letters of the bloodthirsty prominent citizen, but these are "lost" by The Law. In hopes that by telling the truth on one killing in self-defense the cops will believe his denials of Arnder's murder, he confesses to killing Ronnie.

But the plan backfires. Stockton is too late. The Law had already located Bowman and soon afterward, Gates, to save his own skin, tells them of Ronnie's killing. His tale of the killing is different than Stockton's, but detectives never check the discrepancies. He says Stockton drew first, telling Ronnie before he fired that he was tired of him "running his mouth that he was a queer," a comment echoing Bowman's statement. He tries leading them to the body but fails. He says Stockton slit Ronnie's body from groin to breastbone to hasten decomposition, a detail that doesn't square with the autopsy. He says they stopped at a nearby diner, which doesn't square with the owner's words that they never stayed open the Fourth of July weekend.

In his zeal to prove his innocence on the Arnder killing, Stockton confessed to killing Ronnie Tate and led lawmen to the body. That would prove his veracity, he thought. Instead, cops were now able to clear two unsolved murders from the books where before they had zip.

Too late, he learned a lesson: *friends* were all links in the endless chain of evil. There was no breaking that chain.

• • • •

April 18. Three days after "Breakout Day." Once again, the riot squad stormed the pod just as they were finishing breakfast. Once again, the cells were shaken down. This time, however, there was a difference. The guards beat the walls with their sticks, looking for hollowed stashes. They passed the inmates' mattresses and pillows through an X-ray machine. It was the most thorough shakedown yet. But they found nothing.

Stockton and the others gloated silently. They would have swallowed their smirks if they'd known the extent of the state's information. They may have even abandoned their plan. Their fears of an informant were correct. At least two inmates told their lawyers, and the lawyers told officials. To this day, the names have not been released.

The next day, the state attorney general learned of the plot. A snitch leaked a "virtual blueprint" of the plan, officials later said, including the detail that one man planned to hide in the bathroom and take guards by surprise. The AG's office called Mecklenburg, burning up the wires. Even as this happened, Clanton tried entering the guards' bathroom on the way back from recreation. He turned the knob, but the door was locked and he walked on. The guards didn't notice a thing.

April 20 started with little warning that the ante had been upped. Stockton ate breakfast as the squad once again arrived. Again, the search was fruitless. But today something new was added. A white shirt handed each man a memo typed on Mecklenburg letterhead:

MEMO FROM DEPARTMENT OF CORRECTIONS, APRIL 20, 1984

TO: STOCKTON, DENNIS

FROM: W. A. CRENSHAW, ASSISTANT WARDEN–PROGRAMS

SUBJ: YOUR STATUS

This is to notify you that you have been placed on General Detention status pending review by the Institutional Classification Committee because the administration has received reliable information that the security of the institution may be jeopardized.

They were getting put on lockdown, locked in their cells until officials were satisfied the danger had passed. "What's this?" Clanton fumed. "A lockdown? For how long?"

"We gonna get our showers?" Stockton broke in.

"In your cages, boys," said one of the guards. "The only ones you'll smell are you."

That same day, interrogations began. Bunch went first. Three guards came and said he was scheduled for a checkup. "I ain't scheduled for no doctor's visit," Bunch argued, panic lacing his voice.

"C'mon, Tim, don't make us have to come in there or it'll get nasty," the white shirt said. "None of us want that."

Bunch was escorted to the medical building and left inside an empty room with a long table and chairs pushed against the outer wall. After a couple of minutes, a file of prison officials strode in, led by Harold Catron. "This ain't no checkup," Bunch said, looking from face to face. The officials chuckled and said he had that right.

Bunch told what happened when he returned. There are ways to pass such messages even when on lockdown. Neighbors spread the word and pass it from cell to cell. According to Stockton's autobiography, one of the more sophisticated methods is "muling" through the toilets of cells above and below each other on the tiers. Each man places a pillow over the open toilet and sits, then rises quickly two or three times. This creates a vacuum, "knocking" the water all the way down the tiers. Only a tiny amount of water is left in the bottom of each toilet, which can be toweled dry. Voices then carry through the pipes better than through a telephone. The prisoners agree when to talk again, then hang up by flushing their commodes.

Bunch's message was encouraging. "They're scared to death," he said. "They know about the weapons, but don't know where they're hid. They know something's up, but they're unsure if we're gonna escape or just riot and take hostages. They don't know as much as they let on."

Now began a two-way game of cat and mouse. With few other options possible, the prisoners hoped to go through the interrogations and learn what their jailers knew. Prison officials had guessed the broad outline—stockpile weapons, take hostages—but didn't know the details. The lockdown could legally go on forever in the name of prison security. The TV was shut off, the men kept inside their cells for all but a shower every other day. Dennis lay in bed, scribbled in his diary, read *The First Deadly Sin.* But most of his neighbors weren't readers, so time dragged on and boredom soon grew. He wrote in his diary:

> **April 21, 1984** All of Death Row remains on lock up. . . . No showers. . . . I was not allowed out of my cell to talk. . . . Letter from mom in tonite's mail. Doors were not opened for ANY-THING all day.

That same day, Linwood received an August 17 execution date. The next day, JB threw his food tray through the slot. It clattered to the cement and everyone jumped. This was followed by a blazing bag of garbage, shoved through the slot with a broom. Since JB and Stockton were neighbors, it landed in a bloom of sparks before Dennis's door. A guard walked calmly to the blaze and spritzed it with a fire extinguisher. He looked at Stockton and grinned.

Stockton's turn before the panel came five days into the lockdown. He sat in the folding chair and scanned the faces of the officials. They looked tired: one had a tic in the corner of his lip; another had bags under his eyes. Stockton guessed the screws were being turned on them from above. The bright sunlight streamed over their shoulders into his eyes: they could watch his face clearly but he had to squint to see them. All part of the game.

"What do you know of inmates stockpiling weapons, Dennis?" an assistant warden asked. "We know something's up."

Stockton shook his head. He didn't know a thing, he said. Afterward, this report was filed:

INSTITUTIONAL CLASSIFICATION COMMITTEE REPORT, APRIL 24, 1984

INMATE NAME: STOCKTON, DENNIS

SUMMARY STATEMENT OF INMATE:

"I get along with everybody. There is nothing going on. I don't see how there could be any weapons over there. I don't see how there would be any trouble. I don't want to get involved in anything. What other people do is their business."

SUMMARY STATEMENT OF COMMITTEE AND RECOMMENDATIONS:

Dennis Stockton, No. 134466, was administratively assigned to general detention status on April 20, 1984, because of reliable and confidential information received from various sources concerning potential problems on Death Row. The information indicated that the inmates were plotting to cause serious property damage and personal injury to the staff and other inmates. An investigation into this situation has been conducted and appropriate security measures have been taken to ensure that the pod area has been rid of all weapons. Stockton indicates that he is not involved in any plot and that he feels that he can continue to live in an open housing situation. The results of the investigation are inconclusive and will continue until such time as the institution is assured of being able to operate in a safe, secure manner. . . .

The lockdown ended after a week. On April 27, the men were let out for recreation. Virginia's spring was now headlong, a riot of greens and yellows, a sprinkling of white puffballs. The high was in the eighties, the sky a pastel blue. Stockton took a breath and held it, feeling his lungs expand. It was good to be out, good to be alive. The younger inmates went at the hoops like starved men, knocking one another over during dunk shots, whooping and making catcalls as female guards hurried by. The prison knew The Row had been on lockdown, and some of the women laughed. As Stockton watched, Harold Catron strolled up the sidewalk and stopped on the other side of the fence. He watched them, his hands in his pockets, saying nothing until all the players were aware of his presence and a silence descended.

They stared at each other across the fence. Catron looked tired. His shoulders slumped, he chewed his lower lip, studying his adversaries in prison blue. It was a war of wills and maybe this time they had triumphed. But it would be a grave mistake to think they'd beaten this man, Stockton realized. Men like this didn't lose easily.

Still, it was clear the security chief was worried, torn between his fear of disaster, anger at the petty tyranny of those above him and realization that most escape rumors were hot air. "I'm ending the lockdown at supper tonight," he finally said. The men cheered as he walked away.

They'd won the first round, but victory had a cost. The plotters were edgy, ready to lay blame somewhere. JB walked the pod, radiating menace. Linwood stayed in his cell. Clanton itched for a fight, mumbling what he'd do once he found the snitch.

Of all of them, Tuggle seemed the most affected. It seemed unhealthy for Lem to think too much, Stockton decided. All of a sudden the big man's favorite subject of conversation was murder. He wouldn't let it drop, as if working himself up to do it again. Lots of convicts bragged of righteous slaughter, but Tuggle acted as if the act came as naturally as breathing or swallowing food. "They haven't charged me with all my killings," he said one day. "There was a guy in jail with me in Marion. Guy named Jones. They said it was suicide, but t'wasn't so."

On September 15, 1983, six months before Tuggle arrived at Mecklenburg, fellow prisoner James Franklin Jones was found dead in Tuggle's cell in the Smyth County Jail. Tuggle told other inmates that he killed him, but investigators discounted the claim, attributing the remarks to standard tough-guy banter. Tuggle refused to let it drop. Jones was let into Lem's cell to watch TV but started making too much noise, Lem said. This was annoying, so he choked him to death. Then he wrapped a sheet around his neck and hung him from the bars to make it look like suicide.

Except for Turner and Giarratano, Lem was the only conspirator who still spoke to Stockton. They didn't discuss the escape, but Stockton would have to have been blind not to see they were still going ahead with grim determination. As April turned to May, Linwood and Clanton shaved their mustaches, the ones shown in all their mug shots. Clanton stayed in his cell more and more. He wanted the guards to get used to not seeing him out so they wouldn't miss him the night he slipped into the bathroom. Whenever he had a chance, he still tested the door. Sometimes it was locked, sometimes not. They started laying bets whether it would be on the big day.

• • • •

May brought the storms. Black thunder peaks blew across the Piedmont, bringing with them lightning and daylong bouts of rain. The temperature fluctuated wildly, as high as the eighties by day, down to the thirties or forties at night. Stockton liked watching the storms' violence from his small window. All would be black beyond the guardtower lights, the water streaming down as from an open faucet, when a jagged streak of light ripped the dark in two. Sometimes the lightning hit close: he felt the charged *crack,* followed by a white as blinding as pain. The towers were the highest points and the guards who pulled duty those nights said the sudden flash scared the Jesus out of them, the air smelling of ozone and the hairs on their arms standing on end. Even though they knew the towers were grounded, they still stayed away from the sides. Stockton thought: just like the chair.

May also brought with the weather a change in Stockton's fortunes. It started as a bureaucratic snafu. On May 10, the guards rousted him from his cell early for a hearing in Danville. He told them the case had been continued, but word hadn't made it to the right office. Who was he to question the chain of command? Sure enough, no hearing, but the guards said to look on it as a vacation; they even bought him a Big Mac, a treat compared with the green burgers they served at Mecklenburg. They returned shortly before noon. He listened as the radio told of a Florida man executed after eleven years on his Row, then slept the rest of the day.

The storms swept in again. The next morning he awoke to a throbbing in his back. It was so excruciating, he could barely stand. By now, the guards recognized his pale look as the return of kidney problems, so they bundled him off to the urologist in South Hill. "You again, honey?" the nurse said. "I wonder if you're getting stones. I had a kidney stone once, and between giving birth and passing stones, I'd say stones were worse." The doctor prescribed more painkillers, scheduled a follow-up visit and kept him overnight for observation.

Chance, fate, destiny. The fall of the die, the spin of the wheel. Stockton learned on returning that his two consecutive trips Outside were seen as anything but innocent. They had rekindled rumors that he was the snitch. His anger took over. "Fuck you!" he screamed in Clanton's face, jumping from the table. But it was to JB—sitting the next table over, letting his lap dog do the dirty work—to whom the comment was directed. That's it, he thought. If they're calling me a snitch, I might as well deserve it. He stormed to his cell, pulled out his pizza-sized metal seat, plucked a pen from the Jif peanut butter jar and wrote a letter to Harold Catron. He even signed his name.

It was a decision that colored his fate for the next twelve years. The letter was a bombshell. Stockton said he was one of the original planners, that they planned to escape with a cache of weapons stored in hollowed-out parts of the walls. He drew a diagram of stash locations and said they planned to take hostages and kill other prisoners who didn't go along. Yet he refused to tell all. He liked Turner, so didn't reveal the stashes in his cell. He did not reveal the bomb hoax. He revealed just enough to kill the plot. And to get himself killed for violating the code.

He folded the letter carefully and sealed it in an envelope marked with Catron's name. He wrote to a friend in another prison and to his mom, then gave all three letters to a guard not in JB's pay. He noted the letter in his diary, then sat back to await results.

It took four days. Before then, Turner and Tuggle told him to be careful, yet Peterson and Linwood both apologized for their suspicions and asked him to rejoin the conspiracy. Stockton declined, not without a twinge of guilt. He watched one of JB's guards deliver an ounce of reefer and a shank. Evans stopped at his door and once again showed him the $100 bill. "Get lost," Stockton said. "Your plan's bullshit and I don't feel like getting killed."

Crazy, crazy, crazy. These people didn't see how crazy they were. At least a one-sided fight between Willie Turner and Ed Evans provided some normal entertainment. They were out on rec when one of Evans's librarians strolled down the walk. Turner yelled how fine she looked this warm spring day. She stopped and smiled. Evans tried butting in, but Turner waved him off. "Go 'way, Ed, the lady and I are having a conversation," he said. She laughed, having to know he was stripping her mentally, so much eye-fucking was going on. Thirty minutes later Turner excused himself and Evans immediately ran up, hanging to the fence and whispering desperately till the librarian had to go. Evans watched her disappear in her fine blue dress; he looked for all the world like a dog who'd gotten kicked. He glared at Turner and drew him away from the guards.

"You're interfering with something I'm workin' on. That girl came to talk to me."

"Ed, that woman was walking from one building to another and I just got to her first," Turner answered, then laughed derisively. "She's part of your *plan*? *Wil-bert,* your *plan* is bullshit. When you gonna learn?"

Those were killing words. As they lined up to return, Evans moved in close behind Turner. Willie wheeled fast and popped Evans upside the head. Evans pitched backward and Turner moved in, his hand reaching for his pocket where a shank was probably hidden. Clanton and JB grabbed his arms. Turner got the message. Nobody gave a rat's ass for Evans, but a killing now would screw everything.

The shakedown Stockton had been expecting came on the morning of May 17. This time, they brought in a German shepherd that supposedly could sniff out weapons. This time, the men were locked in their cells until their names were called, then cuffed while the dog sniffed around.

The pooch was a joke. Stockton watched as he sniffed for about forty-five seconds, knocking over his orange soda and licking a candy bar. "I paid for that," he said.

"Dog's gotta eat, don't he?" the handler replied.

Once again, the result was zero. Not a single weapon was found.

So that was it, Stockton thought, disgusted. The guards were such bozos they couldn't find the stashes with a map. He started laughing. He'd tried, but now they deserved whatever happened. He never snitched again.

Everyone was in high spirits after the search. For the first time in months, the inmates got high. Stockton halfheartedly wrote a grievance about the dog ruining his junk food, knowing it would do no good. He heard a whisper through the vent; it was JB, telling him to stick his arm out the slot, then passed over a paperback copy of *Love Story.* Stockton opened the book and found four joints. It was JB's way of apologizing. Stockton felt like a heel.

He returned another book, keeping *Love Story.* It had been a long time since he'd seen the movie. He'd gotten all misty-eyed when Ali McGraw died.

The days turned long and dreamy. Richard Petty won his 199th career race. Rick Mears won the Indy 500. Bobby Allison won the Mellow Yellow 300. He and Tuggle were lifting weights in the rec yard, Stockton reminiscing how much he missed those races, when Lem got serious. "It's gonna be soon now, Dennis," he said. "You sure you don't want to reconsider?"

Nobody had mentioned the escape for about a week. It was easy to imagine on these lazy days that it was all a dream. He still felt guilty for snitching, as well as disgusted with prison officials for being so incompetent. "Naw, you guys go ahead," he said. "I made up my mind."

"It worries me," Lem replied. "I mean, what if we get out and the gate is locked. We'll have to come back in the building, and you know what that means. There'll be killing."

"Maybe not. Maybe everything'll go smooth as silk and you'll creep out past their noses. Just do me a favor. If you have to come back, don't kill me."

"I hope not, Dennis," Lem said sadly. "But once things get started, there's no controlling 'em. You know how it is."

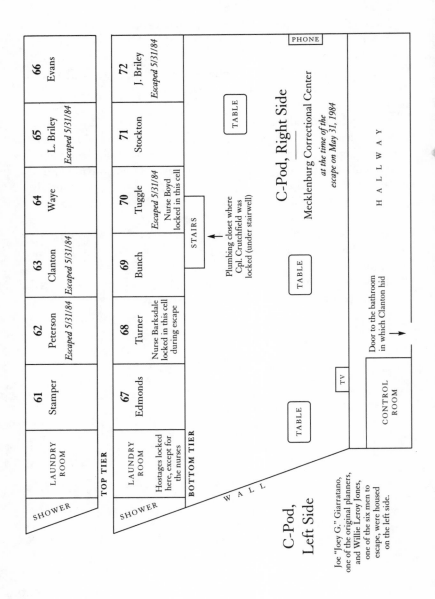

TOP TIER

| SHOWER | LAUNDRY ROOM | **61** Stamper | **62** Peterson *Escaped 5/31/84* | **63** Clanton *Escaped 5/31/84* | **64** Waye | **65** L. Briley *Escaped 5/31/84* | **66** Evans |

BOTTOM TIER

| SHOWER | LAUNDRY ROOM Hostages locked here, except for the nurses | **67** Edmonds | **68** Turner Nurse Barksdale locked in this cell during escape | **69** Bunch | **70** Tuggle *Escaped 5/31/84* Nurse Boyd locked in this cell | **71** Stockton | **72** J. Briley *Escaped 5/31/84* |

W A L L

← STAIRS

← Plumbing closet where Cpl. Crutchfield was locked (under stairwell)

PHONE

TABLE

TABLE

TABLE

TV

CONTROL ROOM

Door to the bathroom in which Clanton hid →

H A L L W A Y

C-Pod, Right Side

Mecklenburg Correctional Center

at the time of the escape on May 31, 1984

C-Pod, Left Side

Joe "Joey G." Giarratano, one of the original planners, and Willie Leroy Jones, one of the six men to escape, were housed on the left side.

The planners of the only mass escape from Death Row in American history hatched their plot in a dayroom like this one at Mecklenburg Correctional Center. Here, convicted killers Gregory Frye and John Joseph LeVasseur—who was on Death Row when the escape occurred—are playing cards about one year after the escape. The secured area behind them is a guard post. UPI

Earl Clanton, hiding in a bathroom near a control panel like this one, helped his cronies take control of C-Pod on the night of the escape. Here, an unidentified officer is shown in a typical control room at Mecklenburg, about two years before the escape. The control panel opens and closes doors in the cell block. AP

A photograph of Mecklenburg showing Building One, which houses Death Row, in the background. *THE VIRGINIAN-PILOT,* BILL TIERNAN

Aerial view of Mecklenburg in an October 6, 1984, photograph. The administration building is the large white structure on the bottom left. Building One, housing Death Row, is two to the left of the administration building. AUTHORS' COLLECTION

Death Row escapee Linwood Briley, with his brother James, committed at least eleven murders during their combined criminal careers. Linwood was the first Death Row inmate that Dennis Stockton met when he arrived at Mecklenburg. They grew a pot plant in Stockton's cell and started a thriving marijuana business. AP

Death Row escapee Lem Davis Tuggle raped and murdered two women in western Virginia. He arrived on Death Row in the weeks before the escape and was the last to join the plot. AP

Death Row inmate Timothy Dale Bunch, the "punk," or homosexual lover, of James Briley, was convicted of raping and killing his lover and then trying to disguise the murder by hanging her. He sometimes had visions of talking with his hero, Gary Gilmore, the first man put to death after executions resumed in America in 1976. THE VIRGINIAN-PILOT

Death Row inmate Morris Odell Mason was once diagnosed as a paranoid schizophrenic and had a very low I.Q. He was convicted of nailing an elderly woman to a chair and burning her house down around her. THE VIR-GINIAN-PILOT, R. L. DUNSTON

Death Row escapee Willie Leroy Jones rode with Lem Tuggle after the escape and made it all the way to Vermont. After Tuggle's arrest, Jones called his mother, who persuaded him to give himself up to police. He was barely ten miles from the Canadian border. *THE VIRGINIAN-PILOT*

Death Row escapee Earl Clanton hid in a guards' bathroom in the hall outside Death Row the night of the escape. On a signal from James Briley he barged past a guard and into the control room, releasing his confederates, triggering the escape. *THE VIRGINIAN-PILOT*

Death Row escapee Derick Lynn Peterson was the first to be recaptured, along with Earl Clanton; they were apprehended in Warrenton, North Carolina, eating cheese and drinking wine in a Laundromat. AP

Death Row escapee James Briley, with his brother Linwood, were the last to be recaptured. They were arrested by the FBI in Philadelphia. The Brileys controlled Death Row through a combination of drug sales, homebrew production, guile and intimidation. UPI

Dubbed "the genius of Death Row" in a *New Yorker* profile, Willie Lloyd Turner was one of the original planners of the mass escape, and the lead weapons maker in C-Pod. He had been convicted of robbing and murdering a jeweler in Franklin, Virginia. He gained notoriety after his execution when his attorney discovered a gun and bullets hidden in the electric typewriter Turner kept with him in Virginia's Death House. *THE VIRGINIAN-PILOT,* JOHN H. SHEALLY II

Randy Bowman, key prosecution witness in Dennis Stockton's murder trial, was the only person to testify that Stockton agreed to accept money to murder Kenneth Arnder. He later recanted to reporter Joe Jackson, then withdrew that recantation after a visit by investigators. Before Stockton's execution in September 1995, signed affidavits surfaced that fingered Bowman as Arnder's real killer, but authorities showed little interest in the new evidence. *THE VIRGINIAN-PILOT,* JOHN H. SHEALLY II

Dennis Stockton, in October 1986 in the Death House at the Virginia State Penitentiary in Richmond. Stockton had let his appeals lapse and was only days from execution when he agreed to renew them. *THE VIRGINIAN-PILOT,* JOHN H. SHEALLY II

Murder victim Kenneth Wayne Arnder was shot in the head and his hands were severed at the wrists in the brutal July 1978 killing. Five years later, Stockton was convicted of his murder. AUTHORS' COLLECTION

Sheriff Jay Gregory of Patrick County, Virginia, was lead investigator in the Arnder murder case. He was later elected Patrick County sheriff, and said that his arrest of Stockton helped to win him votes. *THE VIRGINIAN-PILOT*, JOHN H. SHEALLY II

Frank Coppola, a former altar boy and Portsmouth policeman, was the first man executed after Virginia reinstated the death penalty in 1977. He was the fifth man in the nation to die after executions resumed in 1976. Coppola, defiant to the last, achieved legendary status among many Death Row inmates. *THE VIRGINIAN-PILOT*

Joe Giarratano, one of the original plotters of the mass escape, was convicted of killing a Norfolk woman and her daughter in 1979. Like fellow inmates Dennis Stockton and Willie Lloyd Turner, he chose not to run. *THE VIRGINIAN-PILOT*

Steve Rosenfield, along with Anthony King, represented Stockton before his execution in 1995. He believed that Virginia authorities arrested the wrong man in Arnder's murder. COURTESY STEVE ROSENFIELD

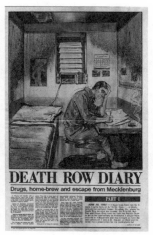

Front-page coverage of the mass escape led with a photo of Dennis Stockton and a special eleven-page section excerpting Stockton's diary, with details of the escape plot, drugs, sex and official corruption on Death Row. This led to death threats against Stockton and caused officials to move him to one of America's most inhumane lockups, Powhatan Correctional Center, ostensibly for his safety, though Stockton and others believed it was retribution for the truth-telling in his diary. AUTHORS' COLLECTION

Cover sheet from Stockton's fateful diary, and a sample page, detailing a meeting on July 28, 1984, with Norfolk newspaper editor Bill Burke. AUTHORS' COLLECTION

Dennis Stockton (standing, second from left), with his 1955 White Plains, North Carolina, high school baseball team. He was a promising left-handed pitcher who idolized the New York Yankees and was later scouted by former Yankees pitcher Tommy Byrne. AUTHORS' COLLECTION

Dennis Stockton, soon after he agreed to chronicle his approaching execution in an extended series of dispatches that ran in *The Virginian-Pilot* in 1995. THE *VIRGINIAN-PILOT*, BILL TIERNAN

7

The close shaves gave it away.

May 31, 1984, dawned no differently than any other day on Death Row. In fact, it was more pleasant than most. Storm clouds had flown off overnight, leaving behind blue sky and brilliant sun. On such a morning, escape seemed the farthest thing from reality. The talk had lasted too long, replacing action with blab, something at which prisoners were expert. At 8 A.M., the control-booth guard threw the switch and let the men out for breakfast. As usual, Stockton scored the pod's single morning paper and grabbed the sports page. Some days he had to race for it, but not today. No one seemed to care. Talk was nearly nonexistent also, but that was fine with him since he could lean back in peace and read the NASCAR results. When he looked up, everyone but Mason and Evans had returned to their cells.

Stockton flopped on his bunk to enjoy the remainder of the cool morning. Suddenly, his door opened and the law-library guard motioned him to follow. He'd completely forgotten that today was library day. As usual, only he and Evans made the trip. All seemed normal when they returned. The others were eating lunch. TV played *All My Children.* Then he saw Linwood.

The older Briley had shaved his beard and combed his hair in a way that made him look years younger. Minutes later, Tuggle asked to borrow a razor. Stockton handed over one of his disposable Good News razors; when Tuggle reappeared, his beard had also disappeared. Neither man looked like his old police mug.

Was today it? Stockton hadn't kept track. How could the guards miss this new look? Yet they trudged through their duties, impervious to all signs.

At 6 P.M., they went to the rec yard. The rain of the last few days had brought the humidity down. Stockton sat near the water spigot, expecting to watch a basketball game. But the inmates paced the yard in small groups and the basketball lay untouched by the pole. Over at a picnic table, Evans told a guard how to prepare seafood. "Naw, if you let the shrimp stay in the water more'n three minutes, they git tough 'n' rubbery 'n' hard to peel."

Tuggle walked his way, looking troubled as he sank beside him. "Don't say anything about this, but we're gonna leave tonight and I need to know how to get away from here," he said. "Can you tell me which roads run into North Carolina and where they are?"

Stockton glanced around, but no one had heard. "I gave Linwood a map with all that on it," he said.

"I know, but he's taking it with him and JB. I'd like to know for myself, 'cause we won't be sticking together."

So it was finally happening, every man for himself. Part of him felt like begging to get back in, another part was grateful to be out of the backstabbing. Still, he felt sorry for Lem, a latecomer and now odd man out. He drew a road map in the dirt, pointing out the escape routes from prison like he had with Linwood.

"I wish you were going," Lem finally said. "Hell, I'm the only white man. I'll stick out like a bad penny."

Stockton laughed. "Just stay out of sight and you'll be fine. And don't go where anybody knows you."

"I know where there's a load of guns near Marion, close to where I lived."

"That's exactly what you *don't* want to do."

"Yeah, I guess you're right."

Stockton figured the dumb hillbilly'd be the first to get caught. They shared a joint in silence, then moved across the yard in opposite directions. Stockton strolled past Bunch, lifting weights, to where Turner paced nervously under the basketball net. "We're going out tonight," Turner whispered. "They just told me."

"I heard. You reckon the guards suspect? Ain't nobody acting normal, you included."

Turner smiled. "Naw, them dumbasses ain't got sense to figure nothing out. Now I gotta go back and get the shanks. They shoulda told me earlier today was the day."

Turner told a guard he was ready to go inside. Stockton went along, figuring it wise to get out of the way. The guard radioed for assistance and in a few minutes Cpl. Harold Crutchfield arrived to escort them back. Turner asked for masking tape to do some repairs in his cell. They stopped at the downstairs control booth and Crutchfield gave him a roll. Stockton remembered the tape was for covering the mouths and eyes of hostages and wondered how Crutchfield would feel when it came his turn.

Stockton went straight to his cell and the control-booth guard, Ricardo Holmes, shut the door. He watched as Turner motioned to Giarratano, who jumped in surprise and looked around like crazy. Turner motioned for him to calm down. Then Willie Leroy Jones walked up and also acted stunned. It was like watching a silent movie. Were all the conspirators so ill-informed?

Shortly after 8 P.M., Stockton heard the others returning from the yard. He stripped away the card from the bottom of his panel so he could see. The prisoners bunched up as they waited in the foyer outside the sally port; Clanton was near the back of the line. The plan's success or failure depended on the next few seconds. Holmes hit the switch and the prisoners jostled forward. The guards told them to quit pushing and wait their turn. In the confusion, Clanton tried the bathroom door. It opened. He slipped inside as the others walked through the gates, dispersing quickly through the dayroom, muddling a head count if one were attempted.

But the guards turned away. The failure to count heads would later be identified as the first crucial mistake. The practice had lapsed after the shakedowns produced nothing more threatening than an occasional joint. Prisoners later gossiped about a payoff to a guard, but this was never proven. Blind trust in the system was the real culprit. Alton Waye turned on the TV; some of the men drifted over. The escape, so long and divisive in planning, had finally begun.

• • • •

Even as Stockton watched, little things started to go wrong. Hadn't Dwight Eisenhower said as much: that plans were great things until the shooting started? Everything seemed normal except for one big difference. The men usually headed straight for the showers after recreation, but now they gathered nervously as though waiting for something to occur. Stockton was nearly trembling with excitement. They'd give themselves away! Even with all that had happened, even with his defection, *he still wanted them to succeed.* He couldn't help but admire Clanton, alone there in the bathroom, his ear probably pressed to the door. He was on his own until Holmes was lured from the control booth. It took a lot of balls.

And now something happened that nearly made him shout. A regular occurrence . . . regular as clockwork . . . but one they had totally forgotten. They hadn't figured the nurse's nightly visits into their plans.

Routinely at eight-thirty, the downstairs door opened and a guard escorted the nurse as she passed out the meds. She stood at the table next to the control room and called out their names, written on envelopes containing their pills. They came up, one by one, and washed down the pills with a Dixie cup of water. She always drew the water from the guards' bathroom where Clanton now hid.

Nurse Barksdale appeared on schedule, escorted by Officer Donald Gentry from the main control room downstairs. A two-year veteran at the prison, she treated the inmates like men instead of animals. She was also the nurse Linwood and Peterson had talked about raping on the way out. They all watched in horror as she suddenly turned the knob to the bathroom door. It didn't budge. "It's stuck," she said, pulling again.

Every man stared. Clanton had had the foresight to lock the door, but now the guards knew something was amiss. An officer pushed against the door with his shoulder. Still no luck. "Ricardo, did you know this door was jammed?" he called to Holmes. "Maybe you should call maintenance." Holmes rose from his chair.

JB had sidled, unnoticed, near the control booth. "Somebody on the last shift said the bathroom was out of order," he said. "They said they was gonna leave a note."

"No note here," one of the guards replied. Another suggested they could get water in B-Pod, down the hall and through the locked door. The nurse and Gentry disappeared briefly to fill the cups, then returned and passed out pills.

JB slumped in relief. But now Stockton thought again of the men standing around rather than taking their showers. The guards might notice. Maybe he could help them out . . . maybe in a small way atone.

Barksdale called his name for his sleeping and kidney pills and Holmes threw the switch, opening his door. "Any pain tonight, Dennis?" Nurse Barksdale asked. "Not tonight, ma'am, thanks," he answered, taking his pills. He liked this nurse. Get out of here, he wanted to warn her. *Save yourself.* But to do so would start a panic, and people would get killed.

As he turned, he saw Tuggle sitting by himself at the middle table. "Things don't look right with no one in the showers," Stockton whispered.

Lem looked around. "Aw, shit, you're right," he moaned. "We're fucked. Why'd I ever let you talk me into this thing?"

"I'll grab my stuff and take a shower."

"Yeah, yeah," Tuggle said hopefully, looking up. "Great idea."

Stockton told the control booth he meant to take a shower. Holmes nodded. He grabbed his towel and washcloth and sauntered to the downstairs shower room, pleased with himself.

In reality, he was messing things up even more. JB was ready to lure Holmes out, but between the nurse and now Stockton's sudden desire for cleanliness, he decided to wait. Yet not everything was on hold. Dana Ray Edmonds, sentenced to die for cutting the throat of a Danville grocery store owner during a holdup, called to Holmes that his cell had a clogged toilet. He didn't plan to escape, but like Stockton was a sympathizer. Corporal Crutchfield, the guard in charge of building maintenance, walked over to the nearby pipe closet and looked inside.

His shower over, Stockton dried off. As he strolled back, he spotted a couple of the plotters hanging by Willie's cell. Turner was passing the shanks through his slot like candy, two per man. They stuck them in their pockets and walked away. Barksdale finished her rounds and her escort signaled to Holmes. He pushed the switch and the sally port shut behind them. They walked down the hall toward B-Pod, chatting. Good, she's safe, Stockton thought. He entered his cell and closed the door. He hung up his towel, grabbed his comb and ran it through his wet hair.

Nearby, Crutchfield leaned into the plumbing for a better look. JB glanced at Peterson and nodded. Peterson leaned close and lovingly pressed his knife to the corporal's throat. "Stay where you are," he whispered. "Don't make a sound."

Stockton looked at the clock: 9 P.M. He grabbed a pen and paper, upended his trash can and sat before the window, ready to take notes for his diary.

He didn't wait long. From somewhere JB had picked up a paperback; as he walked toward the control booth, he asked Holmes to pass it to Giarratano on the other side. Nothing strange in that: as long as Stockton had been here, officers passed things back and forth between the condemned. If a man ran out of matches or needed some Tylenol he'd ask at the window. Whoever manned the booth would open the door, step out and usually do what was asked. They'd noticed that the guard often left the door ajar, thinking he'd only be out a second. What could go wrong?

It was the night's second major error. Holmes checked his monitors and stepped outside to grab the book. Everything happened at once. JB held tight to the novel and yelled, "Now, Goldie!" Clanton burst from the bathroom with a roar. He pushed past the startled Holmes and into the booth, hitting the button that opened the sally port. Holmes reacted quickly, grabbing Clanton from behind and twirling him around, nearly making him fall. But he never had a chance—Linwood and JB pushed into the booth, each holding a long shank. "Give it up, Ricardo," Linwood said. Holmes's eyes grew wide, then he stepped back from Clanton in defeat.

The other conspirators piled from their cells. Officer Sandy Walker spotted the struggle in the control booth and took a step forward, but Giarratano and Willie Jones burst from their cells on either side of him, each holding a shank. Officer James Fitts was captured in a similar way by Turner. The silence was eerie: the shanks and the looks in the eyes of the prisoners told the outnumbered guards all they needed to know.

Fitts, Walker and a third man were marched to a part of the first tier near the stairs with a sunken floor. They were told to strip to their underwear, then their hands were shackled behind their backs. They were ordered to the floor, out of sight of the hall. One of the guards wore candy-red briefs, a gift from his wife. The inmates said he looked downright yummy.

"You know this is crazy," Holmes said as they forced him to strip. "You can't get out of the building. You'll just get killed." But Clanton was still high on adrenaline and kicked Holmes from the booth. "Get down with the others and be quiet," he snarled.

Of all the guards, Corporal Crutchfield was least lucky. He was stripped, his mouth taped with the masking tape he'd given to Turner, his hands cuffed behind his back. Two prisoners picked him up by his arms and legs. He thought they were going to bash his brains against the wall so he started to pray. "Quit blubbering, Harry," one said. "We ain't gonna hurt you, just hide you." Then they crammed him between the dripping pipes and slammed the closet door.

The prisoners had taken control of C-Pod in barely three minutes. Now they had to secure their gains. The guards were hog-tied with sheets and string and manacled with their cuffs. They also planned to tape their mouths like the unlucky Crutchfield, but abandoned that once they realized it would take too long. Watches, keys, rings and money were taken—some of the inmates soon sported new jewelry and a couple wore gold chains. JB ordered all keys piled on the TV table as they were discovered. The guards' uniforms were also thrown in a pile: each inmate dug for shirts and pants, but some of the larger men had trouble finding a good fit. Each man wore an additional layer of clothing under the uniform for a quick change after the escape, but this only made the sizings more difficult. Giarratano, who manned the control booth, looked like a sausage stuffed into a blue shirt several sizes too small.

Except for Giarratano and Jones, all of the inmates on the left side were rounded up and locked in a cramped room without windows. No one trusted the left-siders and now they were hostages themselves; the Brileys were certain they would signal the takeover by flashing the lights of their cells. None resisted except Morris Mason, who clamored to go too. "Shut up, Morris," Jones ordered. He was so nervous he kept dropping his knives.

Turner saw the problem and walked over. "Willie, lemme go," Mason pleaded. "My execution date's this year. You leave me here, you kill me same as the executioner!"

But Turner grabbed the arm of his former disciple and shook him. "See JB over there?" he said. "He still remembers what you pulled with Bunch. Why'd you go and do that, Morris? You'd probably be in this now if not for that stupid stunt. Get in that room with the others and stay back outta sight and just pray JB don't kill you before he leaves."

JB was clearly in charge. He ordered Alton Waye to stand by the TV. A loud TV was the norm for Death Row at night: Waye's job was to turn the volume up as guards approached, so they wouldn't get suspicious, then turn it down until the next victim approached so everyone could hear JB's commands. He ordered Giarratano to release Bunch and Evans, then placed Bunch by a window overlooking the yard and told Evans to answer the pod's phone and sound official if anyone called. Ed was nervous: he didn't rattle on as usual, trying to play the leader. He picked up a black nightstick from one of the guards and hung on to it like a security blanket.

JB was transformed—a distillation of himself, every sense tuned to the sounds of the building, what still needed to be done. He snapped orders to everyone but Linwood, who seemed content to let his younger brother run the show. Even though they had control of the pod, JB said it was still too early to celebrate. They had to take the entire building before hoping to get outside. The trick now was to call people in, one at a time.

But the first fly in their trap arrived unplanned. Barely ten minutes had passed since Officer Gentry escorted Nurse Barksdale down the hall to B-Pod. She passed out her meds to those inmates, then went to the elevator so she could continue to the first floor. But Gentry had misplaced his elevator key. Holmes would have a set, so he left her by the elevator and strolled back to Death Row.

The wall between B-Pod and C-Pod had shielded the rest of the second floor from knowledge of the takeover, yet even as he closed the door behind him, Gentry sensed something strange. The TV was loud as usual, but the men seemed so quiet, no catcalls between sides. As he walked toward the booth he saw a heavyset man in an ill-fitting shirt. That wasn't right—what had happened to Ricardo? Then the man looked up and it was Giarratano.

Gentry went numb. He stopped and in that second saw Willie Jones with a shank in his hand. His heart started pumping; he wheeled and ran back toward B-Pod, but the door in the new wall was locked and he fumbled for the key. If he could get through and lock the door behind him, he could raise the alarm. Feet were pounding toward him. He dropped the key, picked it up, fumbled at the lock. Linwood and Peterson were on either side of him, each carrying a knife.

"Nice try," Linwood said, smiling. They marched him to the dayroom and put him with the others, adding his uniform and keys to the pile.

Meanwhile, Nurse Barksdale was getting concerned. What was taking Officer Gentry so long? She knew the corridors were safe, but she still felt uneasy standing alone. As one of Mecklenburg's few night-shift nurses, she saw the reports of what the men did to each other, things like "running the gears," plunging a knife into another's abdomen then slicing up and across so the victim was eviscerated and his guts spilled into his own hands. They didn't teach things like that in nursing school. She looked at her watch. Three minutes. Maybe he'd been unable to find the key. She'd go back and help him. Anything was better than standing here alone.

As she closed the door behind her, she saw a tall man in a guard's uniform approaching. She smiled. Everything would be fine.

Then she saw the face. It was Derick Peterson. In the same instant, she saw the blade. "Oh God, oh God, what's happening!" she screamed.

"Shut up, now," Peterson hissed, grabbing her by the arm. "You'll be fine if you don't raise a ruckus."

But Barksdale wasn't so sure. She saw Gentry, stripped to his shorts, forced to lie with five others in the sunken alcove. She wondered if she'd be forced to strip: if so, she knew, rape would almost certainly follow. Big baby-faced Giarratano smiled at her from the control room, the buttons nearly popping off his blue shirt. Turner and JB stood by the TV. "There's too few of us and too many of them," JB growled. "Any one of 'em gets loose, they'll raise a warning. We're gonna have to kill some to make sure it doesn't happen."

"That's not what you said early on," Turner shot back. "We all agreed, no bloodshed! That's the only reason I agreed to go along. You can't go back on what you said!"

"Whose side you on, Willie?" JB screamed.

But what really frightened her were Clanton and Linwood. They were smoking joints, then smirked at each other as she was led in.

Peterson dumped her in Turner's cell. He looked at her hard for a second, apparently making some decision, then turned and walked away. She noticed holes in the wall and near the metal seams. Were these the rumored stashes? She could see the rear tower out the window. If she flashed the light, would the guard see? Then a huge shadow filled the door.

"You got twenty seconds to get out of them clothes, Nurse." It was the angry one, Earl Clanton. Behind him she saw Linwood Briley, undressing her with his eyes. "What're you going to do?" she asked.

"Shut the fuck up and do as you're told!" Clanton said.

She tried to steel herself for the inevitable. She unzipped the uniform and stepped free, leaving it in a white pile on the floor. Clanton was on her in a heartbeat, pawing at her breasts, pushing her back onto the bed. Linwood was there too, touching her, his hands everywhere. She tightened to a ball and fought off the hands, rough as sandpaper, pulling at her underwear, trying to pry apart her legs. There was no steeling against this, the nightmare they'd always said could never happen in the escape-proof Mecklenburg.

But then rescue came from the unlikeliest source. "Stop it!" someone called from the door. The pawing stopped, though the hands stayed put as if she were owned. It was Wilbert Evans, the ugly one they called Slobber Jaws.

"What you doing?" Evans cried. "You want to be regarded as a man, you act like a man. A real man don't treat a woman that way!"

"We gotta take her clothes to keep her from running off," Clanton said, glancing away.

"That woman ain't goin' nowhere," Evans said. "Why don't ya get her a blanket she can hide under?"

"You get the fuckin' blanket," Clanton said. "We won't strip her but we'll sure as hell tie her up." Evans ran off, and the two tied her with torn sheets, pawing at her some more.

Evans mercifully reappeared. "There won't be no killing and there won't be no raping," he shouted. "You gettin' what you wanted. Now get outta here and leave this poor woman alone."

He covered her with the blanket and waited for Clanton and Linwood to leave. "I'm sorry this happened, Nurse," he said. His eyes traveled down the lines of her body traced by the blanket. His fingers laced together. His eyes seemed so sad, as if by his past acts he knew that nothing could save him . . . that the most he could hope for was a moment's gratitude. She knew this man didn't mean to rape her, guessed that he was remembering freedom when he'd probably loved a woman. He was probably thinking how he'd never do so again. She felt sorry for him and realized she was no longer afraid.

"Thank you, Mr. Evans," she said softly. "You probably saved my life."

Evans grinned. "You'll be safe now," he said, tapping the nightstick lightly against his leg. "They won't come back in." Then the door clicked shut and she knew she had survived.

Several hostages would later swear that the efforts of Turner and Evans saved their lives. Turner's actions could have been predicted: he'd opposed bloodshed from the start, and his position as arms maker gave him a certain cachet. But what happened to Wilbert Evans that night? He was already vulnerable—a suspected snitch, a thorn in everyone's side. Prosecutors would later call his acts calculated to make a better clemency plea: the reformed man, savior of his jailers. Statements he made after the escape could support the charge. Yet he never could have planned the nurse's rescue. Maybe he felt her vulnerability as he watched, then simply reacted. It was the story of his life: first Deputy Truesdale's murder, now this. Acting on impulse. The grown child.

Once he left Barksdale, Evans approached JB. "What do you want me to do next?" he asked. JB apparently had not yet learned what just occurred with the nurse. He told Evans to take that nightstick and guard the hostages. Evans did as ordered, but kept watch on the nurse's cell.

Now another nurse arrived. Maude Boyd grew worried when Barksdale failed to return from her rounds. She entered C-Pod and an inmate dressed as a guard scooped her up as easily as her friend. She was thrown in Tuggle's cell. No one told her to strip, though like Barksdale she saw the men on the floor. Tuggle took her marked envelopes of medications; she tensed as he led her to his bunk, but Tuggle simply reached over and tuned his radio to his favorite country station. "Relax," he said, adding, "Make yourself comfortable. My home is yours." He grinned as he closed the door.

It was now a turkey shoot in C-Pod. The inmates picked off the guards as they blithely walked down the hall. As quickly as one was taken, another was called in. Turner, posted at the window, called out that a guard was coming. JB, Clanton and Tuggle got ready to grab him. Most tried to run but didn't fight once they saw the knives.

Yet the plotters still needed the white shirts. The shirt imparted authority: guards registered it a second before the face and automatically obeyed.

The first call went to Lt. Larry Hawkins, the shift commander, the most important hostage they could take. Using their phone list, JB called his office but was told he was out on rounds. He left a message to call extension 166, C-Pod's dayroom. At 8:50, Hawkins returned the call. JB forced one of the hostages to answer. "We need you to come assist a wounded inmate," the guard lied.

But Hawkins was still busy so he sent another white shirt in his place. At 9:10, Lt. Milton Crutchfield entered Building One and ran up the stairs to Death Row. He'd barely closed the door behind him when he was nabbed by Peterson and put with the others in the bottom tier. Two minutes later, Officer John Mayo hurried up the corridor to help with the "wounded inmate." He tried to run when he saw the inmates, but the door blocked his way.

At 9:13, Hawkins decided to visit Death Row. Something was going on. He'd sent Lieutenant Crutchfield, but the man never called back. He dispatched Mayo, but he also disappeared. He tried calling the pod, but no one answered. Was the place a black hole? He'd check it out himself. Turner saw him head for the stairs.

Now Hawkins became a victim of the vaunted "escape-proof" design. Just as in the sally port, the stairwell doors electronically locked behind anyone walking through. The theory was that any prisoner trying to escape would be trapped until the control booth released the lock. Clanton and Tuggle lay in wait under the stairs. Hawkins passed them unknowingly, walked upstairs and looked through the glass into The Row. Every door was open. The inmates were out. Peterson waited for him at the top, dressed like a guard.

The two stared at each other in amazement, waiting for the other to break the spell. Hawkins moved first and bolted down the stairs. "Get him! Go get him!" someone yelled. "You can't let him get away!" But Clanton and Tuggle were waiting. Hawkins ran right into their arms. They threatened to kill him if he didn't do as they ordered.

By ten o'clock, the row of about a dozen hostages extended from the downstairs shower room to in front of Stockton's cell. They answered quietly when addressed by one of the inmates. Nurse Barksdale had been molested but no one had been physically injured; there had been few threats, just an understanding of what could happen, thanks to the knives. Stockton heard one guard vow to quit if he lived through this night. Another whispered: "I just hope they make it out. There's no telling what'll happen if they don't."

Of all the hostages, Hawkins was most in danger. Twice, JB dragged him to the phone to order another guard into the trap. The knife was often at his throat. Stockton wondered what kind of revenge would follow once this ended. Prisoners weren't the only ruthless ones in Mecklenburg.

Sudden power is more potent than any drug. All the prisoners felt it, but no one more than JB. His thinking seemed razor-sharp, coming quicker and clearer than ever before. He was a conquering general, a lord of discipline. One thing the lord didn't need was distraction, especially from guards mumbling between themselves. "Ed, shut them up or I'll do it," he cried. How fine it would be to take one of the motherfuckers himself and off him as the others watched, a quick cut across the trachea and a wound that opened like a smile, spraying them all with blood. They'd get the message quick. The whole fucking state would get the message. But that was just indulgence, a load of daydreams. No time for that now. Much as he hated to admit it, Turner was right. Killing was counterproductive, at least at this moment. The simple threat was enough. Of course, all that could change.

By now, Linwood had told JB about the incident with Barksdale. JB suspected that Evans's sympathies lay with the hostages. All that talk of blasting out, the big bad Rambo movie, yet in the crunch the cocksucker went soft. Like Linwood always said, If you weren't with us, you were against us. He told Giarratano to open Evans's cell door. "Get your ass in your cell, Ed," he said. "I'm fuckin' sick of you siding with the hostages." Stockton watched as JB followed Evans to his cell, then stared in hatred through the closed door.

Now Stockton and Evans were the only original conspirators to be locked in their cells. Stockton was just as glad. JB was in his glory, a little Napoleon. He even dressed the part—white shirt, gold bars, walkie-talkie strapped to his side. It felt a lot safer in here.

Stockton went to take a leak, and when he returned Tuggle glanced over to his door. "Here," Lem said, poking a stack of envelopes through the slot. "Enjoy." It was the envelopes with meds, each marked with an inmate's name. There was his, empty. He flipped through them quickly in search of anything worthwhile. All he found was Mellaril, Thorazine—mind-control shit. Tonight was definitely a night to stay sharp, not dopey. He tore up the envelopes and flushed them down the commode.

He returned again to the window and now JB had Hawkins at the phone, the shank once more to his throat. "Stay off the phones, there's an emergency here!" he commanded at the younger brother's behest.

"Bring a van around to the sally port gate. Hurry now, we have a situation here!"

They had to win control of the main booth on the ground floor before they could take over the rest of Building One. At the same time, someone would have to stay behind for insurance. Turner and Giarratano volunteered without hesitation, so quick that both Brileys looked at each other, surprised. Turner would guard the hostages while Joey G. stayed in the control booth in case they needed back in. By now they held about a dozen guards plus the two nurses, their bargaining chips if anything went wrong. The safest thing to do was lock them in the downstairs laundry room where LeVasseur had been raped. Its door was heavy steel mesh; the lights were extinguished in case anyone else strolled by. But the key was missing and that made JB edgy, the last thing the hostages wanted. "Whoever has my uniform will find the keys in the shirt pocket," said one of the corporals. Peterson slapped his pocket and the keys were where he said.

These clowns are gonna be *great* on the road together, Stockton thought.

"This is your last chance, Dennis," Linwood said from outside his door. Stockton hadn't seen him walk up and his friend's voice took him by surprise. "You writing all this down in your diary?" he asked. "Gettin' it down for the movie? Why don't you come with us and you'd know the ending? I'd feel better if you did."

From the start Linwood had been straight with him, even if the others hadn't. He was the first to talk to him when he'd arrived, the one to acknowledge his existence even as they got ready to go. Linwood was scheduled for execution in three months; Stockton couldn't blame him one bit for trying to break free. He hadn't thought of that when he wrote Catron, had he? He hadn't considered that if his letter had been successful, it would be the same as pulling the switch on Linwood. Now his friend offered him one last chance at escape—a chance he didn't feel he deserved.

Yet, to tell the truth, he felt strangely proud. The escape had proceeded professionally, bloodlessly—better than any of them had dared believe. Even if they stopped now, they'd rubbed their keepers' noses in the cherished myth of Mecklenburg's perfection. They'd destroyed the myth for good. They'd gotten inside the system and beaten it: they'd watched, learned and planned, doing the impossible by getting this far. It was a masterpiece of the prisoner's art. He'd helped bring it into existence, then because of his damned hothead-edness he'd almost torn it down.

"Naw, Linwood," he answered. "I hope you make it, though. I really do."

"They'll kill you here, Dennis. They don't care if you're guilty or innocent once they've made up their minds. Once we get out, they'll take revenge on whoever's left."

"I'm betting otherwise," he said.

There was an uneasy silence as they watched the remaining con-spirators choose uniforms from the pile. "Ain't we a sight?" Linwood laughed. "They'll never forget this, will they?"

"Never in a thousand years."

"You take care, Dennis," Linwood said, drumming his fist against the glass.

"You too, Linwood," Stockton answered. "Give 'em hell."

• • • •

Strange things had been happening all night in C-Pod, thought Offi-cer Corlene Thomas, but this had to be the strangest. As the officer in charge of the building's main control booth, it was her duty to hit the buttons letting people in and out of the main entrance and side doors. Ever since eight or eight-thirty, officers and supervisors kept going up to Death Row, but they never returned. A call had come in that an inmate was injured, but no one ever called for paramedics. She watched as one white shirt went up, then another. Finally, Lieutenant Hawkins, the watch commander, went up and stayed. Things must be all right because he called down for a prison van to be parked at the sally port. But then he called right back, fussing for everyone to stay off the lines, saying that they had a *situation* here!

Now came the call that worried her most, simply because it went against standard protocol. An officer had rung to say she'd gotten a call on an outside line. Someone was coming to relieve her so she could return it. The voice sounded like Hawkins's, though it seemed a little strained. To tell the truth, she wasn't sure who it was or even from where it had come. That was the thing about Mecklenburg— for all its state-of-the-art gadgetry, there were still plenty of tiny screwups, a hundred minor miscommunications.

Thomas watched as an officer approached her booth. She didn't recognize him, but officers got moved from other buildings and even other prisons all the time. He certainly looked tall and neat in his uniform. He smiled and said he was her relief. Thomas unlocked the door.

It was the night's third big mistake. The tall officer was Derick Peterson—the minute she opened the door, he lunged against her, knocking her to the floor. She was in cuffs before it registered, long before she had a chance to hit the alarm. Peterson had called from the dayroom, placing a towel over the phone to disguise his voice. He made her sit out of sight, then called back up to C-Pod. He could hear the cheers of the others when JB answered and yelled, "He's in!"

It was 10:35. They now had control of every door to Building One. They finished suiting up in the captured uniforms. They had $783 in traveling money they'd found in their captives' pockets. They were ready to run. JB said he would return for Giarratano and Turner once they had the van. They took Tim Bunch, whose job was to man the main control booth and let them back inside should their bluff fail. Giarratano pushed the unlocking button and the six "guards" trooped downstairs.

Peterson waited for them, Corlene Thomas at his feet. "Bet you never figured *this* to happen," Peterson told her, chuckling, trying to calm his nerves. *What was taking 'em so long?* The phone rang and he picked it up, figuring it was JB. "Yo," he said, "what's up?"

"Who's this?" said the official voice at the other end of the line.

"Uh, well," Peterson stuttered. He looked down at the wide-eyed Thomas. No help there.

"Who *is* this? I'm looking for Officer Thomas. Why isn't she at her post?"

"I relieved her," Peterson answered. "She's gone."

"Where has she gone?"

She's tied up, you dumb shit, he thought. "I don't know," he said, praying for the others to hurry up. "I was just told to relieve her. I'm just doing what I was told." The officer said something that sounded like gibberish. Good Lord, get me outta here, Peterson thought, hanging up the phone.

Then it rang *again*. He touched it like poison, expecting the same caller. Or maybe the marines. But it was Giarratano, asking why his line was busy. Everybody was ready to come down. Peterson pressed the button that opened the door.

JB's excitement could barely be contained. He burst into the control booth and dragged Thomas to her feet. "Where on this board do you open the main exit?" he demanded. When she hesitated, he put his knife to her throat. She showed him the button. They threw her into a nearby rest room and locked the door.

Meanwhile, the others had found a closet where the riot gear was stacked. Each man donned a helmet and shield; they found a green canvas stretcher propped against a wall and Linwood grabbed a heavy-duty fire extinguisher from a crate. There were also gas masks; each man hung one around his neck.

Now all they needed was the "bomb," and that was still upstairs. It would be the pod's TV, covered by a blanket. The stretcher would be a good touch—one of them could follow, spraying it down with the extinguisher.

It was unbelievable—everything had been too easy. "Open the doors," JB told Bunch, expecting the van to be waiting for them, backed into the loading bay. Bunch hit the button and the door whined open. The van wasn't there.

JB dialed upstairs. "Get that fuckin' watch commander," he told Giarratano. "There's been a holdup with the van. We'll take him with us when we all go back down."

"We're not going," Giarratano said.

For JB, it was the night's biggest surprise. "You're what?" he screamed into the receiver. Bunch thought maybe JB had finally lost it. His face seemed to cave in.

"Me and Willie aren't going," Giarratano repeated, his voice trembling over the phone.

JB wiped his forehead with his sleeve. Joe and Willie were chickening out? It was incomprehensible, and for the first time he had doubts. "You seen something through the windows—what is it?" JB asked, confused. "Just let us up, okay, I'll talk to you there."

The six ran back upstairs with the stretcher, leaving Bunch at the main controls. Death Row looked like it had been through a storm. A table and several chairs were turned over; several shanks lay scattered about the floor. Clothing, shoes, baby pictures, family snapshots, car keys, new wallets, old wallets, popcorn, milk, cans of Pepsi and a pair of abandoned eyeglasses were pitched around the dayroom. Nothing moved on the left side, no sound came from behind the locked door. JB opened the laundry room and pulled out the watch commander. "The van ain't down there yet and you're gonna find out why," he said, blindfolding Hawkins with a torn sheet. Those staying behind were ordered back to their cells; Giarratano slammed the doors behind them. They howled with indignation when they saw the TV placed on the stretcher and covered with a blanket. "Use the TV from B-Pod," Waye called from his cell, but the other men laughed.

"Like we're gonna storm B-Pod and take their TV?" Tuggle said.

"You'll just hafta do without *All My Children* a couple a days, Alton," Peterson added.

Meanwhile, JB was arguing with Turner and Giarratano. "We're ready to go," he said. "You're holding us up."

"We're not goin'," Turner said.

"Why?" JB yelled. Turner's refusal was the most surprising. He'd done more than anyone else—he was just as culpable, and the DOC would fry him when they found out. It was like a personal judgment, JB thought, like they didn't trust *him.*

That was certainly part of it. Giarratano had opted out gradually as he became more convinced that perhaps he was innocent of murder. But Turner hadn't made up his mind until just then. He'd watched JB's growing ruthlessness, his willingness to use the shank. He feared worse things waited once they got Outside.

"JB," he said, "we'll wait half an hour after Bunch gives the all-clear. Then we'll release the hostages. That'll give you a good head start."

Linwood touched his brother's shoulder. "That's a good suggestion," he said.

"But . . ."

"James, they're gonna keep their word," he said. "It's their choice, not ours. *Let's go!"*

The van still hadn't arrived by the time they got downstairs; Hawkins, the knife at his throat, called and ordered it done. The voice on the other end said it was coming from the boiler plant. In a minute they saw it pass outside the wire and pull up to the gate. Hawkins was taken back upstairs and handed over to Turner.

It was 10:38. Officer Barry Batillo drove the van to the main sally port gate as ordered. When Hawkins first called and said they needed a van to move a bomb, Batillo had started the first vehicle he came to, a new blue van. Then he considered the potential damage. Why ruin a new one? He switched to an older white van and parked outside the gate.

The six looked at one another. It was so quiet outside, no sirens or shouting, not even wind through the trees. As if the world were holding its breath, seeing how far they could go. This was it: the bluff they'd concocted, the biggest con of their lives. Might as well take it all the way.

"Well, boys," Linwood said, "we'll be remembered. That's for certain."

The six took off for the main sally port—Peterson went first, clearing the way. "Okay, everybody, get back, we've got a bomb here," he cried. JB, Tuggle, Jones and Clanton each held an end of the stretcher; Linwood followed, spraying the TV and stretcher as if they were hot. There was a problem with logic there, but no one noticed. Batillo stood watching as the six ran toward him. JB was in front: he yelled at Batillo to turn the van around and back halfway through the gate so it wouldn't close on them. It was the white shirt Batillo saw, and he complied, figuring it was the shift commander. It was the fourth and final mistake of the night.

Batillo backed up, then threw open the rear doors. "Get back," JB commanded. "We have a live explosive device here and it might go off!" Batillo ran across the road to some nearby trees. He knelt in a ditch and covered his head with his hands.

Linwood climbed in the driver's seat while the other five threw the stretcher through the open rear doors. They piled in behind it. The console was just like Stockton drew it, the two-way radio by his hand, the key in the ignition, the engine idling. He cranked up the seat. He started laughing. They had money, they had a place to go, they had wheels. It was too good to be true.

He keyed the radio and contacted the tower. "Open the sally port gates," he said. The gates swung open and Linwood rolled slowly down the road. As he vanished in the trees, he called the tower again. "Secure the sally port gates," he said. Then they were gone.

Timothy Bunch stood outside Building One's loading bay and watched the sally port gates close. The DOC van rounded a curve and disappeared from view. He rocked back on his feet and looked up at the sky. He spotted Orion, the Big and Little Dippers. He used to do this as a boy on his dad's farm in Indiana. The air smells good, he thought. I bet it smells better where they're going. He couldn't help but envy them, now that they were free.

What if he just walked right out the gate in all the confusion or straight through the yard and mingled with the other guards? It'd be worth it to see their faces, but he knew he'd never last two days outside. He accepted now what Gary Gilmore told him in his dreams, that this was the world to which he was born. It was just like Tuggle's faded blue tattoo said: BORN TO DIE. He remembered his crazy plan to break into a beauty shop and dress like a woman, and how Stockton had said that while he was at it he'd better shave his legs. They'd both started laughing so hard they could hardly stand. It was the only real moment of friendship he'd had in this place . . . what he'd had with JB had nothing to do with friends. Sure, Stockton hadn't wanted to team with him if they broke out, but that was survival. Everyone on The Row understood survival.

Still, if any of them was to escape, he wished it had been Stockton and him.

Bunch looked at the luminous dial of a watch he'd taken from a hostage: 10:47 P.M. They'd done the impossible in little over two hours. They were in the history books now.

He stuck his hands in his pockets and sauntered back inside Building One. He looked outside once more, then closed the loading bay door. He jingled some loose change in his pocket, stopped by a soda machine and got a cold Pepsi. *Ker-thunk.* It landed even with his knees. There was change left over, so he bought another. Maybe he'd give it to Stockton. The old man would appreciate it. A gift from The World.

He called Giarratano. "They are gone," he said, smiling. "They made it."

Then he started laughing. *Maximum security, my ass!* Timothy Bunch, killer and breakout artist, hadn't felt this good in years.

8

A howl of jealous rage rose up when Bunch announced the six were free.

No one had really believed the ruse would work: they'd get hung up at the gate and the whole thing would turn into a disaster. Now they would be part of history and the others envied them—even Stockton, though he did enjoy the fulminations from the surrounding cells. None roared worse than Evans. "Them lucky sons of bitches!" he cried. "It's a million to one—I don't want to hear no more about it!"

But everyone else did, so Bunch told the story in its glory, ending with Linwood's slow, stately departure and the gate closing like the final curtain of a play.

Now the remaining Death Row inmates on Stockton's side of C-Pod—those who hadn't been part of the planning or escape— clamored to be let out of their cells in the brief time remaining before the prison discovered the breakout and they all paid for the fugitives' sins. Giarratano and Turner balked, keeping to their promise to JB, but the others, led by Evans, threatened to alert the tower by flashing their lights. The two reluctantly gave in.

Evans seemed gripped by a hysteria that was equal parts anger and hope. He barged from his cell, kicking away debris. He rushed to the laundry room and yelled to the hostages: "Don't worry, I'll get you out. I protected you during the breakout." He pounded his hands together in excitement. "I'm gonna get a commutation on this," he said. He demanded that Turner and Giarratano release the hostages, but they were more interested in shedding their uniforms and finding their old clothes. Woe to the inmate dressed like a guard when the goon squad arrived.

For a brief moment, Evans had been a hero, surprising them all. Now he returned to the blowhard everyone knew. "They're so dumb they'll get caught in no time," he predicted loudly. Stockton suspected Evans had never forgiven the plotters for choosing the Brileys' plot over his. Worse, it had worked! He figured that somehow Evans would find a way to get revenge.

After thirty minutes, the hostages were freed. The key to the laundry room was lost in the confusion, so Dana Edmonds, known for his strength, grabbed the door at the bottom and bent up the steel mesh. Another inmate crawled underneath and uncuffed their hands. The hostages crawled out, met on the other side by Evans who shook their hands and announced, "I'm Wilbert Evans. I kept people from getting killed." The nurses were released. Turner offered his shank to a white shirt, who cautiously backed off. "You're safe," Turner said, dropping the shank on a table and stepping away.

At 11:15, Giarratano handed the phone to Hawkins. The first officers arrived shortly before midnight. They found Death Row in shambles, shanks on the floor and tables, hostages still in shock, shivering at near-death memories or wearing a thousand-yard stare. Evans was everywhere, shaking hands. "I ain't the only one that's gonna get fired behind this," Hawkins told an arriving white shirt, but moved away when he saw Stockton writing down his words. The inmates on the left side were released: Morris Mason blinked in the lights and smiled, happy to be alive. Stockton heard a shout from the plumbing closet and reminded a guard about poor Corporal Crutchfield, forgotten among the pipes. But no one could find the key, so it was another hour before he too was freed.

The dayroom was a slapstick scene, a bunch of Keystone Kops running into one another and falling down. Stockton couldn't decide what amused him most: the shamefaced guards, the inmates extolling their heroism or the escalating confusion as each new official had to be told everything from the start. There were incriminations, recriminations, excuses. Throughout the prison, word was traveling from building to building. He heard shouts outside his window. He turned up his radio, doused his light, prayed the six got away safely and went to bed.

At 2 A.M., Robert Landon, the DOC's director, was awakened from pleasant dreams. He and his staff were on retreat in Colonial Williamsburg, peaceful venue of presidents and kings. Suddenly, someone pounded on his door. "Landon, Landon, wake up! They've escaped from Mecklenburg!"

Was this a prank? If so, he wasn't amused. Things like this didn't happen in the real world.

Fifty miles away in Richmond, Governor Chuck Robb also got the call. A few hours later, he issued an executive order placing the state's Army and Air National Guard on alert. It would be *the* embarrassment of his governorship and resulted in scores of shakeups, studies and resignations. For up to a year afterward, he would flinch every time the phone rang late at night, hoping to God it wasn't another disaster at Mecklenburg.

• • • •

And where was the source of the uproar?

By 10:48 P.M., the Mecklenburg Six, as they came to be called, were going south. Linwood pulled onto Route 58, the highway running past the prison, then drove the speed limit down Route 4, a winding back road skirting the John H. Kerr Reservoir that dropped into North Carolina. They cheered the instant the prison dropped from sight. "I can't believe they actually let us out the gates like that!" Tuggle said. "Oh, man," Clanton shouted, "we're free!"

Freedom. The reality hadn't begun to sink in. The reservoir, a chain of lakes straddling the state borders, flashed and sparkled in the moonlight. Eighteen months earlier, the Brileys had written a letter to Richmond schoolchildren warning them away from crime: "You can take our word for it, you don't know how precious your freedom is until you've lost it." Now Linwood contemplated that freedom, his arm out the window, a joint between his lips. Behind him, Derick Peterson had fallen into awed silence: he watched the dark woods pass, the stars and horned moon keeping pace in the breaks between the trees. It was the first time he'd been out in two years. Everything seemed cast in beauty: the fields of corn and tobacco, the solitary country store, a pole light its sole illumination, a sign in the window, NIGHTCRAWLERS, 25 CENTS.

The idea was to get out of Virginia as soon as possible and dump the van. Linwood drove across the John H. Kerr Dam, the water around them a promise of something beyond expression, then crossed the border within minutes. They passed Interstate 85 with its assurance of speed and distance but also of state troopers, crept through the darkened crossroad town of Norlina, continued for another five miles to Warrenton. They were thirty miles southeast of Mecklenburg and by now the alarm should be out, all eyes peeled for a dirty white van with a gold state seal. They definitely needed camouflage and discussed ramming another vehicle and taking it when the driver stopped, but that would also make a hell of a lot of noise and draw unwanted attention. Not smart. They were still arguing when Linwood rolled past Marion Boyd School and down a dead-end street called Cousin Lacy's Lane. He drove to the end, behind the school, and switched off the key.

Stockton had told them to hide the van in the woods and cover it with branches, delaying as long as possible the starting point for the inevitable search. But the six were getting nervous—they wanted away from the van and they wanted so *now*. Yet their choice only assured discovery by morning, if not earlier, since cops were always checking around schools for vandals and horny kids. But everyone was yelling at everyone else. Linwood couldn't take it anymore. He flung open the doors, left the keys in the ignition and headed for the woods, JB at his heels, Tuggle and Jones fast after him.

Peterson headed in the opposite direction. "See ya 'round," he said, flashing his familiar grin. Clanton went with him, sullenly. He still wanted to hang with the Brileys, but they seemed eager to ditch everyone. So he stayed with Derick, staring morosely after the two men to whom he'd devoted himself for the last three years.

Ahead lay Warrenton, a sleepy town of about twelve hundred souls. Many were elderly and cautious, perfectly happy that nothing more exciting than local football matches rolled their way. It was a historic town, founded in 1779, boasting the grave of Confederate General Robert E. Lee's daughter. A sign on Main Street proclaimed that newspaper editor Horace Greeley had been married in the town church. Folks occasionally talked about jailbreaks from the minimum security prison outside town, but those prisoners weren't the overly violent sort and no one felt threatened.

All that was about to change. It was a little past midnight when hospital orderly Andrew Davis drove his regular route home from the late shift at a nearby hospital. He'd passed the county courthouse, passed Miles Hardware, when two men called to him from the shadows. Davis knew most everyone in Warrenton by sight, black and white, and he thought he knew these guys too. He stopped his car at a red light and saw he was mistaken when they caught up. But they were dressed in some kind of police or guards' uniforms, so why worry?

"Can we have a ride, mister?" one said, then jumped up front before Davis could answer. His companion crawled in the back. "Where can we get some drugs?" the guy in front continued, a younger man. Unless this was some weird form of entrapment, these guys were *not* The Law.

"I don't know nothing 'bout drugs," Davis said.

"Okay, then, where do people hang out?"

"Mister, this town folds up its sidewalks at ten."

The man in the back grunted in disgust. Davis didn't like his looks—a big, angry-seeming guy. For the first time, he considered he might be in trouble. "Where you want to get off, then?"

"We'll just get out wherever you stop," the talking man said.

Now he knew he was in trouble. Davis lived a few miles out in the country with his wife and four kids, and he sure wasn't about to take these men *there*. A half mile out of town he pulled off on a dirt road. "I'm not going any farther," he said. The words were barely out of his mouth when the man in front grabbed for the keys and the surly guy in back came at him with a knife. He figured he was dead, but at least he could go out fighting. He screamed and threw up his arms, knocking away the knife. He kicked out at the young guy and scrambled backward from the car. He ran screaming to a nearby house and called police when the sleepy owners let him in.

It was the first hint Warrenton officials had that the escapees had arrived. But there would be others. It didn't take a patrolling officer long to find the van. It wasn't hard. Not only had Linwood pulled behind the school, he'd parked in the playground.

Police believed the two who'd hailed Andy Davis were the Brileys, but they were really Clanton and Peterson. When Davis ran off, they figured his car was too hot to take so they loped into the woods. Before dawn, officials had already set up a command center in the fairground, and search parties ranged throughout the woods. From their hideout, Clanton and Peterson saw flashlights. They heard groups of men calling back and forth, the baying of hounds. One group drew close and they tensed. Then, miraculously, the searchers turned and faded into the woods.

"Is that all they're gonna do?" Peterson whispered.

"I hope so," Clanton said, looking sick. He was eaten up with mosquito bites; the damn things kept whining round his ears. At least in The Row he could sleep without turning into one big welt. "They find us, they're gonna shoot us, no doubt about it," he said. "You heard 'em—they're scared shitless. We're out in these woods all by ourselves. Ain't nobody gonna say different. They might even plant a couple guns on us, say we was armed and dangerous."

Suddenly, this escape didn't seem like such a good idea.

Friday, June 1, dawned on an armed camp. More than two hundred officers were brought in for the ground search: the agencies included the police departments of Warrenton and nearby Henderson, the Virginia State Police, the North Carolina Highway Patrol, the North Carolina State Bureau of Criminal Investigations and the National Guard. The FBI even arrived, brought in since the fugitives had crossed state lines. The feds began monitoring all phone calls in and out of town. Roadblocks cordoned off a ten-mile area. Helicopters churned overhead with infrared equipment. Pontoon boats checked the reservoir. Four bloodhound teams roamed the woods. The confusion just got worse as the media and other sightseers pulled in.

In town, the residents were terrified. In addition to the van and the attack on Davis, a pickup truck was stolen in nearby Afton. People who rarely locked their doors now barred them, while others went armed. By midday, town merchants had sold out of ammunition and weapons. The middle school principal paid $17 for the last box of .38-caliber slugs at Miles Hardware. A guy at the tire store told everyone how he had two guns at the head of his bed and one under the pillow. A newsman snapped a granny rocking on her porch with a shotgun across her lap. And at the elementary school, students were not let out for recess and parents appeared in droves to pick them up at last bell.

There was one tragedy: a man in nearby Halifax County, observing the helicopters overhead and the roadblock at the end of his street, left his loaded pistol on the nightstand. Two days later his nine-year-old son was playing with a three-year-old neighbor girl. When she asked if the pistol was real, the boy removed the clip and, assuming it was now safe, pulled the trigger. But there was still a round in the chamber and he shot her between the eyes.

Those most at risk turned out to be the searchers—and more from the citizens than the escapees. A DOC spokesman warned that if he were a black man living around Warrenton, "I wouldn't walk in the woods and I wouldn't wear a blue shirt." Some black residents wore shirts with the words I'M NOT ONE OF THE BRILEY BROTHERS. The same applied around Mecklenburg. Many of the searchers were young, black prison employees dressed in prison blue. Their job entailed knocking on doors in Boydton, the nearest town, and elsewhere in the county, asking if anyone had seen anything suspicious. They were scared to death they'd be killed by the panicked white citizenry. Guards told of one wealthy Boydton resident who had come home for lunch when their van pulled up. Two black guards got out. He ran to grab his shotgun, but no one was killed.

Meanwhile, Peterson and Clanton were getting hungry. They abandoned their guards' uniforms in the woods, then headed into town to buy food. Peterson wore a sweatsuit, Clanton a T-shirt and sweatpants. He kept his guard's jacket, but thought it safe after ripping off the Mecklenburg patch. They jogged down a side street to Willoughby's Convenience Store and Laundromat and bought cigarettes, wine, cheese and bread. They could see the county jail a block away. The people inside the store were friendly, talking about the escape. They went into the Laundromat, where they helped one woman carry her laundry then dug into their wine and cheese. Clanton made a call on the pay phone, then Peterson tried to call his mom.

The calls were their undoing. The FBI picked up two suspicious calls at 4:15 and 4:54 P.M. They came from Willoughby's, near the center of town. Some officers entered the store, but failed to check the Laundromat. A few minutes later, the commander of the North Carolina prison SWAT team was riding with another officer when he glanced through the laundry's plate glass windows. A man wearing a uniform coat with the patches ripped off was standing inside.

It was nearly 6 P.M. The police surrounded the Laundromat. They ordered a cleaning lady to stand back, then stormed inside. The two were still having their wine and cheese. They didn't resist when the police crashed in, guns drawn, screaming for them to raise their hands.

They had been out for little more than nineteen hours. Their short-lived freedom was over. As they were marched from the Laundromat, Peterson turned to Clanton and snapped, "You wanted to come back in here like a damned fool!" When asked why he was re-captured so quickly, he groaned, "Damned if I know."

Peterson shook his head and wondered which was harder: escaping the escape-proof prison, or escaping your own damn nature.

• • • •

Since Peterson and Clanton were picked up so quickly, the searchers assumed the others were somewhere nearby. The next seven days witnessed a manhunt few would see the likes of again. The searchers marched through the woods, shoulder to shoulder, hoping to flush the four like deer. The work was hot and sticky: ticks and mosquitoes attacked as if siding with the fugitives. They trekked through beaver ponds, marshy stands of cattail alive with water moccasins, spooky wildernesses of rhododendron so thick you couldn't see the man a few yards ahead. They bought all the bug repellent in Warrenton, then sent to the state capital for more. After every search, they rushed the showers and pulled out the ticks still embedded in their skin. All to no avail. By June 2, Governor Robb posted a $40,000 reward for information leading to the fugitives' capture. By June 4, sightings were coming from throughout North Carolina and Virginia. Each call had to be checked. A Warrenton man called police about a stolen shotgun, only to call back that his mother had taken it for her own protection. Police rushed twenty-five miles away to Oxford, North Carolina, after a clerk reported that a man resembling one of the Brileys had stolen two cans of beans.

By June 8, they learned they'd looked in the wrong part of the country the whole time.

The other four had stuck together soon after Clanton and Peterson took off. They headed up Main Street in search of a car, Linwood and Tuggle riding stolen bikes while JB and Jones walked. Tuggle was too big for his bike and his knees kept banging the handlebars. They checked from house to house, looking for anything with keys. Finally, four miles out of town, they spotted a blue Ford Ranger pickup with North Carolina vanity plates PEI-1 parked beside a darkened welding shop. The keys were inside. They squeezed in the cab and filled the tank. Once again Linwood drove, heading north on the interstate until that met I-95 just below Richmond. They drove the speed limit through the capital city at about the same time the governor was awakened so rudely. They passed the exit for The Wall, where hopefully they'd never keep their dates with Old Sparky. Just a few miles away sat the tan stucco house with the neat lawn and trimmed hedges that the Brileys called home. "This where you guys gettin' off?" Tuggle asked.

"Like to," Linwood answered, "but it's the first place the cops'll come."

By dawn, the four were north of Richmond. They stopped for breakfast, changed from their guards' uniforms to sweatshirts and jeans, filled the tank again. By now, news of their escape was on the radio. They laughed and smoked some reefer from a plastic bag of nearly two hundred joints the Brileys had brought along. Mecklenburg seemed miles distant and years ago. They continued north on the interstate, past D.C. and Baltimore, up the Delaware Turnpike. At Philadelphia, they pulled off the highway and into North Philly, one of the poorest, meanest sections of the City of Brotherly Love. The Brileys bought some clothes at a thrift shop and dumped their prison uniforms in a park. Linwood gave Tuggle and Jones $25 and kept the rest of the nearly $800 taken from the hostages for themselves. "Let me go with you," Jones begged. Linwood said he was on his own.

For his part, Tuggle was already in the driver's seat. This was one tough-looking neighborhood and he sure as hell didn't want to get robbed of his wheels *here*. What would he do, call the police? "So," he said as Jones climbed back in the passenger seat looking dejected, "where d'ya want to go?"

Jones shrugged, feeling lost and sorry. He didn't really care.

"So how about Canada?" Tuggle continued. "They'll never find us there."

He had it all planned. He'd gotten the idea from Stockton, dreaming like he did of heading to the jungle. That was crazy—you needed a boat or plane for that, but the idea of another country was brilliant and from what he'd heard the Canadian border was a sieve. He'd slip up there and live in the woods for the next twenty or thirty years. He'd build himself a little cabin, live off hunting and fishing and what he caught laying traps. He'd rather be in the country than the city, and after two murder convictions he knew that the farther away he was from others, especially females, the better. He had no control around women, especially when drinking, which was an impossible situation since for him the two went hand in hand. But out in the woods he wouldn't have that temptation. He'd just be another law-abiding citizen who, at worst, indulged in a little poaching. Was that so bad?

Willie Jones agreed. He'd probably agree to anything, Tuggle figured, since he had no plan of his own. He didn't give Jones much chance when the two would finally part ways, but until then at least he was an agreeable traveling companion. Maybe he could drop him off in one of the big cities, Montreal or Quebec City. Shoot, from what he'd heard those Frenchies *loved* American black guys. Jones just shrugged, a gesture that was fast becoming his trademark. Tuggle felt sorry for the guy, but he wouldn't let it spoil his good mood. No matter what happened, whether he was caught or built his log cabin, this was a dream come true. He'd never been this far north before; hell, he'd hardly been out of Virginia and Carolina, and here he was on the way to another country. He was discovering a pleasure of the seasoned traveler: the anticipation of the unknown, the rootless illusion of starting anew. He stopped to help a woman whose battery had died and he hauled out jumper cables. He and Jones ate at fast-food restaurants and bought a cheap bottle of scotch. He asked two troopers directions back to the New Jersey Turnpike. There was some question later how two escaped murderers could tool along one of America's busiest roads without being spotted, yet Tuggle drove the speed limit or under, his arm across the back of the seat.

Once "Free Bird" played over the radio and he remembered Stockton. Dennis called it his anthem. Tuggle wondered what was going down at Mecklenburg. Probably on lockdown for the rest of the century. Stockton should have come along, he thought. The two of them would've got along fine in the woods.

Not much could spoil this drive, unless it was the fact that these Yankees didn't believe in country stations and he had to settle for oldies rock and roll. That and the money situation. Damn greedy Brileys—the $25 wasn't going far. Once off the Jersey Turnpike they sold some spare parts from the flatbed for $17, then headed north on back roads until they reached Woodford, Vermont, a small town just north of the Massachusetts border in the heart of the Green Mountain National Forest. They camped for three days to save money, sleeping in a tent they bought and roasting weinies over a fire. Across from the campground's main entrance, Tuggle spotted the Red Mill Gift Shop, a little souvenir stand that looked like cake to rob. The owner, a friendly enough woman, was usually by herself and he chatted her up, learning her name. But for once Tuggle resisted temptation, close to the border as he was. No need to give himself away.

They headed north again, bought clothes at an army-navy store, drove the back roads through the trees. By the morning of June 8, they were camped in Jay, a tiny resort town ten miles south of Canada. They were also low on pocket change. They needed something to get a start in Canada, just a couple of hundred was all. Tuggle remembered the old lady and her gift shop back in Woodford. It seemed a cinch. He left Jones in the tent and headed south, promising he'd be back late that afternoon.

At about 1 P.M., Ursula Spika was alone in her store when the man from the campsite wandered in. She'd had lots of tourists this season but she remembered this one because of his accent. She didn't get many southerners this far north: he was funny with his ball cap and hunter's vest with no shirt, his gut rolling over the top of his green pants that looked newly bought from some surplus store. "Good ole boys," she'd heard them called, though to tell the truth there were plenty of characters like him also living in the Vermont and New Hampshire woods. "Can I help you?" she asked, smiling. He returned the smile, put a knife to her throat and told her to give him all her money and she'd be okay. Then he just as calmly walked away.

She was shaken, but not so badly that she didn't note the North Carolina plate on the back of his truck. She gave the license number to police when she phoned them.

Tuggle had gotten $100. That'll do, he thought, cruising back through Woodford when he suddenly saw the lights of a state trooper in his rearview. He hit the gas, barreling through this Palookaville and its twin, called Stamford, then down some side roads and back on the main highway. He lost the state trooper but somehow in Stamford picked up a second tail, a part-time constable whose previous cases involved little more than stolen bikes. The constable, the town's only officer, was thinking how Stamford was such a quiet place that there'd not even been a robbery since he took office and now here was this wild man in a North Carolina truck who'd just robbed that nice Miz Spika. Tuggle rounded a curve, and straddling the road was yet *another* trooper's car. Why fight it, he thought. It's been fun, but he was going back to Death Row.

Tuggle pulled over and raised his hands. "I'm Lem Tuggle," he said when the constable nervously approached, gun drawn. "I think

you'll find I'm wanted pretty bad by the people back in Virginia."
He'd been a fugitive for ten days.

It was 1:30 P.M. By then, Willie Jones had decided that Tuggle
wasn't coming back. He didn't know why, he just *knew*. He left the
campsite, broke into a house and called his mom long-distance. He
was ten miles from Canada and ready to leave the country, he told
her. Instead, she urged him to turn himself in.

Jones left the house, walked around a little and thought about
what she said. He walked up to another house and knocked on the
door. He asked to use the phone and called a Vermont State Police
station near the border. He told them who he was and that he was
turning himself in because his mother wanted it. He said he was un-
armed and would be waiting in the middle of Route 242 through
town. At 5:30 P.M., four hours after Tuggle's capture, the police found
him right where he said, good to his word.

It is not known what was said in the conversation between the
twenty-six-year-old Jones and his mom. But it can be imagined. He
was hungry, he was lonely, he was covered with bug bites. This
wilderness stuff might be okay for Tuggle, but not for him. He'd
failed at everything in life—lost his job, killed a friend's parents after
they'd only tried to help him, stolen their life savings and blown that
in Honolulu, where he was finally captured. He'd go to Canada and
fail there too, probably end up killing someone else who only showed
him kindness. As always, he was scared.

So he called his mom. He told her where he was, what he planned
to do. He probably started crying. Without a doubt, she cried too.

Give yourself up, Willie, she told him. You'll be running all your
life if you don't.

They'll kill me if I go back, he answered. They'll put me in that
chair and throw the switch. They'll never forgive me for what I done.

His mother agreed. Man never forgives, she told him. But God does.

• • • •

That left the Brileys.

The brothers were everywhere. Nowhere. They were sighted in
Virginia, North Carolina, New York, Boston. Once Tuggle and Jones
were captured, the sightings spread to Canada. A delivery man in
Montreal ran off screaming when the people who ordered chicken
turned out to be two black men.

But calls didn't just come from panicked citizens. A few hours after the capture of Clanton and Peterson, a policeman in Portsmouth, Virginia, said he saw Linwood strolling down the main part of town. At about 6 P.M., Officer George Michalsky was driving home for dinner when he paused at a stoplight and noticed a man walking alongside with his hands in his pockets. Michalsky stared and the man gazed back with what the policeman considered a "dead-evil" stare. When Michalsky returned to duty at seven-thirty, he saw a newspaper photo of Linwood and identified him as the man on the corner. The brothers had once lived in the shipbuilding city and were believed to still have relatives in town, so an APB was issued. At 9 P.M., another officer thought he spotted both brothers tampering with a car near where the first man had been seen. He called for help and started chasing the pair; a detective nearly hit them as they ran in front of his car. As they disappeared around a building, one of them reportedly fired from behind the corner. The detective fired back. No one was hit, no one arrested. The two Briley look-alikes were never found.

The fear was worst in Richmond, the brothers' home and scene of their crimes. Former neighbors locked their doors. While some did not believe the two would be stupid enough to show their faces, what with all the cops watching, others figured there were scores to be settled with those who testified against them at trial. If they didn't get even themselves, they'd send someone. The family of Duncan Meekins, the gang member who'd turned state's evidence, was given police protection. The assistant commonwealth's attorney and former city attorney who had teamed to prosecute the brothers were also given protection, but they were "too mad to be scared," one said. Richmond police rushed to surround an empty house where the two were supposedly holed up; four hours later, they broke in and found it empty. A panic-stricken woman claimed a Briley had demanded sex from her daughter; the daughter explained to police that her overexcitable mother had misunderstood.

The brothers soon became the subject of popular culture. Two Lynchburg, Virginia, disc jockeys penned "The Ballad of the Briley Brothers" and played it on the radio as the search dragged on. "The rooms are small, the food ain't great, the guards are big and burly," crooned songwriters Matt McCall and Randall Graham. "So Lin and James, and four more guys, checked out a little early."

It seemed that the only place where there were no panicky calls was Philadelphia, where JB went as Slim and Linwood as Lucky. The two lived quietly as watchmen in Dan's Custom Car Factory. Dan Latham, the owner, had just opened the garage specializing in installing vinyl tops when a friend introduced the two as out-of-towners and said they needed a place to stay. Latham agreed in return for their help in fixing up the place; the three lived and worked in the North Second Street garage, sleeping at night on cots or in one of the cars needing repair.

The man who introduced the two to Latham was Johnnie Lee Council, their uncle. The park where they separated from Tuggle and Jones was only a few blocks from Council's home. At first glance, this did not seem the ideal situation for men who'd anticipated their executions and now wanted to enjoy life. North Philly was a tough place, where many houses were boarded and others gutted by vandals. Vacant lots separated the ruins, overgrown with tall weeds hiding mounds of trash and rubble. The summer sweltered, and most residents were too poor for air-conditioning. Most spent their nights leaning out windows, hoping to catch a breeze.

Besides all this the two weren't even being paid, just given a place to stay and an occasional meal. But they seemed happy. In addition to acting as watchmen, they served as handymen, fixing things for the new shop, washing cars, cleaning up and doing various odd jobs. Latham was grateful: Slim and Lucky were quiet, hardworking, cheerful and dependable. If he didn't know their pasts, that was fine: in North Philly, it was often wiser not to. They didn't ask for much, yet enjoyed life to the hilt. They roller-skated, watched videos and movies, walked openly around the neighborhood, making small talk and sharing reefer. They were big eaters and loved pink champagne. JB met a New Jersey woman who asked him to come home and live with her. Pursuit seemed distant, everything cool.

But the FBI had developed leads, and while the rest of the nation looked elsewhere they had quietly concentrated on the neighborhood. Johnnie Council was the key. Soon after the escape, agents checked Mecklenburg's phone records and discovered several calls were made from Council's house to the Briley residence in Richmond. When Tuggle mentioned after his arrest that he let the brothers off in Philly, interest quickened. Agents set up surveillance and spotted Council leaving his house with a man in his car resembling Linwood. They shadowed Council and he eventually led them to Latham's garage.

They sent in a plant, variously described as a bounty hunter, emissary or street person: whatever he was, he fit in the neighborhood and hung around the garage. Soon the Brileys befriended him. They drank beer together, bantered about women, discussed JB's fine new hairdo. At the end of each day, the plant reported his findings to his handlers. Spotters surrounded the garage. The FBI laid its plans.

The evening of Tuesday, June 19, was as hot as usual, and it drew many in the neighborhood outside. A man in the house by the garage finished barbecuing chicken and went inside to eat. Another group gathered around a broken armchair on the sidewalk. The Brileys, their uncle and some friends milled around the front of the garage, shooting the bull, drinking beer. At just before ten, a spotter gave the signal and six cars and a large white van wheeled around the corner, screeching to a halt outside Dan's Custom Car Factory. Twenty officers jumped out, yelling "Freeze! FBI!" Agents popped up along the rooftops, weapons steadied. The partiers froze: everywhere they looked, lawmen pointed rifles, shotguns, M-16s. This was a tough neighborhood, but damn!

As they watched, the brothers were ordered to drop. They did not resist, but stayed composed. "What's goin' on?" JB demanded, both men denying they were the Brileys. The lead agent lifted JB's shirt and saw the old bullet scar on his chest. The two admitted their identities and were led off in cuffs. Each was ordered held on $10 million bail.

The nationwide manhunt was over. The last of the Mecklenburg Six were recaptured. They had been free for nineteen days.

That night, at least one person would miss them in North Philly. Shaken by the arrest, Latham left his business and spent the night with his family in another part of town. The garage was locked up, the lights extinguished. Long after the agents led off their captives and the curious left the streets, thieves broke in through a skylight and shimmied down a chain. They took a small television and about $5,000 in tools. They broke open the lock and stole the car Slim and Lucky sometimes used as a bed.

Four months later, as Linwood neared his execution, he smiled behind the glass partition as he remembered North Philly. "I had my nineteen days," he told an interviewer. "They couldn't take that away."

Part II

THE
RETRIBUTION

"On Death Row, life not only copies
art, it creates a grotesque art form all
its own that makes life its slave,
death its master."

—Caryl Chessman,
Trial by Ordeal

9

Now began the long season of revenge. The escape kindled fuel that had built up for years. Prisons across the state erupted in takeovers, riots, blood. Members of the conspiracy would be executed, inmates isolated, prison officials fired. What started as an escape, the most basic human response to impending death, turned into a reflection of American penal life. Guards, wardens, inmates, politicians and tax-payers—all looked into that mirror and saw a world tiered, like the cells themselves, on reprisal and retribution.

As predicted, Death Row was locked down. Stockton and his neighbors were confined to the packing-crate dimensions of their cells, no releases for anything but a five-minute shower, three times a week. It was Stockton's second muggy Piedmont summer and he glistened with sweat till his pores ran dry. His first execution date came and went, disappearing with barely a notice under the weight of all the automatic appeals. At least a trip to the Death House would bring some variation, he thought cynically. Visits from lawyers and family were restricted, a move ensuring further isolation. The DOC claimed that the men's lawyers were security risks and at first refused them entrance. The attorneys fought back in federal court and when, about one month later, they were finally allowed entrance, they were shocked by what they saw. The inmates looked skinny and pale; their minds seemed affected as well. It took Marie Deans fifteen minutes to convince Roger Coleman that she wasn't a hallucination, while others, like Dennis, had problems concentrating. Prison officials were caught tapping The

Row's phone calls, a violation of state law, yet county prosecutors refused to press charges, saying the officials were guilty at worst of bad judgment or overzealousness in their desire to prevent another escape. The state asked the courts to throw out the appeals of the fugitives and speed their executions even before they were recaptured, but the request was denied, deemed unconstitutional.

The inmates' only means of escape now was vicarious, listening to the radio for news of their fugitive comrades. They hoped they'd beat the odds and get away, yet one by one that hope failed. Stockton wasn't surprised by the quick capture of Clanton and Peterson—both were helpless without someone telling them what to do. He couldn't understand Jones for giving up when so close to freedom, but was proud of Tuggle for making it so far. That left the Brileys. It was obvious to Stockton that the feds wanted the brothers so bad they could taste it. They even contacted his mom. She said in a letter that a man identifying himself as an FBI agent came to the house and asked what she knew about the escape, but she sent him packing, saying that all she knew was what she'd seen on TV. Stockton chuckled. Good ole Mom.

So it was all the more depressing when the radio crowed of the brothers' capture in North Philly. Like everyone else Stockton had doubted they'd be taken alive, yet they gave up without a fight. Now all six were thrown in A-Basement in the Richmond penitentiary, just a few steps from Old Sparky. Linwood's execution date was next, and he'd probably stay there until he died.

The escape was over, but the impact didn't end there. Stockton merely had to glance out his window to see what they had done. Mecklenburg was at war, the Great Escape lighting a fuse that burned the rest of the summer and into the next year. Death Row was quiet, but the inmates in the other buildings taunted their jailers, asking guards to lend them their uniforms. They yelled to the towers, "In the name of God, open those gates!" Eleven days after Tuggle's capture, a Mecklenburg prisoner stabbed a guard. On June 29, a shakedown uncovered homemade weapons and severed window struts, signs of another escape plan. On July 12, a full-fledged riot began. It started that morning when four inmates refused to leave the rec yard. Others joined in, blocking the gates, arming themselves with barbells, metal bars, slats torn from picnic tables. The SWAT team arrived, spraying Mace, wielding batons. Yet even as they drove back these inmates, others watching from Building Two—home of the top performers in the prison's "phase program"—wheeled from their windows and attacked their own guards. The officers screamed for help via radio and fought back before the exhausted SWAT team came to their rescue. By the time it ended, six prisoners and nine guards were hospitalized.

The state's vaunted behavior-modification program lay in shambles. Two weeks after the first riot, a massive shakedown resulted in the discovery of even more arms. This was reinforced by guards brought in from another prison—they asked for the cells of those inmates deemed troublemakers, then beat them around the groin and buttocks with their batons. Twenty-six inmates were injured. Ten days later, the inmates in maximum security struck back, overwhelming guards with hidden weapons, taking nine hostages, occupying three control rooms and the entire second floor. The DOC moved two hundred guards and state troopers onto prison grounds. The rioters demanded an end to brutal treatment and released two guards stabbed in the head and a third suffering from diabetes. The state agreed to look into their complaints and the inmates gave in.

Meanwhile, the state bureaucracy devoured its own. Three weeks after the escape, Warden Gary Bass and Chief of Security Harold Catron were suspended for ten days without pay and moved to new jobs. A state report blamed the Great Escape on the mistakes of guards, ruling out institutional problems like inadequate staffing, low morale, poor training and flawed design. Some employees resigned, including the chief nurse and two assistants, who revealed they'd written the governor a year earlier about the prison's dangerous conditions but never received a reply. Soon afterward, five officers taken hostage were fired, including control-booth guards Ricardo Holmes and Corlene Thomas. The DOC chief, Robert Landon, told prison officials they would also lose their jobs if the chaos didn't end. That November, he resigned instead. His replacement, Allyn Sielaff, quit one year later, as well as his boss, Franklin White, the state secretary of public safety.

Stockton and the others watched through their windows as the madness grew. Their roles in the escape led directly to the blood and takeovers, the riot troops at parade rest, the *whop-whop* of network helicopters, the night sky lit like fire. They were to blame for the unwanted attention, national embarrassment, firings, shakeups, resignations. They listened as the radio told of a hostage crisis in Staunton, a prison about one hundred miles to the northwest, of riots at The Wall in Richmond. A man escaped from The Wall's print shop by packing himself in with a shipment of envelopes. It was like Attica in miniature: the unseen fuse ran from prison to prison, the violence its own escape, an incinerating apocalypse wreaking revenge on The Man and The World. The men on Death Row knew that when the dust eventually settled, the state's revenge would turn their way.

One inmate thrived, and he was Wilbert Evans. A story in *The Richmond Times-Dispatch* dubbed him a hero, overlooking the parts played by Turner and Joey G. in protecting the hostages. Their reward for participating in the escape was to be thrown in solitary, while Evans was treated like a king. The guards brought coffee and the morning paper to Evans's cell; while everyone else in Death Row sweltered through June and July locked down in their cells, Evans was released to the relative freedom of the dayroom for hours at a time. It made Stockton furious. Here Evans had preached shooting his way out of prison, and now the guards gave him the deference they once reserved for JB.

One person seemed angrier, and that was Willie Lloyd Turner. Giarratano seemed philosophical about his time in The Hole, but Willie came out wanting revenge. He watched as the guards brought Evans shaved ice to beat the summer heat, stewed as the guards brought him other treats and chatted like old pals. Willie had been the weapons maker, and until the fugitives were captured, the bulk of Mecklenburg's retribution fell on him. On the night of July 5, while being released from his cell for a brief shower, Turner stopped before Stockton's door. He was tired of watching the bullshit, he whispered. He'd made a bomb and planned to blow Evans away.

Stockton didn't believe it at first, but knew Turner was capable of miracles and so was intrigued. He recorded the conversation that night in his diary:

> **July 5, 1984** 7 P.M. [Turner] said he would have it [the bomb] ready before the weekend. I'm curious as to *how* he is going to do it. He said he would let me know before he actually did it. . . .
> I don't know what [Turner] is doing in his cell but he's sure making a lot of racket making "SOMETHING." I've heard a knocking, pecking noise all nite tonite. . . . Whatever it is, I

think he's keeping to himself and not telling the truth when he says a "bomb" because I never heard of making a bomb with that particular noise. . . .

Three days later, however, Turner proved good to his word. He showed Stockton the contraption when he passed again for a shower. Stockton thought it was closer to an "electrical zip gun" or spear than a bomb, but he was still impressed. The little arms maker had sawed away a hollow chair leg and packed it tightly with match heads. A wire was attached and to its end was fastened a projectile shaped like an arrowhead. The packed matches would fire with enough force for the arrowhead to pierce a brick, Willie claimed. He pronounced a day of execution, but when that day came and went, Evans was still breathing. Stockton asked what happened. Turner just smiled and answered, "I decided to save it for better things."

Soon Stockton would have his own chance for revenge.

• • • •

Quick reverse to the morning of June 1, 1984, a few short hours after the Great Escape. It was 6 A.M. when the phone rang, and a newspaper editor in Norfolk was startled from sleep.

"You're not going to believe this one," said the voice on the other end of the phone. "Six guys have broken out of Death Row in Mecklenburg."

The editor was still groggy. "Broken out? From Death Row? Escaped?"

"They're gone. Biggest manhunt you ever heard of. You'd better get in here."

It was first light and the Norfolk newspaper and every other media outlet in Virginia were gearing up for a story that would lead the network news that night and would make headlines for weeks, even months to come. By the time the editor was in the downtown office of *The Virginian-Pilot,* then the state's largest newspaper, reporters and photographers were being dispatched to Mecklenburg. How could six condemned killers flee Death Row, making a mockery of the DOC's boasts that the prison was one of the nation's most advanced repositories for dangerous criminals? As the media frenzy built, there were more questions: Who were the six men? What crimes had they committed? Would they leave a path of mayhem and death, or somehow try to disappear into anonymity? But the questions that most intrigued the Norfolk editor were the nuts-and-bolts of the escape, the same kinds of questions that had intrigued him during his eleven years as a newsman: How exactly had they done it? How could that story be told?

As others pursued the breaking story—the massive manhunt and mounting fear as the six eluded capture—the editor took another tack. He contacted the harried DOC and got the names of the men who still remained behind on Death Row. There were eighteen, he learned, and one, Albert Clozza, was from nearby Virginia Beach. Clozza was on The Row for raping and murdering a teenage girl. The editor called Clozza's lawyer and asked if his client would talk. The lawyer said Clozza was a private and peculiar man who almost surely would not talk to the press, but go ahead and write a letter, you never know. If nothing else, the mail would still get through.

That gave him an idea: Why not write every man who remained? Ask what they saw and knew of the escape. He included stationery and a stamped envelope addressed to the newspaper. The letters went out the day after the escape. A few days later, responses began to trickle in. Seven of the eighteen responded. LeVasseur said that he knew of Willie Jones's hideout, but would only give the story to a pretty reporter with a North Carolina TV station and wanted the editor to arrange a meeting. Timothy Bunch wrote: "The full capacity of what shall be exoteric will have to remain esoteric until litigating procedures are taken into consideration by my lawyer. Do have a fine day!" The others were somewhat more lucid, providing enough details, some conflicting, for the newspaper to run a page-one story about what may have happened on the night of May 31.

But the most intriguing letter was short and to the point. The inmate said he could tell the story better than anyone else. He had been keeping a daily diary for almost a year. It told all, he said, and he wanted it published as a book. Was the editor interested?

The letter was signed by an inmate the editor knew nothing about: Dennis W. Stockton. He sat down and wrote back to Stockton. He was interested, *very* interested, he said.

• • • •

Stockton read the editor's letter, put it down, picked it up and read it again and again. Its arrival seemed unbelievable. Things like this didn't happen in the real world. He'd already toyed with the idea of using his diary for revenge. The question was, how? He too had grown disgusted with the preferential treatment for Evans. He'd grown more and more convinced that the incompetence and corruption that allowed the escape to occur in the first place would never be widely known. His ruled pages laid it all out: who planned the breakout, who wanted bloodshed, which guards were in JB's pay. He'd hinted as much to officials and even read the March 5 entry detailing the first meeting in the dayroom of the conspirators to a startled state police detective in a light summer suit. But once the detective got his wits about him, the old cop games started, the ones that never changed and never seemed to end. The state police tried to get him to hand the diary over to them. He refused. They hooked him to a polygraph and played the good cop/bad cop routine, saying that he'd lied. The diary was a sham, they yelled—the only way to prove otherwise was to hand the whole thing over and let them check it themselves. He laughed, well aware of that line. Once he handed it over, he'd never see it again. Slap that tag "Ongoing Investigation" on the cover and you could kiss it good-bye, the state effectively burying a document that made them look like fools.

But the newspaper's offer . . . now this was something different. It brought together so many threads. He'd finally get published, at least in a paper, and that might lead to a book or movie. He might make some money and repay his brother and mom. He could get out the story of his innocence, draw some attention to his case. He would be a kind of historian, having the only written eyewitness account of the breakout. He could tell the truth about this hellhole and maybe end the hypocrisy.

He plucked a pen from his peanut butter jar. "I have been here at Mecklenburg since June 15, 1983," he wrote the editor. "I have kept a very detailed diary since I've been here, in hopes of writing a book one day. It has grown quite large, especially with the events of last week. Why don't we work together in making this book a reality? That way you will get *much* more than you asked for." The letter was in the mail the next day.

Despite prison surveillance, phone calls soon started between the inmate and the editor. Stockton realized he was edging closer to the role of a whistle-blower, the ruined and ruinous messenger of incompetence, a message that often boomeranged. Sometimes just thinking

about it made him pace his small cell. A man is prey to his truths—
once released, they stalk him forever. This happened when he led detectives to Tate's body. How can the truth hurt me? he'd asked his
lawyers. They shook their heads and suggested he wise up. The Law
was not about *the truth,* they replied. He'd learned the hard way that
there are many truths, and the one made public is often the most ex-
pedient or least damning to the status quo.

Still, he decided to give publication in the newspaper a shot. But
first he had to meet the editor, put a face to the voice, see if he could
trust him. The two arranged a meeting for late June.

By the time they met, every member of the Mecklenburg Six had
been recaptured, but the shock waves of their escape still reverberated. The editor had made the three-hour drive from Norfolk
through rural Southside Virginia, past long stretches of pine forest,
fields of soybean and corn, modest homes with spacious carports, to
Mecklenburg. As he drove, he wondered what he would say. Stockton wanted the diary published as a book and was convinced there
was a made-for-TV movie here. The editor was convinced that,
movie or not, this was one hell of a story.

Newspapers are driven to get *inside* closed systems. Prisoners are
driven to break *out,* and if Stockton couldn't do that in the flesh he'd
find another way. Soon the editor sampled what it took to get in or
out of Mecklenburg by legal means. He signed his name in a visitors'
book, as well as the name of the prisoner he came to visit, then sat and
waited in the small reception area of Mecklenburg's administration
building. A guard called his name and told him to hold his arms out
from his sides for a pat-down search before the interview. All personal effects—keys, wallet, loose change—were placed in a plastic
container. The guard let him take a notebook and pen, nothing more.
He riffled the pages of the notebook, looking, the editor supposed,
for contraband.

A short van ride away was the building inside the prison complex
where the editor would finally meet the man whose voice on the
phone—a sonorous, back-country Carolina drawl—had intrigued
him. Now that inmates could finally receive visitors, the editor could
see at last what this guy looked like and find out if the diary was even
real. He was led to a room in which a row of plastic chairs faced a
wall that was metal at the bottom, Plexiglas above waist level. A series of phones hung along the wall. The interviewer would talk to the

inmate by phone as the two sat face-to-face, no more than five feet from each other, separated by the soundproof glass. The editor took a seat and waited.

The man who appeared behind the glass wore a denim shirt, his hands shackled in front of him. He was gaunt, thin and angular, older than the editor had expected. His black hair was cut short, slicked down and neatly combed. Dennis Stockton took his seat on the other side of the wall. He had brought a large manila package and a flip-top box of Marlboros, which he placed on a ledge beneath the phone. He sat down, lit a cigarette and picked up his phone.

The first thing that struck the editor during the awkward introductions was the man's eyes—deep-set, piercing, haunting. When he looked into them, he could see why people believed the man was a killer. In time, he would get to know virtually every detail of the life of this middle-aged man who sat before him, dragging on a Marlboro. But for now, he wanted to know just three things: Did the package that Stockton brought with him contain the diary? If so, would the editor be able to get it during this no-contact visit? And once he did, would it provide details and tell the story of the men who pulled off the escape and how they did it?

Stockton answered the first question right away. "I been here almost exactly one year, and I've wrote down everything that happened," he said, his voice low and hushed. "This is it right here." He pulled out a thick sheaf of papers bound by a large rubber band. The hand-lettered cover sheet read NOTES FROM DEATH ROW, BY DENNIS W. STOCKTON. THIS IS PRIVATE PROPERTY.

A guard passed by Stockton's side of the wall. Stockton quietly pushed the package back into the envelope. He waited until the guard took a seat in a plastic chair out of earshot before speaking again. "You can check all this out if you want to," Stockton said. "I think you should. You'll see that what I've been telling you is all on the level." Then he made his proposition: he wanted the diary published, but only in book form—not in the editor's newspaper.

The editor said he would have to read the diary before he could make any judgments on whether there were book possibilities. He explained that publication in some form in the newspaper could generate interest in the book.

Negotiations between the inmate and newspaper editor had begun. There would be no resolution of the issue that day. The two men said good-bye. When he got up to leave, it seemed to the editor that the piercing eyes of the inmate seemed not so haunting as haunted and sad.

In fact, the editor did not see the diary until mid-July. Lockdown of the prison as a whole was over, but investigations into the escape and security at this and other state prisons were just beginning and would drag on for months, some for years. There was no way the editor could get the package that first day. Instead, Stockton concocted a plan. Dennis would mail the diary to his lawyer as "legal mail," then the lawyer would mail the package to Dennis's brother, who now lived in southwestern Virginia. The brother would then ship it to the editor.

When the editor received the diary by Federal Express, he read it in one sitting. The entries had been made in pen in clean, legible script, written with painstaking care. Stockton appeared to leave nothing out, including references to guards whom he had seen deliver contraband to the Brileys. He named them as well. Stockton also included dozens of pieces of supporting documentation of what had happened during that year inside and outside The Row: memos from the DOC, grievances he had filed complaining about mistreatment and lack of medical care, letters and postcards from relatives, news clippings. Reporters dug in; new questions arose; the summer dragged on. The editor and two members of his staff spent weeks reviewing the accuracy of the diary's contents, down to the ball scores and NASCAR results peppering individual entries. It seemed to Stockton that the journalists talked to everyone, including his mom, who said she was interviewed by the nicest Italian boy. For the journalists, it seemed too good to be true: this condemned man with a seventh-grade education had kept a meticulously detailed and accurate record. Nothing was amiss. Everything checked out.

Finally all was ready and a date was set for publication: Sunday, September 16. The editor asked Stockton point-blank about the dangers of revealing all these secrets and gave him a last chance to pull out. There was a moment of panic, but Stockton fought it down.

"Every man's got to row his own boat," he said.

• • • •

Sunday, September 16, 1984, started like any day. Stockton ate breakfast, flipped on the radio, waited for some word. Nothing. He read

Philip Caputo's *A Rumor of War.* Nada. He ate lunch, clipped coupons from Saturday's paper for his mother, wrote letters, scrubbed his cell. Zero. He ate supper, finished his book and dropped to sleep, exhausted, around 9 P.M.

He woke to shouting. People calling his name. He looked at the clock and saw he'd slept two hours. A man on the left side screamed that he'd just heard about Stockton's diary on the eleven o'clock news.

"What's this about a diary?" Turner asked excitedly from the cell next door. "Am I in it?"

Stockton didn't see a copy until the next day. There he was, in a black-and-white photo, facing the camera with his hollow-eyed stare. Over that, the banner headline—DIARY DETAILS LAX PRISON CONDITIONS: DEATH ROW INMATE WRITES OF DRUG ABUSE AND ESCAPE PLAN. Half the front page, plus eleven pages of a special section, most of that devoted to his diary entries from June 20, 1983, to July 15, 1984. "A 43-year-old inmate with a sharp eye for detail and a self-taught ability to write has provided a rare look at life on death row in Virginia's toughest prison," said the introduction. "His chronicle tells of the planning and success of the only mass escape from death row in United States history."

The guard took it away and passed it on to the next cell.

Stockton's pride was short-lived. He began noticing how neither the guards nor other inmates spoke unless absolutely necessary. Turner, the lone exception, was obsessed with whether he'd made any money on the deal. "Not yet," Stockton said. Televangelist Pat Robertson requested an interview for the *700 Club,* but Stockton declined, not trusting his motives, fearing Robertson would twist the story to push his own religious views.

Then Stockton heard the talk. That he was the snitch, though his diary clearly showed there'd been undiscovered snitches before the letter he sent to prison authorities; that he'd broken the prisoners' code. The new warden apparently heard too, and told reporters that Stockton would be locked away from other prisoners for his own protection. What might be harder to prevent, he added, was retaliation from the guards.

Soon Stockton got a sampling of the warden's fears. Two days after publication, a guard he'd never seen before brought his supper tray. The man wasn't wearing a name tag, a breach of protocol. From what Stockton had heard, the only guards to remove their tags were those involved in executions, but at the moment he didn't pay it much mind. To his delight his drink was filled with crushed ice, a luxury around there. He tipped back the cup and something sliced his tongue. He spit it all out and picked through the mess—a sliver of glass. He dumped the rest down the commode.

Soon something scared him even more. It was late at night and the guards had made their rounds. Stockton kept his window open to catch any breeze. Suddenly he heard Turner and Waye talking out their windows. They were talking about him.

"Speak louder," Turner said. "That dope he takes for pain knocks him right out. He won't hear."

Waye's answer was garbled, then Turner spoke again: "You know what would hurt that bastard most? If three or four of us got together and said he said he killed that guy he's always saying he didn't."

Stockton felt sick. After the newspaper published his diary, Turner was the only one of the condemned prisoners to still remain friendly, but that was all a sham. He moved closer to the window and tried to take notes, but his hands were shaking so badly he had to put down the pen.

The guard's footsteps approached again, and Turner and Waye stopped talking. Stockton lay on his bunk and closed his eyes. A flashlight played over his face and lingered; the guard moved on to Turner's cell. Stockton heard whispers, then the guard moved on.

Stockton sat at the edge of his bunk, his arms crossed over his chest as if to hold himself together. The panic came in waves; he fought to keep it down. He'd been scared of no man here except JB, but this was something else. Willie knew exactly where to stick the knife, that spot where he placed the most hope, his innocence plea. Outside he heard the cadenced cry of a man from B-Pod, called the "Fool's Block" since that's where they kept the crazy guys. *Whoo . . . whoo . . . whoo.* He heard a rustle by his door and saw the scaly tail of a rat. There were two of them running around the pod. He made a sound and the rat moved on.

His isolation became more complete. Governor Robb called him a liar in the press. Stockton's requests to see the warden got lost. Money vanished from his canteen account. Mail he was expecting never turned up. The phone didn't work. The newspaper bypassed his cell.

19758002775993

Meanwhile, Linwood's execution drew near. Stockton contemplated writing Linwood a letter but decided it might somehow be used against him. On June 21, 1984, the Brileys had arrived at The Wall's A-Basement together, both a few steps from the chair. From the beginning, officials were terrified there would be another escape. They had good reason for concern. A letter sent to Linwood from another Richmond inmate contained the words "hostage," "killing," and "weapons," all in code. A shank was found buried in the yard where the brothers took recreation. On July 31, JB refused to leave A-Basement when guards tried moving him in anticipation of Linwood's execution, originally set for August 17. They shot him twice with a stun gun and carried his limp body to a waiting van. He and the other four escapees were then taken west to Powhatan, the notorious lockup west of Richmond.

Linwood received a stay, but the wording left open the possibility that the execution could still go as scheduled. He was baptized by his preacher, Reverend Odie Brown. The death squad proceeded as if his execution were still a given until minutes before his thirteen-hour death watch began. He watched the guards prepare, rushing back and forth to the death chamber, testing the chair. "I got a stay," he cried out, but they didn't seem to hear.

A new date was set: October 12, 1984, at 11 P.M. They prepared the chamber again. His lawyers told him no legal remedies were left. His execution seemed assured this time.

On Death Row, the inmates passed around a petition vowing to protest with a fast. Sixteen signed, including Stockton. Five did not, including Evans.

October 12 dawned gray and cold. Several hundred inmates at The Wall donned black armbands. Radio talk shows in Richmond were jammed with calls. Shows with white audiences supported the death penalty, while those with black listeners seemed opposed. Catholic Bishop Walter F. Sullivan, scheduled as a witness, withdrew after Briley said his presence would be "cooperation in an evil." Later that night during a worship service, Sullivan thanked Linwood for sparing him "the horror," a comment that marked the first shots in a battle between the diocese and the state over the morality of the death sentence.

At Mecklenburg, most of the condemned fasted through breakfast. But not all. "Is that pork sausage?" Evans asked loudly when the guard wheeled the food cart past his cell. "Let me have the whole container. I sure am hungry this morning."

In A-Basement, Linwood seemed calm. He met with his ten-year-old son, who'd learned his father's identity only after his capture. The boy asked to hug his father, but was not allowed. Others who visited included his mother and father, his lawyer and prison activist Marie Deans. Shortly before 6 P.M., he talked over the phone with JB. Later that night, the younger brother wrote a poem, later run in the inmate-published *FYSK* magazine. One verse read:

> I spoke to my brother at 5:55 P.M. on October 12th
> He was holding real strong
> even though he was being done wrong—
> He told me he love—love me which I already knew,
> but to hear it straight from him was really something new.

Not everyone regarded Linwood as a martyr. Richmond law enforcement officials reminded the public of Linwood's and JB's victims, especially the rape and murder of Judy Barton and the execution of her son. Hundreds of demonstrators, both for and against the death penalty, gathered a block from the penitentiary, facing each other on opposite sides of the road. They were separated by a thin line of police. About 150 opponents marched from the Cathedral of the Sacred Heart singing hymns and carrying candles or signs that read NO MORE VIOLENCE and NO STATE MURDER. An even greater number of supporters opposed them, many carrying Confederate flags or signs reading FRY THE COON, KILL THE NEGRO and BURN, BRILEY, BURN. Others shouted taunts. "The people he killed didn't have a choice," one man cried.

Briley ate his last meal at 7 P.M. He asked for fried chicken, what everyone else ate that night. Instead, he was given grilled steak, baked potato, green peas, rolls, salad, cake, peaches and milk. At Mecklenburg, most of the condemned abandoned their fast, though Stockton and a few others still held to theirs. Stockton tuned to a Richmond talk show. "Fry the nigger," a man said.

The death squad came for Linwood at 10:55 P.M. He wrote a note to his preacher, part of which read, "I don't want my life to end at Eleven! But if it does, I know we will all COME TOGETHER in *HEAVEN*." He walked the forty feet to the death chamber and sat down in the chair. The warden read the execution order and asked Linwood if he had anything to say.

"I'm innocent," he replied.

The guards adjusted the leather strap across his face, strapped his legs and arms to the chair, attached an electrode to his right leg and fitted the metal helmet to his head. DOC Chief Robert Landon stood by a phone to Governor Robb's office. He nodded, and a fifty-five-second surge of 2,500 volts of electricity coursed through Linwood's body. He jerked forward against the straps. His hands clenched, then relaxed. The executioner waited five seconds, then zapped him again.

It was 11 P.M. Although he was probably dead by then, the prison doctor waited another five minutes before listening for a heartbeat. Muscular reaction pressed Linwood's body forward against the dark leather straps as if, for one last time, he could break away.

10

Things went from bad to sinister. The others started blaming Stockton for Linwood's death. There was no anticipating this since Briley's date with the chair had been scheduled long before publication of Stockton's diaries, yet four days after the execution he got his first hint. He arose as always in the morning to get his painkillers when he noticed that someone had slipped an envelope beneath his door while he slept. He slit it open and four playing cards fell out: a pair of black aces and eights. Wild Bill Hickok's poker hand when James McCall shot him in the back in Deadwood, South Dakota.

The Dead Man's Hand.

The rats came next. It was 4 A.M. when he heard Turner calling out his window. "Dennis," he hissed. "Dennis, you awake? Come to the window and talk."

It was the first time Willie had spoken to him since the execution. Stockton never mentioned overhearing his plan. "Did you know about the two dead rats that were found in front of your door the other night?" Turner asked.

It was the first he'd heard of it, he said.

"I'm surprised the officer didn't tell you. He accused me of doing it. Said they had name tags tied around their necks. The tags had your name on 'em. The guard said I threw 'em there, but Bunch told me it was him."

"Why you tellin' me this, Willie?"

"Because I'm your friend, Dennis. Friends watch out for each other."

Stockton almost laughed, but he held it in. Still, killing rats and tying name tags to them was just Bunch's speed. He thanked Willie and waited until everyone was awake before calling to the guard. "I would appreciate it if you will wake me up the next time you find something outside my door with my name on it." His voice echoed in the dayroom. "It took a punkified bastard to do something like that, but I know who sent 'em and all he's really after is a ten-inch dick, something he ain't had since his daddy went to Philly!"

The guard stared at Stockton in amazement. A little later, Bunch told his neighbor they'd have to quit talking so loud.

Then the five surviving members of the Mecklenburg Six came home.

At first he didn't know. A week after Linwood's death, The Row expanded. The murder rate was going up; more juries voted for execution; The World was becoming meaner all around. He was moved to B-Pod and Alton Waye was placed in the cell next to him. They were opposite the Fool's Block: the inmates started banging their doors and screaming as they were led in. It was the filthiest prison block he'd ever seen: shit was smeared on his cell walls and the dayroom floor; the thin mattress smelled rancid. He watched as the guards brought in each new resident: Dana Edmonds, who'd just become a Christian; Eddie Fitzgerald, a new guy; others he didn't know. The face of each fell as he entered. One or two gagged from the smell.

Stockton yelled for cleaning equipment, but the guards paid no heed. They were a different breed here with a solid rep for violence, brutalized by their supervision of the shit-slinging "mentals," as they called their charges. He noticed they took off their name tags when they came up to talk. "So this is the famous Dennis Stockton," said one. "You gonna write about us like over in C-Pod? Get us fired like them?"

"Sorry if the accommodations ain't up to your standards," added his partner. "Maybe you'll be happier when Briley and the others arrive."

That was how he heard. That night, as each new guard arrived for his shift, he asked, "Where's he at?" The others would point to Stockton's cage. They'd beam lights in his door every fifteen to twenty minutes. He'd drop off to sleep, only to have another light shone in his eyes.

But it was hard to sleep anyway, thinking about JB's return. They were as good as signing his death warrant by bringing the younger brother here. Stockton asked to see the warden, but the guards said he was busy. He tried to call his lawyer and they said they couldn't get an outside line.

On October 24, 1984, the celebrities came home. Willie Leroy Jones was brought in first and housed in the tier overhead. "Where's Stockton at?" he yelled. An inmate pointed to his cell. Peterson, Clanton and Tuggle were taken to C-Pod. JB arrived and was taken upstairs near Jones.

That night, the visits to JB started. It was like the escape had never happened. The guards still treated him like a dangerous god. At 3:15 A.M., a lieutenant and another guard walked by Stockton's cell and shined in their lights. "He's asleep," the lieutenant said. They went upstairs and talked to JB for twenty minutes. They shined their lights again on the way back down.

"The son of a bitch is scared to death," the lieutenant said, laughing.

"He'd better be," the other guard agreed.

October 26 was Stockton's birthday. Happy forty-fourth, he thought, wondering if he'd live to see another. He was washing up when a guard said in a loud voice that the investigator he'd requested was ready to see him. "I didn't ask to see no damn investigator," Stockton said.

"You said something about being in danger."

"The only danger I'm in is from you idiots announcing to the cell block that I'm going to see an investigator! You sure you said it loud enough for your boss to hear?"

"My boss?"

"Yeah. JB!"

It was déjà vu all over again, just like Yogi Berra said. He watched the guards here making the same fatal mistakes they had in C-Pod. He watched as the control-booth guard stepped from his post and locked the door behind him: they weren't even supposed to have keys anymore in the belief, after the escape, that this gave prisoners less incentive to attack. Sometimes they even left the door ajar, as Holmes had done on the day of the escape. As a test, Stockton asked for a Tylenol. Sure enough, the guard came over and gave him a pill, the door standing open the entire time. They were just asking for another takeover but were too blind to see what was so plain to him.

Everything seemed to center on JB. That night, Bunch was allowed to visit him for thirty minutes. "If anyone asks, you were sick and been to medical," said the guard escorting him back to C-Pod. "You got it," Bunch replied.

The next night, Stockton woke to loud voices. JB was talking out the window to Peterson, who lived all the way over at C-Pod. They were analyzing the failed escape attempt in 1981. They're planning again, Stockton thought. This time, I won't be left alone in my cell.

On Halloween, Clanton was brought for a visit. The fugitives were being treated like royalty. "Stockton's diary was the cause of Linwood's execution," he heard JB say. Clanton paused as he left and shouted: "Dennis Stockton, you take good care of yourself, hear?"

Two hours later, JB and Peterson were again talking at the windows. JB repeated what he'd said about Stockton's diaries. When Peterson asked what he planned to do, JB answered, "I'll see to it that he suffers."

On November 1, Stockton's notes to the new warden finally got through. He told him what he'd seen and heard. "They'll kill me if I stay," he said. "The guards are setting me up for the kill." The warden looked sick. Ostensibly, he was in charge but he'd discovered how little control he actually had. Each pod was a feudal kingdom. He could insist that every precaution be taken but he wasn't there twenty-four hours every day. Something could happen and the story would never come out, true guilt never be proven.

Stockton returned to his cell and buried his head in his hands. The tension was too much. He was so tired. Maybe he should just end it, but he couldn't give them the satisfaction, couldn't let them think they won. Suddenly he heard a noise and looked up. JB's face was in the glass door. He'd been let out to prowl the dayroom. The two men stared at each other, their eyes never breaking contact. JB sneered and moved on.

There were small mercies. Some of the newer men felt sorry for Stockton, yet were afraid of JB. The story of Linwood and Stockton growing the pot plant had become a Death Row legend. One of the new guys sent him a joint in an unmarked envelope. He smoked it down to nothing, the first he'd had in too long.

There was one slim hope. His lawyers said an agreement was in the works between the governors of Virginia and North Carolina to send him back home to stand trial for the killing of Ronnie Tate. If that happened, he'd finally get a copy of Robert Gates's interview with police, the one with all the inconsistent statements—the one suppressed by police or prosecutors during his own trial. If he could show that Gates had lied on the stand, he could start the long road back to show his trial had been unfair.

One rainy evening, a guard came to his cell. "Pack your stuff," he said. "You're leaving."

"Leavin' where?" The guard didn't know but it didn't matter. He'd lasted them out. He'd survived Mecklenburg! He threw his belongings together and stood in shackles as they loaded them in a hand truck. "Stockton's leaving!" someone shouted and he started laughing. "You got that right, motherfuckers," he cried.

"Where's he going?" Waye demanded. Others echoed the question till the dayroom rang. One voice was missing. Stockton looked up at the top tier and JB's face was in the glass. His eyes were filled with hate. Stockton's laughter came in waves, rolling out after all the days of tension. "Too bad, JB," he called. "You missed your chance." JB smashed the door with his fist and turned out of sight into his cell.

He was escorted downstairs, processed out, placed in the back of a dirty white van—the reverse of the order a year and a half ago. I'm free, he thought. I'm going to Carolina. He waited impatiently for the state trooper, a new policy after the Great Escape. The cruiser arrived and the gun towers slid behind the trees. But when they reached the interstate, the van turned north toward Richmond instead of south toward Carolina. "Where we going?" he said, pounding on the window. The driver answered: "The penitentiary. A-Basement. I thought you knew."

The next morning in Richmond, a prison official told him what had happened. One of his neighbors, Eddie Fitzgerald, had revealed a plot by JB and others. They'd bribed a guard to leave Stockton's door unlocked. In the middle of the night, they would come and kill him.

Stockton remembered JB's face outside his window, his hatred as he was taken away. He'd never suspected how close to death he'd come.

So where was he staying, he asked. Here in A-Basement?

"Oh, you won't be staying here," the suit-and-tie answered. "Not long, at least."

"Where then?"

"The state's not too happy with your diary, you know," he said, shrugging. "They intend to bury you somewhere and forget you."

That place was Powhatan.

• • • •

Powhatan Correctional Center lies twenty-five miles west of Richmond on the south bank of the James River. It sits on a rise like a medieval fortress, commanding a view of all approaches and surrounded by open fields. The address is State Farm and many of the inmates spend their days tending the fields, picking cotton or whatever else is planted that year. A visitor drives from the highway on the north bank, rolls down a hill past the buildings of a neighboring medium security prison with their faded antebellum facades, through shade trees by the river and over a rickety bridge. As his car climbs the south bank, prisoners straighten from their labor, running a sleeve or kerchief over their faces, mildly curious. Many of the faces are black. Huge fields, black laborers, white houses—images the state doesn't publicize in tourist ads.

Powhatan already had a bad rep before the Great Escape. Among inmates it was rumored to be tougher than even Mecklenburg or The Wall. According to a 1981 court order compelling the state to improve its prisons, conditions at Powhatan were unsuitable for human habitation, its services were inadequate, its safety nil. Powhatan officials had their own way of dealing with threats to the established order. Before conditions degenerated to those of everywhere else in the state, examples would be made. One such chance came on March 3, 1985, as inmate David Wayne Dunford sat alone in his cell. Dunford, rumored to be a snitch, looked up just as his assailant threw a quart of paint thinner between the bars. This was followed by several lit matches. Dunford screamed for help, then just screamed as flames ate into his skin and a sweet-sick smoke filled the tier. When guards finally cut through the lock, burns covered more than 70 percent of his body. Nine days later, he died.

Powhatan officials were desperate to solve the crime. The inmates wouldn't take over here, they vowed. "I cannot think of a better signal . . . than someone being convicted of capital murder," Warden William P. "Buck" Rogers wrote in a letter to his boss. A realist, he noted how difficult it would be to get inmates to break their code of silence and suggested cutting the sentences of those willing to testify. His bosses agreed.

Internal affairs men fanned through the cell block, interviewing inmates, repeating Rogers's offer. Joseph Payne, sentenced to life for the 1981 murder of a store clerk, was soon charged for Dunford's killing and sentenced to death. Several inmates gave circumstantial evidence during the trial, placing Payne near the scene, but there were credibility questions that didn't come out on the stand. After Payne's sentence, several swore out affidavits saying that investigators isolated inmates, offering to cut their sentences. One man said officials beat him to get his cooperation. "About five or six guards came into my cell one time," William Miller said in an affidavit. "There were guards on my arms and legs. The sergeant had his knee on my head. He told me . . . 'You're going to testify or you're going to be sorry.' "

Only one man said he saw Payne toss the matches and this was Robert Francis Smith. Known as a snitch, his nickname was "Dirty Smitty." But there was a problem—some witnesses said Dirty Smitty was the real killer. After Payne's trial, three inmates swore they saw Smith throw the matches, while a fourth said he heard him say, "I'd testify against my own grandmother . . . to get the hell out of jail." Nevertheless, Dirty Smitty was the state's main witness and as a reward got ten years knocked off his forty-year sentence for robbery. When he recanted a year and a half later, he outlined promises made to him by officials and said he'd perjured himself for fear of prison investigators. But Virginia's courts refused to hear the recantation, citing the twenty-one-day rule, saying the new evidence came too late to be used.

Stockton arrived at Powhatan in April 1986, spending the interim in The Wall's "Animal House," so named by the guards for the psychotics kept there. State Farm would be his home for the next nine years. Most of that time was spent in M-Building, a prison within a prison, dumping ground for those troublemakers and crazies deemed too bad for even Mecklenburg. M-Building had ninety-eight single-man cells, back to back, three tiers high. More than a quarter of these were set aside for Isolation. This would be Stockton's home, then Willie Turner's and then that of a third man, Joe Wise, condemned for killing Mecklenburg's groundskeeping chief and dumping his body down a privy. The three would dub themselves Virginia's "forgotten Death Row."

Stockton arrived first. His initial reaction was to go numb. He stood in the well beneath the tiers and listened to the din echoing around and above him, the screams and threats, the radios turned full blast to drown out other sounds. The barnyard smell hit him like a fist to a speed bag. The inmates threw shit and urine from their cells—it rained from the tiers, slicking the floor. In fact, throwing shit had become a hellish art form. Inmates kept containers of the stuff, doctoring it with urine, aftershave and eggs so that it held together in flight. Some let it ferment, increasing both the stink and cohesion. They called this concoction "brew" and would spend hours arguing who was the best "brewer." Not surprisingly, roaches and rats thrived. The guards wore plastic face shields and would sometimes pick up the stuff and throw it back. If the meals arrived during a brew-sling, the food containers would be pelted with the stuff.

Death, like brew, was a big part of life at Powhatan. David Dunford's death occurred before Stockton's arrival, but at least three others died in M-Building during his stay. One occurred on the other side of the building and he never learned the details. One was the prison barber, killed with his own shears. The third was a man called "West Virginia" who lay in his cell for four hours before his body was found.

Some attempted suicide to get free. Near the end of Stockton's stay an inmate named Mark Witt tried cutting his throat. A prisoner on his way to the showers saw blood pooling under Witt's door. He peeked inside. "It looked like someone had poured a bucket of red paint over Witt's head and body," he said. Amazingly, Witt lived.

It struck Stockton how easy it would be to disappear in a place like this. No one would ever know what happened. Then again, maybe sudden death was preferable to the slow kind experienced by the majority. Stockton would dwell on this as the others involved in the Great Escape followed Linwood's path to the executioner. The World was glad to see them go, but The World was not their stage. They played to the system—other inmates, their keepers, themselves. He began to envy them the longer he hung on.

JB went first. It happened while Stockton still lingered in the Richmond penitentiary's Animal House. April 18, 1985. Officials expected trouble, but nothing at all like what occurred. At 7:45 that morning, a group of inmates jumped four guards in the rec yard in hopes of taking hostages and stopping the execution. Guards rushed in with nightsticks but were outnumbered as even more cons rushed in, pulling shanks. Soon the guards stood back to back as the inmates circled, ducking and slashing inside their swings. By the time reinforcements saved them, the battle had lasted twenty minutes and nine guards were injured, six seriously.

But the execution would not be stopped. A few hours after the riot, JB was visited by his mother, daughter, brother, aunts and new wife, a former TV show host who had married him forty-nine days earlier. He requested a last meal of Sprite and fried shrimp. He spent his final hours talking on the phone and listening to tapes of Reverend Al Greene.

As nearly six hundred death penalty protestors and proponents faced off outside the prison, JB walked to the chamber. He smiled defiantly as he entered, twice asking witnesses, "Are you happy?" He sat on the polished chair and refused to give a final statement. The switch was thrown and his death officially recorded at 11:07 P.M.

JB's death whetted the executioner's appetite. The next visitant was a man Stockton didn't know, name of Michael Smith, chilling in his anonymity. He was followed on June 25 by Morris Mason, saved from JB's wrath to die sixty-nine days after him in the chair. There were no crazy giggles as Mason walked to the chamber. His eyes were dark and scared. He turned to Russ Ford, the Death Row pastor, and said, "Don't forget to tell the men back on The Row that I was a big boy." When his knees started to buckle, the minister put his hand on Mason's shoulder. "You'll be okay, Morris," Ford answered, which seemed to calm the little killer. He walked to the chair and sat; the electricity roared and he lurched against the straps. His hands raised straight up and fluttered like dark doves.

The guards let Mason sit for thirty minutes to cool down. Exhaust fans were tripped, sucking the smell of microwaved flesh from the room. The death squad stuffed their nostrils with Vaseline and some donned surgical masks. Mason's joints had fused and the guards had to break his arms, legs and back to load him flat on the gurney. The sound was like that of cracking crab shells.

Other condemned men in addition to Stockton followed the accounts of the executions too. Some made a kind of peace with Old

Sparky. Others made different plans. After Mason, the state quickly scheduled executions for Tuggle, Turner and Giarratano, but all were saved by last-minute stays. Stockton wondered how his former friends withstood the pressure. He got his answer when in November 1985 the three—aided by Eddie Fitzgerald, who'd warned authorities of JB's plot against Stockton—tried escaping again.

They used Willie's pipe bomb, the same he'd made to finish Wilbert Evans and shown to Stockton. It was two days after Thanksgiving 1985 when William Reese, the guard in C-Pod's control booth, answered the phone. To his shock, the man on the other end was Tuggle, his voice cold. "Reese, we're right behind you and there's a gun pointing at your head," Lem said. "If you don't crack the doors, you're a dead man. We're Death Row inmates, and we got nothing to lose."

Reese turned and saw Tuggle sitting at a table about seven feet away. He had the phone in one hand and what looked like a 9mm automatic in the other pointed at his head. The chamber looked dark as steel, the handle mahogany. There was nowhere for Reese to hide. If that wasn't bad enough, Turner appeared and placed a small tube by the window, and Tuggle said it was a bomb. "Wait a minute! Wait a minute!" Reese cried. "You don't want to do anything like this."

Tuggle looked at him calmly, almost sadly. "You don't understand," he said. "We ain't got nothing to lose." But Reese refused to open up, knowing it would be the Great Escape all over again and this time people might get killed. The four inmates stepped back from the window and the bomb exploded in a flash of white and red, splintering the glass. Turner, Giarratano and Fitzgerald reappeared, holding chair legs sharpened like spears. As they jabbed and hacked at the cracked glass, jagged shards fell away. As Reese screamed in the phone for help, the crack widened, becoming large enough to insert the gun. He backed as far as possible from the crack, remembering how he'd had a choice between early retirement and this madness. He'd worried that if he retired, he'd probably get bored.

Reese braced himself for the gunshot that never came. Instead, he watched the escape attempt end as suddenly as it started. To his amazement, the four stopped pounding at the glass. They huddled, then stripped to their shorts and lay on the floor until the SWAT team arrived. These reinforcements showed up ten minutes later and found twelve very real shanks, but said the gun was fake, made from cardboard, paper and soap. Reese laughed in relief, but his hands shook as he filed his report. He took lunch, then went to administration, where the warden profusely thanked him for keeping his head.

For once the DOC was lucky, but they knew they might not be next time. These men were proving too dangerous, and almost too smart, to safely keep anywhere. They'd become embodiments of escape, symbols of freedom, worms boring at the foundation of the entire DOC. Turner, the arms maker, was the worst and they sent him plunging through the same Dantean rings to end up beside Stockton in Powhatan.

For the other conspirators, the machine quickened. Clanton was next, meeting the executioner in April 1988. Alton Waye, who earned the name of The Row's meanest inmate after Clanton's death, came next; to the surprise of many, he went against his badass image and was baptized the night before his execution, singing "Amazing Grace" with the Death Squad. John LeVasseur went to meet his old master, Linwood, but not with the help of the state. He was found hanging in the shower, and, after an investigation, the DOC announced he had committed suicide. But LeVasseur's lawyers weren't so certain. Shortly before his death, LeVasseur told them that he had started fighting back against those who tried to rape him. Yet the little man still refused to snitch on his tormentors. In the end, LeVasseur's lawyers never knew whether he died at the hands of another, or simply gave in to despair.

On October 17, 1990, it was Wilbert Evans's turn. To the very end, Evans thought his protection of the hostages would save him. Mecklenburg guards and officials, the nurse he'd shielded from rape—all wrote affidavits asking the governor for clemency. But Evans's timing was as bad as could be. L. Douglas Wilder, the state's first black governor and Chuck Robb's successor, had once been an opponent of the death penalty. Yet he campaigned for office as a supporter of executions and now was running for the presidency. He had reason to believe he would be Willie Horton–ized if he spared a black cop killer. In addition, the national campaign to save Giarratano, whose execution was scheduled soon after Evans's, made it politically difficult for Wilder to grant two clemencies back to back. Giarratano's defenders included Amnesty International and columnist James J. Kilpatrick. Evans had his lawyers and family.

Evans remained hopeful, even when the U.S. Supreme Court turned down his appeal without comment early in the evening. The lone dissenter was Justice Thurgood Marshall, who called the execution "dead wrong." Evans ate his last meal of pigs' feet, collard greens, potato salad, bread and Sprite. He stroked the stubble on his head, cut close to better conduct electricity, wishing they hadn't shaved him so close. The TV was tuned to the World Series. The batter swung and there was a crack. "There goes another one," he said.

It must have been strange serving on the Death Squad that night. For the first time in memory, they were carrying out an execution that fellow guards were begging the state to stop. Four of the guards taken hostage—Ricardo Holmes, Harold Crutchfield, Lt. Milton Crutchfield and James Fitts—told investigators that they probably would not have survived if not for Evans. E. B. Harris, a sergeant at Mecklenburg, wrote Wilder a month before the execution that Evans "saved some of the officers from harm and almost certain death" and, after the escape, "has shown me and the majority of the staff nothing but respect." Even the warden brought in after the Great Escape told Wilder that commuting Evans's sentence to life might sway other prisoners to follow his example "in the eventuality of a riot or serious hostage situation."

Wilder considered the arguments and his answer came late, at 10:52. Six minutes later, big Ed Evans died. He leapt backward against the leather straps as the first jolt of 2,500 volts blasted through his brain. Blood spilled from under his mask, turning his light blue shirt deep red. Bloody foam bubbled from his lower lip. The witnesses recoiled in horror. Some said blood streamed from his ears; others heard air sizzling from his stretched lips, followed by a moan.

The irony of Evans's death didn't slow the executioner. Derick Peterson made his final walk in August 1991; he wheezed and moaned after the first jolt failed to do the job. On May 20, 1992, it was Roger Coleman's turn. Of all the prisoners he met in Mecklenburg, Stockton most identified with the quiet coal miner who maintained his innocence to the very end. Like Stockton, Coleman chose not to escape, thinking it would hurt his chances for justice. He uncovered evidence raising questions about his guilt, including the affidavits of six neighbors who said another man bragged about raping and killing Coleman's sister-in-law. One woman was found dead a day after naming the man on TV. But the courts were unmoved and he was led to the chamber and strapped to the chair. A guard put his thick-rimmed glasses on his face and he read from a handwritten statement: "An innocent man is going to be murdered tonight. When my innocence is proven, I hope Americans will realize the injustice of the death penalty as all other civilized countries have. My last words are to the woman I love. Love is eternal. My love for you will last forever."

On December 10, 1992, Tim Bunch finally got his wish and met the Reaper. Stockton wondered what Bunch thought in those final moments. Did he imagine a meeting with his hero, Gary Gilmore? Or was everything blotted out by fear?

A strange thing happens to Stockton as he watches this march. The anchors that hold him to earth pull loose, a common phenomenon among the pre-dead. He feels weightless, insubstantial, unreal. The last anchor is his family, but they begin their own last walks even as the Death Row celebrities take theirs.

In 1987, his grandmother dies. Her last letter said, "If I don't see you anymore, meet me in Heaven." In January 1993, it was his father, dead at seventy-two. He died suddenly in Holly Hill, Florida, with his second wife, for whom he left Ailene in the late sixties. Stockton never forgave him for that, just as he never forgave him for other things. But the first to go, and the most important, was his mom. In the summer of 1986, she was diagnosed with lung cancer and given her own death sentence: one year. She didn't last that long, dying the night of December 2.

When he heard, he sat alone in his cell. He cursed himself, cursed those who put him here, cursed God. He remembered the time in Shelby he came home from school and Mom was lying in bed and Dad said she was sick. It was the time of the nervous breakdowns from all the long hours at the failing diner, but Dennis was too young to understand. All he knew was that he desperately wanted her well. He saved up his desserts from school lunch and brought them home. Mom smiled when he brought them to her in bed and she ate them all down. Tapioca pudding. Cherry pie. A couple of peanut butter cookies. It became a game—she'd try guessing what he brought each day. "I got a little doctor in the house," she beamed as the two shared the sweets. Soon she was better and went back to work. He was sure then that he'd saved her. But now he thought that no one is ever saved.

He thought more of his mom as the actors in the Great Escape marched, like her, to their ends. In 1993, it was Willie Leroy Jones, convinced by his mother to return when just miles from the Canadian border. Of them all, he probably came the closest to staying free, yet he turned around.

Jones smiled as he entered the chamber, then bent to kiss the chair.

• • • •

Time assumed a different meaning as Stockton watched so many die. He entered prison time, a stream of thought and being alien to The Outside. In The World, there was a presumption of direction, a march to some end. Even in Mecklenburg, bad as that was, he lived in The World's time, forced into its stream when planning the escape. But in M-Building at Powhatan, there was no flow of events, no beginning and end, the punctuation most people used to measure "normal" time. There was only the eternal present, which drained a person white and threw away the husk unless he somehow learned to endure.

Prison time was purest in a single-man cell. Stockton spent his days in the six-by-eight box. His meals were brought to his door. The door was double locked, then padlocked. He counted seventy-one bars in front of the cell, these covered with a steel mesh forming 1,812 tiny diamonds. Like a miser he counted the diamonds again and again.

He collapsed into himself, the years of prison time stretching him out of shape more than he cared to admit. But visitors could see the change. His temper became hair-trigger. A deep hatred built up, not only for his keepers but for all in the system, even those who might help: lawyers, death penalty opponents, journalists, Amnesty International. They were all part of that separate stream of time. He aged, black lines cutting deep into his face. He stewed in the nothingness of this world, convinced the whole system was designed to personally drive him mad.

Prison time is much like the stages of grieving—first come rage and disbelief, then resignation and lethargy. It entwines itself like a strangler vine around every thought or physical activity, tightening with years. It squeezes until the only challenge left is to fight the paralysis or give in. He no longer did push-ups or paced the floor. He easily lost his train of thought, his mind glazing over in midsentence. Even erotic memory disappeared. He couldn't get an erection; he experimented, remembering every woman he ever slept with, even some he didn't, reconstructing every moan and touch, but all to no good. He started to feel that every effort would be wasted, that he'd never prove his innocence, never get free. Time fell around him like a shroud until the solitude actually seemed a protection from The World. Any noise penetrating the shroud was a threat. He drowned out the noise with noise of his own, turning the radio as high as possible. It made no sense, but little did.

He was always tired. People in The World think prisoners just lie around and sleep, but nothing is further from the truth. Stockton wished he *could* sleep in the eight-hour blocks he once took for granted, but sleep here was stolen in bits and pieces, those rare unannounced moments when the uproar stilled. He adapted by catnapping and got used to feeling tired, learning that survivors had to function this way or go mad.

The clock still intruded, but its presence seemed fleeting and unreal. There was the time in 1986 he dropped his appeal and became, like Frank Coppola, a "volunteer." I'm turning forty-five, he thought. The future just holds another forty years of the same kind of life. He had begun reading the Bible at the suggestion of friends, but what he found only depressed him. "So life came to mean nothing to me, because everything in it had brought me nothing but trouble," lamented the preacher in Ecclesiastes. "It had all been useless; I had been chasing the wind."

So he petitioned the court for an execution and it obliged, setting his death for October 6, 1986. He fired his lawyers and told friends he welcomed oblivion: there would be brief pain, then a silence more merciful than Powhatan's loud, protracted torture. The court assigned new lawyers and one, an attractive Asian-American woman, convinced him to fight. He told them he was not interested in delaying his execution unless it was to prove his innocence. They said there might be a chance, then filed petitions interrupting the smooth flow of his demise. They attacked the case from several angles: the dismissal of the charges against Tommy McBride; the court's failure to change venue because of pretrial publicity; prosecutorial misconduct for suppressing evidence; evidence that Randy Bowman lied on the stand. The only attack that worked was jury misconduct. A Mount Airy woman overheard jurors say they wanted to hurry the case so they could convict Stockton; the owner of a restaurant near the court told jurors, "I hope you fry the son of a bitch." Less than two days before execution, he was granted a stay to file new appeals.

A federal judge granted a new sentencing hearing, but that was all. No new evidence would be allowed. That didn't seem promising, yet as he awaited the hearing there was a respite as his death sentence was temporarily overturned and he was moved from M-Building into Powhatan's general prison population; from 1987 to 1990 he reentered the company of other men. He worked in the prison print shop, enrolled in auto mechanics school, spent his afternoons in the library reading books that had been unavailable in M-Building, went to church again after so many years. He rediscovered the joys of reefer, buying the smuggled weed from other prisoners in $10 and $25 bags and regaling them with tales of the pot plants he and Linwood had grown.

But soon he could see that the cruelty and corruption of M-Building permeated all of Powhatan. He bumped into two men having sex in the shower, heard of stabbings and rapes, but in many ways those moments were endemic to prison life, the same everywhere. The first hint of something worse were the tales of Joe Payne's death sentence for the murder of David Dunford and the overlying sense he got from guards and officials that they could do whatever they wanted in Powhatan and no one in The World would know or even care. The cruelty became more apparent the time he watched five older cons, veterans of Powhatan, crowd around a new arrival. They acted like predators. The kid was a "fish," and even though he tried playing tough it was obvious he was terrified. That night he was gang-raped by all five, forced to perform oral sex on one man while a second pumped him from behind. He was left on the ground, bleeding from the rectum, until discovered the next day and rushed to the hospital. The guards laughed when they heard the cause.

During this time the state offered Stockton a deal: life imprisonment if he abandoned all future attempts to prove his innocence. He figured that meant spending the rest of his life in Powhatan and thought of the kid raped by the five old-timers. Maybe some things were worse than death, he thought. He refused the deal, telling the state that he would rather die than accept life in prison for a crime he did not commit. In 1990 the second jury obliged him, recommending death. He returned to Powhatan and the other Death Row in its M-Building.

Now the only escape was within, where he painted his cell to hide the filth but couldn't stop the roaches; where he woke at night as a rat ran across his bed and scratched his back; where he cracked a boiled egg and found a tiny chicken within. Where the most violent arguments began and ended with death threats over the nature, or very existence, of God.

The typical day was the typical week, which was the typical year. It started long before dawn. He woke on his side, the same position in which he dropped to sleep the night before. His radio—tied to the bars with a torn sheet and tuned to the late-night Trucker's Network—played Faron Young's "Four in the Morning." The song ended and the DJ said, "It's four fifty-seven A.M." He stepped to the commode and peed; he washed his face and hands. From the tier overhead came the clink of cups in tray slots. The guard set a cup of juice in his tray. He rolled two cigarettes from a can of Bugler tobacco. A can sold for $3.15 in the prison canteen and came with 240 thin paper leaves, another way of marking time.

Now more commodes flushed, announcing other wakings, and breakfast arrived. Eggs, grits, a dab of grape jelly, two sausages reminding him of dog turds and two pieces of bread. He grabbed the meal before the ants attacked. He replaced the tray and rolled another cigarette, wishing for a joint instead.

The tiers were home to an entire animal farm—roaches, rats, flies, an occasional silverfish or mouse. But in the battle for survival, the ants won hands down. They were the tiny black kind that never seemed to visit alone. In fact, they couldn't be stopped. You killed one and they multiplied. Once he found two boxes of Rice Krispies in his food tray: a treat. He poured on milk and turned to wash his face and when he turned back, four ants were floating in the bowl. I've been waiting years for Rice Krispies and I'm not about to dump 'em 'cause four ants committed suicide, he thought, so he spooned the cereal down, ants included. Afterward he itched inside and imagined them chewing their way to freedom. He admired their tenacity, but war was still war. His flyswatter became an antswatter and one day he spotted nine on the wall and another four charging under the door. He swatted them quick but others kept coming and he envisioned a huge nest, the tunnels thick with ants like a pulsing black intestine, its corridors stretching beneath the whole prison, beneath the wire and gun towers, beyond the fields of flax and soybean, on to Richmond where the governor lived.

Even worse than the ants were the birds. Sometimes one would get into M-Building and he would watch it fly back and forth outside his cell. He had no idea what kind it was, just a bird with lots of gray and brown feathers that was big enough to fly into M-Building then forget how to get out. He could sympathize. Sometimes one would panic and put on speed, finally hitting a glass pane with a *bang!* It would then perch on a ledge and shake its head like a punch-drunk prizefighter. Some prisoners would strew bread crumbs before their bars and put out cups of water, but Stockton left the birds alone. He didn't want their droppings around his cell. The recreation yard was thick with guano, the sides of the building and tops of walls caked white like a second skin. Guards and inmates had long suspected something deadly and unseen lurked around M-Building—they just weren't sure what. People would suddenly start coughing, their temperatures would rocket to over 100, they had to be hospitalized. But they always got better, so nothing was done. Everyone suspected the rec yard, a mecca for sparrows, pigeons and blackbirds. Prison officials tried scaring them off without success. Large ceramic owls were attached to the rails atop the walls surrounding the complex, but the birds used them as perches. Soon the owls were so slick from droppings that the birds slipped off when landing and guards patrolling the walls kept having their uniforms fouled. They replaced the owls with fishing wire strung around the buildings. The birds left, but the guano remained.

The first real hint of something infectious occurred in 1989 when ten inmates and employees fell ill with high fevers. They recovered, however, and the mini-epidemic was passed off as a bad flu. Then, in 1993, doctors at the Medical College of Virginia, a teaching hospital in Richmond that also treated inmates, started noticing that a number of Powhatan's inmates who'd tested HIV-positive were also testing positive for histoplasmosis. They warned prison officials, explaining that the disease was a potentially fatal fungal infection characterized by coughing, high fever, headache, dizziness, chest pains and pneumatic lung patches. The fungus, *Histoplasma capsulatum,* was unleashed into the air when decayed bird or bat droppings were disturbed and inhaled. The disease then spread to the liver, spleen, bone marrow, skin or lining around the brain and heart. First noticed among cave explorers, miners and tunnel workers, it was sometimes blamed for the "pharaoh's curse" that befell archaeologists excavating ancient Egyptian tombs. They advised cleaning the affected area with a formalin solution, but Powhatan officials waited another eight months to act.

On June 8, 1994, two unsuspecting maintenance men plunged their shovels into a pile of dirt contaminated by the droppings and shoveled the dirt onto the back of a flatbed trailer. Within an hour, one of the men had to be helped to doctors. Two weeks later, he was on a respirator, and three inmates in M-Building came down with high fevers. The next day, eight more were sick. From late June to late July, Powhatan was in the grip of a full-blown epidemic. One inmate's fever shot so high he had to be rushed to a hospital in a body bag packed with ice. Another went into seizures. Inmates and guards watched as victims were carried out on stretchers, and everyone wore surgical masks. M-Building was quarantined.

The Atlanta-based Centers for Disease Control and Prevention was called in, and a lung biopsy of the first maintenance man to fall ill tested positive for histoplasmosis. The CDC ordered blood tests of three hundred inmates and employees—by the time the epidemic ended, twenty-two inmates and six employees were hospitalized, their temperatures soaring as high as 105. Another 151 came down with less severe cases, Stockton included. His infection was considered low-grade and never treated. The recreation yard was washed with bleach; something was sprayed to kill the remaining birds. Stockton could see two small carcasses atop a wall and neighbors reported others strewn about the building. Their last perches were too high for workers to reach, so they lay in the sun. As the summer progressed, their bodies swelled.

Another hazard was fire, started by inmates out of boredom or to get a rise out of the guards. They torched their mattresses or waste paper with cigarettes, then stood aside as the guards barged in, stripping the contents and chaining the firebug to prevent a repeat performance. As often as not, a second fire would erupt in another cell just as they were extinguishing the first. Stockton would put a shirt to his nose and mouth, but the billowing smoke still made it hard to breathe.

Stockton once figured that if there was a serious fire, there would be no way to evacuate all seventy-two of M-Building's inmates before they died. Prison procedure was for each man to be led from his cell in restraints. His cell door was padlocked, and even after opening that door each man passed through six or eight more locked doors before getting outside. It took ten to fifteen minutes to evacuate each inmate this way. Stockton figured it would take a minimum of 720 minutes—twelve hours—to move them all.

Yet there apparently was another way to handle a serious blaze. A fire started one summer and the smoke swirled in thick, choking clouds. It was a true panic, everyone screaming to be freed. Stockton stuck his mirror out the slot to see what was happening but the smoke was so thick he seemed alone in a dense fog. He could smell the brew being thrown and heard a guard yell, "Let the sons of bitches smother!" He wet a rag and covered his nose and mouth. Soon he learned the other side of the building was flooded, the side where the fire began. Guards in full riot gear stormed from cell to cell with dogs. The dogs barked furiously and he heard the smack of night-sticks on flesh, the screams of the inmates. He heard guards tear a sink and commode from the wall. A guard told a con not to choke or hurt his dog after it bit off the man's finger. "That's a capital offense and your ass is going to Death Row if you kill our officer dog."

The only way *out* was by sinking inside. He read after breakfast, then devoted late morning and all of afternoon to his writing. There was his autobiography, two novels, some stories and a monthly newsletter about Death Row and prison life alternately called "Death Row Diary" or "Passin' Thoughts." His lawyers told him he was the first condemned inmate in the country to regularly publish such a newsletter. By October 1993, his mailing list was up to sixty-one recipients, including racing great Dale Earnhardt.

Sometimes he was interrupted by Joe Wise, his best friend on The Row, the best he'd had since Linwood, maybe better. Like Linwood, Joe was black. Most everyone in M-Building was black, inmates and guards alike; whites were spread few and far between. It was a mystery to him that his two best friends of the past decade were black, since there were times he thought he hated every black ever born. It was all because of the noise. There was lots of hatred and prejudice in M-Building, lots of loud talk about exterminating all whites by the year 2005, revenge for conditions Outside. They talked of hooking white girls on drugs, getting them pregnant, making them slaves. In the general population, disrespecting a con's woman, black or white, could end in killing, but here the noise just ratcheted up. He tried shrugging it off but that wasn't always possible and then he was "at the gate" screaming like the rest. "Shuddup, you fuckin' niggers, ain't you got no sense?" he would shout, then suddenly remember Joe next door. "I'm sorry, Joe," he said. "I didn't mean it. They just drive me crazy."

"Don't worry about it, Dennis," Joe answered. "They drive me crazy, too."

Nonetheless, Stockton knew that he hurt Joe. He loathed his Jekyll-and-Hyde existence, the one side that wanted to improve himself, the enraged opposite that could suddenly take control. Joe was the same, at times sitting in his cell mumbling simple prayers, one of the most tranquil people Stockton had ever met, at other times the hatred building in him till Stockton got a glimpse of the man who killed the chief of Mecklenburg's groundskeeping crew and dumped his body down a privy. Wise used his religion to try to overcome that frightening and overpowering Other. It was Joe's form of escape, but not Stockton's way.

Once in 1984, soon after the escape, the Norfolk editor asked Stockton in a letter whether he believed in God. The question surprised him. He'd heard it before, but only from the church volunteers who came to The Row and they only irritated him, seeking conversions as a feather in their cap or a good mark in Saint Peter's ledger. He just told them to go away. He especially hated it when they quoted the Bible. The whole damn book seemed an homage to fear, guilt and despair. Take Psalms 13: "How long, O Lord? Will you forget me forever? How long will you hide your face from me? How long must I wrestle with my thoughts and every day have sorrow in my heart? How long will my enemy triumph over me?" Or Job 9: "I am innocent, but I no longer care. I am sick of living. Nothing matters; innocent or guilty, God will destroy us. When an innocent man suddenly dies, God laughs. God gave the world to the wicked. He made all the judges blind."

But the editor was someone he respected who tried hard to understand him, and as Stockton dwelt on the question, he found he did have faith, if just a little. He wrote back:

Yes, I believe in God . . . [but] I'm not going to be a hypocrite and tell you I'm a good Christian. I'm far from that. I do not talk to any of these ministers who come here because 1) they seldom come, 2) they can't remember your name from one visit to the next, and 3) they are always in a hurry. I do pray for my mom often and always feel better when I remember to do so. She worries about me and I simply ask God to give her rest and peace of mind. My mom has been through a lot. Life has not been easy for her and not for

one minute can I recall she has ever lost her faith. There has to be a
true God. If not, then we are all lost.

God and Mom. Stockton heard the theme echoed by many Death
Row killers, though not all. Few of the condemned expressed sorrow
for the victims whose deaths put them here. Some went so far as to
say the victims deserved what they got. Yet it seemed a different matter when speaking of the victims' families, especially their mothers, as
if, because of the pain they'd seen in their own mothers' faces, they
could for the briefest moment empathize with another's sorrow, perhaps feel guilt. Motherhood as a symbol is still a powerful social force,
but among killers it sometimes approaches the mystical. Stockton felt
sorry for Kenny Arnder's mother, Wilma, even when she testified
against him. Willie Leroy Jones, so close to the Canadian border, returned to Death Row at the urging of his mom. Frank Coppola supposedly chose execution to spare his mother further humiliation. The
connection even transcended national boundaries: Nobel laureate
Gabriel Garcia Marquez observed the same when writing of the
teenage killers who guarded hostages during Colombia's war against
the drug cartels. The boys "knew they were going to die
young . . . and cared only about living for the moment," he wrote in
News of a Kidnapping. "They made excuses to themselves for their
reprehensible work . . . [the money they made] ensuring the happi-
ness of their mothers, whom they venerated above all else in the
world and for whose sakes they were willing to die. They venerated
the same Holy Infant and Lady of Mercy worshiped by their captives,
and prayed to them every day with perverse devotion."

The longer Stockton and Joe Wise stayed neighbors in M-Building,
the more their friendship grew, and the closer they drew, the more Joe
badgered Dennis about talking to members of his church. Get right
with yourself and get baptized, he said. Wise reminded Stockton of
how he'd prayed for his mother, so he must have *some* belief. Dennis
said he'd been baptized when he was nine or ten, a kind of hometown
fashion, but Joe kept on him, saying that didn't count. Finally he
talked with the ministers of Joe's church, the Worldwide Church of
God, and asked one of the volunteer ministers, Ron Smith, about
being rebaptized. Smith said it was done all the time, but must be entered seriously. "You mean it's not like taking out insurance?" Stockton replied.

So he was baptized on March 1, 1991, a cold, wet day. A prison baptism can be a jury-rigged affair. Smith was with him throughout. Dennis stepped into the hall and said he was ready; the guard cuffed his wrists in front of him and the three—Stockton, Smith, guard— marched to a sheltered area near the front of M-Building, out of the range of thrown brew. Dennis wore a clean orange jumpsuit, several sizes too big. A plastic pool had been set up and filled with water. It sat on the concrete, surrounded by bird droppings. The guard remained, but Stockton liked him so he didn't mind. Smith touched the water with his fingers and said it was too cold, but the guard answered: "That's all we got, Reverend. Hot water's out today."

Stockton shrugged and stepped inside the pool anyway, and Smith stepped in after him. He sat as Smith recited the baptismal passage from John. Smith pushed him back in the water but the oversized jumpsuit filled with air and billowed around him like a big orange balloon. His legs wouldn't stay down but popped to the surface every time he tried to dunk his head. Wasn't the whole point to get completely covered? Stockton thought. Did it still count if one part of you popped up every time another part of you sank down? The guard was grinning but tried to cover his mouth with his hand. "It's all right, Dennis," Smith finally sighed. "It's the thought that counts." Stockton stood up and Smith put his hand on his head and prayed. When Dennis returned to his cell, he dripped water all the way.

"Did you do it?" Joe asked, all excited. "Don't you feel better?"

"I did it," Stockton answered. "But all I feel right now is wet and cold as hell."

• • • •

So he was baptized, but the symbolic act didn't work the same magic on Stockton that it had on Joe Wise. M-Building continued to rage around him until he thought he would go mad. He discovered that his only escape was writing: the only way to flee the madhouse was by creating another world. People who knew him said, *Dennis, write a novel about Death Row. You could write another* Cuckoo's Nest. But how was that an escape, he wondered. Just as well call such a novel *Frustration* as all around him rose the indecipherable bellows of the mad and raging, the stench of human shit. Why did he want to immerse himself in that any more than he already was? Instead, he could escape this madness by weaving stories of people living free and happy where there was blue sky overhead and green earth underfoot, and it tasted like ice water when a person inhaled the mountain air. Where the hero didn't die and there was a happy ending. His imagination wandered far from M-Building at such times: ideas came one after another and he learned to jot them down. The sensation was better than drugs. His characters were idealizations of what he might have been; to perfect his characters' folksy dialect, he spoke the dialogue aloud. His favorite project was the Horatio Alger tale of a twelve-year-old baseball phenomenon named Joshua growing up in the Great Smoky Mountains. The boy, a left-handed pitcher with a 114-mile-an-hour fastball, is discovered by the New York Yankees and is invited to New York by George Steinbrenner to play in an exhibition game between the Yankees and the Mets. In this fragment, Josh and the narrator, his teenage cousin Jeff Clayton, a catcher and switch-hitter, have just arrived at their room in the Waldorf-Astoria on the day of the game:

A whole passel of news men and women were waitin' for us. Some carried picture-show cameras and set in to filmin' us for later showin' on a bunch of New York television shows. Since Josh is good at talkin' I let him do the talkin' for both of us. Right then I was feelin' the urge to use a bathroom and looked around for one. Nowhere did I see one. I was hoppin' from one foot to another, in a bad way, when Josh took notice and brought his interview to a close. By the time the elevator had elevated us up to our room my eyeballs were floatin'.

The big game was set to commence at 7 P.M. which gave us 6½ hours to get rested up from our trip up. Now us catchers are in many ways—have to be—psychiatrists. Pitchers, especially left-handers, are . . . temperamental, and that bein' so means it's us catchers that have to do the thinkin' for them once the game gets to goin'. In Josh's case that fact is doubly so. . . . What all this means is that it's me that has to do the worryin', thinkin' and signal givin' during the games. Also, I have to keep a supply of blowgum on hand in case Josh runs out. He goes through anywhere from 11 to 15 pieces durin' a game. Anyway, as soon as I finished up in the bathroom I suggested to Josh that we get in a nap. He was checkin' out the what-was-ons on the television when I said that. One of the what-was-ons was a Durango Kid picture show that was just gettin' goin'. It was *Desert Vigilantes,* one that we'd not seen in several months so we were awhile before gettin' that nap in. . . .

A-time we got to the ballpark, suited up and out on the field the stands were might-near full. . . . I found out right off that Josh was in fine form tonight—could tell by the way his fastball wiggled around and the pop it made when I caught it. And his yoyo ball—what I call his sinkin' curve—was breakin' magnificently too. I never said so but I'd have bet Josh's last cent those Mets were in for trouble. Soon, Josh was ready to go and we walked back to the dugout. A few minutes later, we took the field. Everybody stood for the music and soon after that the umpire was yellin', "Play ball! . . ."

Now I could go on and on, give you all the details, but was I to I'd just be repeatin' myself and wastin' words. One interestin' item I better tell though is about the last batter Josh faced. When the umpire called the second strike this hitter asked him, "Whur was that pitch?" Now the pitch was one that coulda been called either way, maybe a half inch off the plate, but the umpire gave a satisfactory answer to the hitter by sayin', "I ain't too sure, but it sounded like a strike." When the hitter swung and missed the next pitch he swung his way right into the record book for he was the 27th'n Josh struck out that night, a major-league one-game record.

Stockton was always seeking advice on writing techniques from the Norfolk editor. In the very first diary entries, there often were misspelled or misused words—Stockton spelled the adverb "too" with only one *o,* for instance. He eventually learned from his mistakes. After he was moved to Powhatan, Stockton wanted more help in developing as a writer, and the editor suggested he read writers other than Louis L'Amour and borrow ideas and themes from them. Stockton seemed especially interested in creating characters who seemed authentic, whose language was true to the Great Smoky Mountains and his favorite literary fantasies. The editor told Stockton when the dialogue rang true, and Dennis took great pride in the compliments. He also told Stockton when the writing did not work, and Dennis would grow testy and prickly when he did not agree. But over the years, Stockton's writings *did* improve, and a friendship flourished between the inmate/author and the editor.

As Stockton wrote more over time, a strange thing happened: the line between fact and fiction began to blur for him. Friends noticed that his speech grew folksy like his characters'. Danny Revels, a character in his first novel, popped up as a regular commentator in the newsletter. Stockton petitioned the Powhatan county clerk to change his name to Mark Anthony Revels, Danny's fictional brother. The change was granted, though Stockton kept it secret. Maybe it looked crazy, but it was a craziness he preferred to M-Building's mad reality.

• • • •

By afternoon, that reality was in full swing. The frustration of those who had no escape built to critical mass. Two inmates on his tier were challenging a man on protective custody. "Get off protective custody, motherfucker, and come outside on our rec yard." One man down the hall couldn't speak, could only bark like a dog. Others mimicked him. From another cell came high-pitched wails. Most of the uproar came from young guys on the bottom tier. Most of them were "cell gangsters," guys who acted tough in solitary but were the "wives" of other men in general population. The most common topic was sex: who fucked whom. Some tried sounding like women, others dressed and walked that way. When going to the shower, some shouted so their lovers could see them naked. Others paid in candy and cigarettes for love letters. Physical contact did occur in M-Building, but unlike the rest of the prison it was between guards and inmates, usually on the graveyard shift.

One night Stockton heard a noise on his tier and stuck his mirror through the tray slot. The reflection showed a guard being serviced by an inmate. The guard's penis was inserted through the slot and his hips were moving. He grabbed the door and slumped, then zipped up and continued on his rounds. Fifteen minutes later he was back, his mouth at the slot. "Quit that shit," Stockton yelled. The guard jumped up, looked around in panic, then hauled ass off the tier.

Late afternoon was shower time, a welcome break. The guards would cuff his hands behind him, then escort him down the tier. He could smell the shower stalls the closer he got. There were about a dozen stalls, all alike, none quite as big as a phone booth and each with a button one pushed to start the water. The temperature was usually cold to tepid. Once Stockton pushed the button, the water ran for a minute or two then stopped, so he had to keep pushing. But the stalls were rarely cleaned and the drains clogged by hair, underwear and sometimes shit, and if he pushed too long the water level rose and he stood ankle deep in the murk. It flowed out and onto the floor. Stockton always washed his feet in his sink after returning to his cell.

Yet even with all this, the trip to and from the shower and the occasional trip to the rec yard were his only times to leave his cell. He eyeballed new inmates, scoped out changes. They were important breaks in the routine. Any reason for variation better be damn important or the whole building would ring with the angry shouts of inmates. Like, for instance, the memorable day of the man on the pole.

That day, the guard informed Dennis there would be no rec trip. A prisoner had climbed atop a basketball goal and refused to come down. He sat out of reach of the goon squad. He'd climbed up in midmorning and it was now late afternoon.

Stockton spotted the man during his trip to the showers. He figured his position had to be uncomfortable and as he watched, the man stood from his perch and stretched, then scratched that part of his anatomy used for pole sitting. He twisted to one side, hauled out his penis and peed. Two guards near the gun tower hurried along the top of the wall until they were opposite. They leveled their guns on the rail and watched. When he was done and resumed his seat, one guard went back to the tower while the other walked to a shady spot at the other end of the wall.

Stockton returned to his cell. In a few minutes he heard what sounded like a helicopter hovering outside. Maybe a TV station had heard. The sound lasted perhaps ten minutes, but the man never made the evening news.

When the shift changed, a fresh group of guards tackled the problem. A guard told Stockton that the shift commander decided to ignore the man. He'd come down sooner or later. He'd better enjoy his freedom while it lasted, the guard added, since he'd never get any again.

Stockton discovered that by looking out the front of his cell and to the left, he could see the guy on the post, the backboard and the distant sky. As he watched, the man was trying to get the kinks from his legs. He'd shake them one at a time, then sit back down. Stockton drifted to sleep, then woke for supper. The man was gone. A guard told him he'd finally grown tired and climbed down. "Where is he now?" Stockton asked.

"In his cell, where he'll stay."

And then there were interruptions that he didn't want to remember—ones that reminded him why he was here.

The guards came to take Joe Wise from Powhatan to the Death House on August 3, 1993. The move was unexpected. Wise's appeals were nearing an end, but another man had been scheduled to die before him. Each man on Death Row had a sense of when his own execution would be held based on the progress of the appeals of the man scheduled before him. But in Joe Wise's case, there was an unwelcome surprise. The man scheduled before him had cheated the executioner: guards found him in his cell in Mecklenburg, dead by heroin overdose, the needle still sticking in his vein.

The apparent suicide brought them all a step closer to execution, and now they were taking Joe. Stockton was just about to catch up on sleep when suddenly his friend called over: "Dennis, they just told me to pack up." He was being moved to the Death House, he said.

Stockton was instantly awake. *"What?"*

Joe repeated his words. Stockton rose and glanced outside. A guard stood on the tier before Joe's cell. He seemed impatient. Joe gave the guard several items to hand to Stockton: some were gifts, others things to pass on. "Good-bye, brother," he said as they shackled his hands.

And now Stockton found he was at a loss for words. What do you say to someone going to the house of execution? he wondered. What was the best thing to say? Nothing seemed appropriate. It wouldn't work to try to make him laugh. "Good-bye" and "I'll be praying for you" seemed so hollow. Did any words fit something like this? He didn't want Joe to see his tears but suddenly he couldn't stop them and turned away from the door. He didn't want to watch Joe loaded down with forty pounds of chains, a guy so simple some called him half-retarded, yet smart enough to find a way to deal with the horrors of Powhatan. It was all so pathetic, and now the guards were marching him down the tier. A voice came from each cell as Wise passed: "Good luck, Joe," "Take care, Joe." If Stockton didn't say something quick it would be too late and his best friend would be gone forever. But if he called out, the others would notice the tremble in his voice. Suddenly he didn't care.

"Good luck, Joe!" Stockton shouted. "It's been a privilege knowing you, in more ways than you'll know."

In his handheld mirror, Stockton could see Joe Wise glance back over his shoulder and smile. Then a guard nudged him forward, and he was gone.

Joe Wise was executed slightly behind schedule on September 14, 1993. It was considered an uneventful execution, no bloody glitches, no embarrassing breakdowns in the machine. He died peacefully, walking on his own into the chamber, sitting in Old Sparky, meeting the gaze of the witnesses. They later said Wise didn't seem scared.

Stockton heard about the delay in Joe's death months later through a prison chaplain. It was 11 P.M. and Joe and his lawyers were waiting for the warden to come and read the death warrant, but there was an unexpected delay. The guard checked the clock, picked up the phone, checked the clock again. Joe's lawyers and ministers waited in a surreal silence. They stood at attention, no one knowing where to look, no one making a sound. Finally, Joe cleared his throat. "Are they ever going to do this thing?" he said.

• • • •

But this was not a special day, no memories that came back to haunt him as Stockton lay in his narrow bed. It was a day much like every other during his isolation in M-Building. The sun went down, Stockton ate supper and a guard passed out mail. An insurance company offered him life insurance at reduced rates. The nurse came by with his sleeping pill. He shaved with his electric razor: after his typewriter, this was his most prized possession. It was either buy your own or shave with the one guards passed from man to man. Some used it to shave their legs, others around their anus. Stockton was grateful he had his own.

By now it was nearly 10 P.M. Some nights, before he went to sleep, he stood at his cell door and stared out the windows. He could see the top of the wall and the treetops beyond. He liked it best when there was a full moon. The trees beneath glowed silver.

He'd lose track of time as if, for these endless years, he hadn't really been here.

11

On the morning of January 30, 1994—Super Bowl Sunday—a guard walked quietly past Cell B-10 in Powhatan's M-Building and heard a strange noise. Snitches had reported odd sounds on this tier, and sure enough the guard heard a metallic grating from the cell of Willie Lloyd Turner. At five-ten and 150 pounds, with a soft voice and benign features, Turner seemed harmless, but the shift captains were warned not to be fooled. Turner was a jailhouse Houdini, and rumor had it he'd been planning a breakout a long time. Now on this cold morning, as other inmates slept or considered the evening's face-off between the Dallas Cowboys and the Buffalo Bills, and as Stockton lay in bed two cells over, listening to the chips and chinks from Willie's cell, the guard peeked through the slot and saw Turner bent over his metal toilet, gripping both sides with his hands and straining as if he meant to rip the toilet straight from the floor. The guard gave the alarm and he and others stormed the cell.

So began Willie Lloyd Turner's last song of revenge. It unfolded slowly, but by the end once again brought national embarrassment to his jailers and earned its composer the title "The Genius of Death Row" in a *New Yorker* magazine profile by Peter Boyer published in December 1995. As the first notes sounded, guards found hidden in his cell a stash of weapons, homemade keys and fake guns. In the end, a year and a half later, Turner's lawyer found a real gun, bullets and two hacksaw blades stored in his typewriter. Taped next to the weapons was a handwritten note with a happy face and the message, "Smile."

Super Bowl Sunday should have been a warning—and a reminder of May 31, 1984. But memory is short and prison officials watched in awe as weapons poured from Turner's cell. A hacksaw blade. Several shanks. A three-foot-long Samurai-type sword. Two fake guns of plastic and wood.

There were also two hatches that couldn't be locked and which officials hadn't even known existed, and homemade keys. The latter scared them most. As Willie was led from his cell in his underwear, he boasted that he could have sprung half of M-Building. The guards laughed. Soon they found he wasn't lying. The keys unlocked several cell and hall doors.

Stockton watched as the DOC suit-and-ties converged on Willie's cell. They followed every move as guards measured the cell's exact dimensions and took picture after picture, as maintenance workers dragged heavy steel into the cell and blocked the hatches, as locksmiths changed the locks on cells and hall doors. "How do you think he did it?" one suit finally asked.

"I wish I knew," his friend answered. "He sure is a smart little nigger. Musta took him years to do all those things."

• • • •

It had. By Super Bowl Sunday, Turner had the dubious honor of being on The Row longer than any Virginia inmate, cheating the executioner for nearly fifteen years. He'd received several execution dates, heard his death warrant read three times and once came within five hours of electrocution before the U.S. Supreme Court granted a reprieve. He was moved from prison to prison, and at every one managed to breach security. Yet he always pulled back at the brink of escape, as if the mere attempt was more important than any brief freedom he might gain.

Turner was born on December 9, 1945, and grew up with his sister and three brothers in rural Southampton and Isle of Wight counties, the historic Southside site of Nat Turner's slave rebellion of August 1831. Willie never spoke of Old Prophet Nat, and unlike the Brileys, did not blame racism for his fate. In many ways, he had better cause. He grew up in almost unimaginable poverty, the family living in a succession of tarpaper shacks where blankets were strung to designate rooms. The children burned sulfur to drive away bedbugs and drank turpentine and sugar to combat trichinosis from bad pork—when there was food. Their father, Elbert Turner, was an alcoholic day worker who sent his children to the fields to pay for his booze. Photos showed a haggard man with bulging eyes, who died at forty-four. Turner's mother, Gussie, also drank. Esmon Thompson, his sister and a psychiatric nurse, remembered Gussie as a "whiny and needy" woman who rarely rose from bed and suffered from chronic asthma and probably depression. In deference to her ailments, there was little talking in the house, few visitors.

Yet for all the surface quiet, it was a violent home. When Willie was seven, his mother choked him unconscious for telling his dad of her sexual fling with another man. This immediately became a vicious circle. If he told on his mother, she beat him; his father beat him if he didn't tell. At times, Willie would blank out and stare into space, and by age fifteen had an unexplained seizure. All the Turner children fled the household in their early teens, and the four boys warred with society. The oldest brother died young after convictions for burglary, armed robbery and forgery; of Turner's remaining two brothers, one was charged with rape and the other with malicious maiming, but both served their time and turned their lives around. Not so with Willie. By the time he reached his teens, court records suggest, Turner had developed both considerable personal charm and a penchant for breaking the law. He had many girlfriends and a way of convincing them, and himself, that he could do anything he wanted, when the truth was the exact opposite. Willie was poor, black and illiterate in Southside Virginia. At seventeen, his future probably seemed hopeless to him.

It quickly fulfilled these expectations. In 1963, he was arrested for impregnating a fourteen-year-old girl and sent to Nansemond County Jail, his first time behind bars. He was the smallest and youngest in a cell filled with violent men, and he was terrified. When a cellmate walked up, Willie jumped the man and beat him with a hairbrush as the man's friends laughed. It was Turner's first sense of what counted in this harsh new world.

Turner was convicted of contributing to the delinquency of a minor and sent to reform school where, three days after arrival, he picked a lock and fled. Although he was soon recaptured, it was the beginning of a lifelong pattern: once jailed, he'd start looking for

218 | *Dead Run*

ways to break free, yet once out, it was as if he'd always find a way back. In 1966, he shot a man in Washington. In 1968, he threatened a girlfriend with a gun in Boston. He was sent to federal prison and escaped, and by 1970 was back in Franklin, Virginia, where he shot a friend five times over an insult. "I hope he dies," he told police. The friend lived and Willie went to The Wall in Richmond.

The state penitentiary in those days embodied just about everything nightmarish and brutal in prison life. Riots. Guns among the convicts. Old Sparky. Corrupt guards. It would be *the* most cited reason for prison reform later that decade, the exact opposite of what Mecklenburg was built to be. In 1970, Turner learned the prison class system: there were predators and prey. He especially feared the homosexual predators, knowing that his size and good looks made him a target. When a con announced his intentions by sending a "gift" of smokes and candy, Willie traded these for a lead pipe, then beat the man.

It was the first episode in a litany of prison violence. Turner was transferred to a road gang and hit a prisoner in the face with an ax. He escaped with the help of a girlfriend and they lived in Washington off money-changing scams. He was recaptured and sent to Powhatan where in 1973 he stabbed an inmate. The next year, he stabbed another man, who died from his wound. Turner was convicted of second-degree murder and sent back to The Wall.

But now, instead of further violence, there was a change. Turner worked in the prison kitchen and learned to read, haunting the prison library. He enrolled in the prison voc-tech program and earned a barber's certificate. He became a prison barber, a badge of trust because of the potentially deadly tools of his trade. It seemed to prison officials that he might make it in The World and so, on January 9, 1978, he was paroled to his hometown.

Six months later, he committed the murder that sent him to Death Row.

• • • •

Turner was thirty-two when he returned to Franklin, and much had changed. His father died before his release and his mother lived in a housing project. His sister and brothers had left town. Except for the fields and Union Camp, whose giant sawmill rose beneath a plume of smoke in the center of town, there were few opportunities for young black men. Turner worked briefly as a barber, hoping to open his own shop, but the respect he'd gained in prison didn't transfer Outside. In Franklin he was still one of the Turner boys, son of the no-account Elbert, and he soon upheld the label, drinking and chasing women by day, sleeping on his mother's couch at night. One day he tried picking up a white girl at a local Dairy Queen, a risky proposition in that time and place. He kissed her hand and got her phone number, but never called. Yet, the two would meet in even stranger circumstances seventeen years later.

During this period, Willie also got hold of a sawed-off 12-gauge shotgun. His mother tried to get help for him, without luck. On the morning of July 12, 1978, Turner wrapped the shotgun in a green towel, stuck it in a paper sack and headed downtown.

Turner would later testify that what happened in the jewelry store owned by William "Jack" Smith, Jr., a longtime Franklin fixture, was a combination of bad luck and accident, but every other witness at his trial would say otherwise. According to them, Turner barged through the door at about eleven-thirty, unwrapped the shotgun and laid it on the counter. Jack Smith, a clerk and a customer were in the store. Smith had been robbed before and knew it was best to stay calm, so asked, "What can I do for you?" When Willie motioned with the gun, Smith filled bags with cash and jewelry, and tripped a silent alarm. When a second customer entered, Turner motioned his hostages behind the sales case, kicking some when they didn't move fast enough. Then began a weird chain of coincidence. A Franklin police officer named Alan Bain walked in, his .38 Special strapped inside its holster, and told Smith his alarm was ringing. Willie took the stunned officer's revolver, fired a shot into the back of the store, and threatened to kill everyone if another cop arrived. Just then a siren sounded outside and Turner panicked. He aimed at Smith and fired, grazing his scalp. As Smith fell, the clerk and one customer fled. Bain pleaded with Willie not to shoot again, promising to drive him from town if no one else was hurt. Willie assured Bain he wouldn't hurt him, but added, "I'm going to kill this . . . squealer," then leaned over the counter and squeezed a round into Jack Smith's chest. Smith made a gurgling sound and Willie shot him again; as he did so, Bain jumped him from behind and wrestled away the gun. As Willie was led away, he said: "Well, I guess I'm on the way back."

Turner was thrown into the county lockup for the next year and a half as his capital murder trial dragged through court. The wait served as his school for escape. He watched the behavior of jailers who practiced an unchanging routine, studied the mechanics of his imprisonment. With the help of a trustee he obtained a hacksaw blade, and while other prisoners slept, cut through the lock of his cell block. Once past that, he entered the hall and sawed at the bars of a nearby window. He replaced the bars, hiding all signs of his progress with an early version of a homemade paste, then settled back and waited for the right time to run.

It came soon. Turner was found guilty of capital murder and the jury gave him death. One snowy night in December 1979, days before the judge officially confirmed the jury's death sentence, Turner and a partner left dummies in their bunks and slipped away. The ruse was not discovered for hours. Willie thumbed to a friend's house and finagled a ride to his great-aunt's across the North Carolina border, one of the first places authorities checked after discovering the breakout. By 3 A.M., Turner was recaptured, fast asleep on a couch in the front room.

Others didn't sleep so well. One was Jack Smith's son Billy, whose own imprisonment began the day he was working as a groundskeeper at the Franklin hospital and saw the ambulance bring his father's body to the ER. On the night that Turner escaped, Billy Smith was home from college for Christmas when the phone rang. It was the local sheriff, calling to warn the family that Turner had broken free. All night long Billy Smith slept on a couch in front of his mother's bedroom, shotgun in hand. At 4 or 5 A.M., the sheriff called to say Willie had been recaptured. Yet Billy Smith had never known such terror like that night, and he wondered if, in his final moments, his father had felt the same fear.

It was a kind of prison Billy Smith had never imagined, but one in which he would live for the next seventeen years. He had hoped to see the world, but the family business fell to him. He returned to Franklin after college, married, started a family. Not a day dawned without some thought of the man who killed his father, and some nights, in his dreams, he saw himself standing over the electric chair, ensuring that his was the last face Turner would ever see.

But the appeals dragged on and everyone grew older, until at times it seemed he was the last person demanding justice. When he felt his resolve weaken he'd trek upstairs and read through the accumulated documents of Turner's many hearings. "Billy, when is this going to end?" his wife would ask. It won't end until it's over, Billy thought—until justice finally claims the man who killed his father and his own dreams.

• • • •

Turner arrived at Mecklenburg in February 1980 as he had every other prison, filled with terror at the thought of living among murderers. Instead, he was welcomed with open arms. There were seven other inmates on The Row when he arrived, and news of his jail escape preceded him. He had instant respect, and maintained it by refusing to slip into the vegetative state he watched come over others. He stayed in shape, running in place in his cell each day for two hours. He taught himself the law and mentored others. His position as Death Row grievance clerk gave him insight into the mind of almost every prisoner there. And he became an inventor, setting aside time each day to work on his "de-ending shears," a barber's tool for removing split ends. He sent a rough sketch of his idea to the U.S. Patent and Trademark Office, but was told that all applications required detailed drawings and descriptions before a patent was granted. The guards hooted in derision: "Ain't no nigger on Death Row gonna invent nothing," one said. This only stiffened Turner's resolve. He studied art books to learn shading and perspective, sketched out the design using an illegal hacksaw blade for a straight-edge. In 1985, he was granted U.S. Patent No. 4,428,119, making him the only Death Row prisoner in the country with a patent. He offered to share the profits with Jack Smith's family, but Billy Smith turned him down.

Yet for all this, it was in making and hiding weapons, what he called his "unauthorized projects," that Turner excelled. He wrote in his memoirs that, within days of arriving, Frank Coppola showed him a .45-caliber automatic and bullets he'd somehow smuggled inside. It was the ultimate security breach and ultimate symbol of freedom: a prisoner could cheat the executioner while taking some keepers along for that final ride. Guns among inmates are one of the prison system's greatest embarrassments, more prevalent than jailers are willing to admit. Stockton himself mentioned seeing guns in the hands of inmates as far back as a 1972 Christmas riot at The Wall.

But this was Turner's first and he would remember it like teenage sex. Coppola wanted a hiding place—the payoff would be that Willie also had access. The solution was both simple and ethereal: the two men's cells were stacked one atop the other so Turner suspended the gun between his and Coppola's cells. Turner picked the lock on their plumbing closet, attached the gun to a wire and strung the wire to Coppola's air duct. But the gun was never used and after Coppola's execution, all mention of it faded into thin air.

Now truth gets thrown a curve. In his interviews and memoirs, Turner assigned himself the central role in planning the Great Escape, claiming he had veto power over the Brileys. They were claims that were never substantiated by other inmates' accounts of the events preceding May 31, 1984, and at best spoke to Willie's pride. When Turner refused to escape with the others, he said it was because he feared a bloodbath, yet his foiled attempt a year later came much closer to bloodshed. One gets the feeling blood itself was no deterrent. He walked away because the Brileys planned the breakout, not him.

Power struggles among prisoners are a fact of life, but even for an inmate, Turner cast a cold eye on others. He was a sharp talker, or "slicker" in prison slang, and Stockton once heard Turner brag that he was the "master of the double- and the triple-cross." Stockton sensed that Willie divided the world into those who could be manipulated and those who could not. Those who could, like Mason and Giarratano, were allies. Those who could not, like the Brileys, were the enemy. His estimation of Stockton seemed more complicated. At first they were friends. But Stockton's published diary assigned leadership to the Brileys, which may have wounded Turner's pride. It was at this point that he started his own autobiography, in which he rewrote events, and it was now that Stockton became a bitter rival. This rivalry intensified as their executions approached, a contest that drove both to "succeed" in strange ways.

There was also a sense that, until this point, Turner believed he could leave Death Row any time he chose. His first brush with the Death House changed that forever. Soon after JB's execution in April 1985, Turner was led to A-Basement, scheduled to die scarcely two weeks later. The first thing he saw was clothing JB wore on the night of his death. He suddenly saw his own fate. "As I walked in I could hear and see hundreds of fat green flies fighting over something stinking in a box sitting on the inside of the door," he wrote. "The stuff in the box consisted of a white death row prisoner jump suit which was spotted with blood, burnt marks, human feces, vomit and some white and other awful looking stuff. And the entire area had a strong smell of burnt flesh combined with the even stronger offensive smell coming from the stuff in the box. Though I had never in my life smelt anything like it, I knew it was the smell of death."

His own death rushed closer and there was no way to stop it, his fate truly out of his hands. He watched the guards practice the death rituals, heard the roar as they tested the chair. He later claimed that he had a gun hidden nearby, but there is no evidence of this. If anything, there was blind panic until, at the last moment, like a scene in a movie, he was given a reprieve.

Yet Turner knew it was only temporary. He returned to Mecklenburg and planned his escape in earnest, unearthing his pipe bomb for the failed escape attempt in November 1985. In 1986, the court overturned his sentence and ordered a new hearing on the grounds that the original hearing may have been tainted by racial bias. He was released into the general prison population and thought of the future. He took classes and dreamed of freedom, but when the new jury again imposed death, he went to M-Building at Powhatan, the neighbor of Stockton and Joe Wise.

Now there was a new urgency. Turner gained the reputation as M-Building's Mr. Fix-It, ingratiating himself to others with quick repairs that would have taken days or weeks to snake through the prison bureaucracy. He secretly returned to his arms making, covering the sounds with his legitimate repairs. He refined techniques learned during the Great Escape, making the Samurai sword from pieces of his metal bed frame, stashing his sword, shanks and saws in holes chiseled from the wall and inside the toilet where aluminum had been removed. Turner covered the holes with a paste made of toothpaste and soap, then let it harden and colored it the same institutional gray as the walls.

Yet Willie was proudest of his keys, hidden in peanut butter jars and watch cases with false bottoms. They were the apex of his art and, like his patent, seemed to spring from his mind. He watched as guards used their own keys to let him out for showers or other trips, memorizing each key's shape and size. He stripped aluminum from the toilet, the metal soft enough to bend and shape with tools but strong enough to hold firm against the tumblers. If a key didn't work at first, he fiddled with it until it did. He made keys to every cell he occupied in M-Building, each taking about a day once he fully visualized its shape and size. There was a purity to this unlike any other project. The key itself was an afterthought. *He* was the key.

Then, once again, Turner got hold of a gun.

It was not Coppola's cannon, the cumbersome .45, but a .38 revolver, a polished blue-black beauty with four bullets in the chamber. As usual, Turner had to brag, so he passed it next door to Joe Wise. Joe turned it over in his hands, then passed it on to Stockton. "He says he's got an escape plan, Dennis," Wise said.

Stockton shook the bullets into his palm. He felt light-headed, as if drunk. Here was power, clenched in his fist. It would be so easy to squeeze the trigger at the next guard who passed, just let fly for all he'd endured, then save the last bullet and press the steel against the roof of his mouth, leaving the executioner behind. But he caught himself, noticing that his hands were shaking, the bullets rattling in his palm. He wiped them clean of prints and replaced them in the chamber. "Why's he showing you this?" he asked Joe. "Willie's no friend of yours." This was true. Soon after his arrival, Turner set about attracting followers by passing around copies of Stockton's diary from the newspaper, painting him as a snitch. Joe was the only one to stick up for Stockton and as a result Turner and Wise were often at their cell doors, spitting their hate at each other while the rest of Isolation tuned in.

"He's trying to set you up," Stockton said. "Leave the gun with me, least for the next few hours." Sure enough, both times that Willie passed his gun to Joe, the guards appeared within hours and shook down his cell.

Wise was executed on September 14, 1993, and after that Stockton never saw the gun again. Yet one day, Turner offered him another trade. Turner wanted to swap his expensive electric typewriter with memory for Stockton's old manual. Stockton had often envied Turner's typewriter, but the warden didn't allow the trade. It was only later, when the same typewriter became the center of so much controversy, that Stockton wondered whether Willie had been trying to set him up too. It chilled him when he thought of it. Had Turner planned to turn him in, then use the discovery as leverage in a bargain for clemency?

Turner's time was running out. His last appeals were shutting down. By January 1994, it was almost certain he would be executed within a year or two. He grew desperate, spending every moment on his projects, even declining time for showers. He started to stink and screamed at the least interruption. Stockton and the other inmates saw him as some strange, cave-dwelling gnome.

It was then that rumors started about Willie's escape plan. He spread the rumor himself, passing it among his followers. They would go out the front, he told them. It seemed unlikely, but some of his disciples appeared to be aware of the gun. Yet his believers grew more impatient the longer he preached, and after Wise's execution they began to turn against him. At such times he'd go off, screaming and shouting, raging like the Screamer or the Dogman at the end of the tier. It came to a head one night when a well-liked inmate learned he was being moved to some federal hellhole like Marion or Atlanta. "Make it happen, Willie," he cried. "Make it happen tonight!"

Can't do it, Turner replied. The plan's still incomplete. Everything's not in place.

"It never was in place, you motherfucking liar!" yelled the inmate, joined by his friends. "You been stringing us along! Meet us on the yard!"

A few days later, Super Bowl Sunday, the guard heard the scrape of a file or hacksaw against Turner's metal toilet. They broke in and Willie took it calmly. He wasn't trying to rip out the toilet, he explained. He was trying to make a new stash. He showed them his armory, pulling out weapon after weapon, showing them a hole in the ceiling he'd dug with a replaceable cell bar. He broke open the vent and pulled out the samurai sword, fake guns, shanks, then proudly showed off his keys.

Turner was moved to the newly opened maximum security unit in Greensville, fifty miles south of Richmond—the state's new home of the Death House and Old Sparky. He was denied all calls and visits until the DOC completed its investigation, yet once again he slipped the knot and called Stockton's friend, the newspaper editor. There was no escape plan, Willie bragged. The keys and weapons just proved to the keepers who was the smartest man around.

Turner had escaped another tight spot, Stockton thought, simply by giving himself up. But the revelation had a price, bringing Turner that much closer to the executioner.

• • • •

Now love found Willie Lloyd in the unlikeliest of places.

Her name was Caroline Schloss, a thirty-four-year-old counselor with Correctional Medical Services, a private contractor providing medical and psychological care to inmates. Correctional Medical had a strict rule against fraternizing with inmates, but Schloss broke it in June 1994 after three days on the job. The rapidity with which this happened surprised even her. As a psychologist, she knew the mind games inmates played with newcomers, the small favors that grew larger with each request. As a woman in this sealed-off world of men, she felt especially marked. Scoring sex with a staffer was top prize in the prison game, second only to escape or release. She'd heard the tales of murder groupies and knew that the DOC considered every woman a potential security risk. With her compact good looks and dark features, she figured come-ons would be frequent. But Caroline Schloss had driven an eighteen-wheeler, worked on bridges, been an aerobics instructor, and competed and won in arm wrestling and kickboxing competitions. She figured she could take care of herself.

Thus, she was more surprised than anyone the day she made her rounds and felt someone staring her down. She turned and saw a small, handsome man, shirtless, arms folded across his chest. Although the stare was standard inmate mind-fuck, she still felt something electric and confronted him. He introduced himself. A Franklin native herself, Schloss had heard of Willie. Almost everyone there had.

Willie claimed he acted menacingly because one couldn't seem weak with so many tough guys around. Incredibly, she watched herself flirt back. Before she left, Turner asked her number so he could phone. She didn't think anything of it then, but one day she was struck by an overpowering sense of déjà vu. She remembered how, as a teenager, some handsome black guy had sweet-talked her out of her phone number outside the Franklin Dairy Queen. He promised to call but never did. Now, incredibly, she watched the same act play out again. They spent hours together, the cell bars between them. Prison officials and her employer frowned on the affair. Correctional Medical Services gave her an ultimatum: stop the visits or quit. She chose the latter and joined Willie's defense as a paralegal.

His execution, scheduled for May 25, 1995, was coming down to the wire. Almost all of his appeals were exhausted: he watched his rumpled attorney, Walter Walvick, struggle and grow hopeful with each new argument, then grow even more disheveled as they failed. Walvick was Mutt to Turner's Jeff, friendly and open next to his client's famous wiliness. Criminal law was not even Walvick's first choice in the law. A partner at Washington's Dickstein, Shapiro & Morin, he'd specialized in the more esoteric world of telecommunications law, but when his firm responded to a plea from the American Bar Association for major firms to donate time to Death Row cases, Walvick stepped in and stayed with Turner for the next seven years.

It all made Willie think. He'd been on Death Row for fifteen years, longer than any man in the state, even that damn Stockton. He was forty-nine; his sister Esmon, who'd fought so hard in his defense, forty-four; Billy Smith, whose life he'd ruined, thirty-five. He'd brought grief and pain to too many people. He'd wasted too many lives, including his own.

He was moved to the Death House. Some days he facetiously practiced death by lying on the floor. Other days it hit him how he'd be the state's second inmate to die by lethal injection—the law had come into effect that January. How would it feel, he wondered. A quick cocaine rush, or sleep's deep creep? In the week before his execution, he said he wanted no more visits by chaplains or family members. It was hard enough taking care of himself, he said.

One hundred miles away, near Norfolk, his sister Esmon started having dreams. The sound of doors closing and locking followed her through darkness. The dreams had to do with Willie, but what did they mean? She'd visited him until 1989, then it got too hard and Willie thought minimizing contact would be easier for everyone. Her brother was wrong. It was actually harder. As they entered the last week, she took time off work to be alone. She thought of Jack Smith's family. Of her own.

In Franklin, Billy Smith went into seclusion too. That year, a bill allowing victims' relatives into the execution chamber failed to pass the legislature, so the governor signed an executive order. Unseemly and bloodthirsty, critics cried. But Billy Smith didn't feel particularly triumphant or bloodthirsty. He just wanted it to end. He and a sister signed up to watch the execution, becoming the first victims' relatives allowed into the chamber in state history.

In the Death House, Turner and Schloss spent time together. They prepared for the end, sometimes fantasizing about what life could have been like on The Outside. But more than anything else, they finished his memoirs, which he wanted published posthumously. In the process, Schloss learned of the Mecklenburg breakout and read about his brush with the executioner in 1985, of how he'd planned to kill as many guards as possible when they came to walk him to the chair. Caroline said she figured he had some escape plan now. If she ever learned the details, she told him, she would have to tell authorities.

By then, all he had to do was stretch out his hand to the Smith-Corona typewriter kept within reach on a table just outside his cell. He hinted to Caroline and others that a surprise awaited inside it, but did not give further details. He told an uncle, "I'm not gonna put y'all through nothing else, but I'm gonna let you know they couldn't do this to me if I didn't let 'em." He told Walvick to check the typewriter after he died.

Now it was the final day. Turner and his lawyer spent the last three hours talking about good and evil, life and death. The warden came and read the death warrant. Willie turned to Walvick as he was led off. "I love you, man," he said.

Turner came through the death chamber doors at 8:53 P.M., wearing the standard-issue blue shirt and crisp new jeans rolled at the ankles. Six members of the Death Squad formed his cortege. He lay upon the gurney and was secured with leather straps. He'd decided against a final statement, but as the IVs were inserted into his arm he seemed filled with nervous energy. "When will it start?" he asked, his lip trembling. "How will it feel?" He raised his head and looked at the witnesses. The intravenous tubes began to jerk as the chemicals started pumping. At 9:04, he closed his eyes.

Billy Smith and his sister watched in the separate room for family, across a narrow hall from the state witnesses. Billy was too nervous to sit. He stood the whole time. He wondered if Turner had seen him when he looked up. It was just like he'd dropped off to sleep, that's all.

A hundred miles away, Turner's sister watched the clock, knowing it would all happen around nine. It's been a hell of a life, she thought. At least he's free.

At 9:07, a doctor declared him dead. There was silence in the witness room until a DOC official grumbled, "The damned bastard escaped the electric chair."

• • • •

There was one more act, and it made national news. After the execution, Walvick walked from the prison into the yellow glare of the halogen lights, passing the black-suited guards standing at parade rest. He wanted out of there, back to his motel room in nearby Emporia, back with his patient wife and a bottle of Jack Daniels. He gave his brief statement to the press, which treated him with strange gentleness. He collected Willie's typewriter and his few other effects, then loaded them in his station wagon and drove away.

He thought about that typewriter. What had Willie hinted at? *Check the Smith-Corona when I'm gone.* Turner was proud of the thing, the most complicated piece of machinery he'd owned in all these years on Death Row. He probably wished he'd invented it himself. It had internal memory and wherever he went he told the guards, "Keep your hands off. You touch the wrong thing and erase my pleadings, I'll haul your ass to court." They snorted but stayed away.

So Walvick arrived at the motel and, watched by his wife and two female journalists, opened the casing with a screwdriver. "Son of a bitch," he cried. Tucked inside a cutout space was a loaded blue steel .32-caliber Smith & Wesson revolver, a different pistol than the one in Powhatan. Next to the gun lay a plastic bag filled with bullets, and beside this the handwritten note with the single word, "Smile." Everyone gaped like they'd seen the impossible—which, in a way, they had. He phoned Emporia police and when the officer arrived his jaw dropped. "My goodness," he said. "That's unique. I'm in awe."

It was a final testament to his client's ingenuity, and when the state dismantled the entire typewriter, they also found two hacksaw blades. Turner had cut away a rectangular piece of plastic from the paper support, then held a match to it until it was pliable enough to mold. This covered his secret compartment, an enlarged area that had originally been the storage space for the power cord. Deep inside he cut two small holes, perfect fits for the gun barrel and the butt. The cover fit tight and snug. The hacksaw blades were stuck inside, glued by another of his strange pastes.

He'd fooled his keepers again. Willie's career had gone full circle, from Mecklenburg to death and beyond. It was as though his life had been scripted, a fable of invention and incarceration. For the next ten weeks, state police interviewed guards, visitors and other inmates to track down how and where he'd gotten the gun. Test-firings proved it worked; fingerprint tests revealed no clues. They traced it as far back as 1954 to a sale in Galax, Virginia, but the buyer was now dead. Prison officials said the typewriter and his other possessions had been X-rayed when he was moved from Powhatan. Although that could have been a lie, Stockton's report that the gun in M-Building was a .38-caliber revolver tended to support it. Turner spent a year and a half in Greensville before his execution—plenty of time to work his magic.

Prison officials initially tried to blame Walvick, but the legal community jumped to his defense. When Walvick dared them to come forward with evidence, the state backed down. Investigators next focused on Schloss, but she pointed out that as Willie's girlfriend she'd been subject to so many body searches that gun smuggling would have been impossible. Investigators grudgingly agreed. When the state police published their report in August, they could not prove how the gun reached Turner. What was left unstated was the strong suspicion of yet another corrupted guard.

That left a bigger mystery. Why would Turner obtain and hide the gun, then choose not to use it? There were several theories. He wanted to show his jailers who was smartest, a monumental "gotcha" nailed solid with a smiley face. His family believed he realized there was no other place for him but prison. It was the only place he'd gained a modicum of respect, the place where he'd become a kind of legend. Even if he did escape, where could he go?

Finally, there was revenge. It would have been sweet taking the Death Squad with him, then saving the last bullet for himself, but what would it prove? That he was the mad dog they'd always called him? The state's revenge would have fallen on Walvick and Schloss, the very ones who'd stuck by him to the last. The state would gloat that they were dupes, victims of the biggest con job of all.

So he left the gun alone, making sure it was found. A personal message to his jailers: *This is our world. You're wrong if you think we're beaten.*

Like many geniuses, Turner's greatest creation was himself.

12

Then it was Stockton's turn.

Barring a miracle, 1995 would be his year. He thought of others
who had preceded him, how they'd walked the last few steps on their
own terms. Linwood went with poise, Joe Wise with simple grace,
Willie Jones by kissing the chair. Turner had turned his Walk into an
elegant vindication—the possession and rejection of the means of
death in the house of death. In that way an execution could be an
ironic boon. How many people had the chance to shape their own de-
partures, turn death into a personal statement? How many were
granted such mastery?

He decided to leave Death Row the same way he'd entered.

Publicly.

Just as his diary had chronicled the Great Escape at the beginning
of his tenure on Death Row, now he would describe what it meant to
walk to death. The newspaper editor fell speechless when Stockton
suggested the project, intrigued by the idea but knowing it would be
a hard sell among his top editors. There would probably be a cry of
outrage from readers, especially among conservative Bible Belters in
a state where people overwhelmingly favored the death penalty. How
dare the newspaper give a condemned killer the opportunity to publicly plead his case? But Dennis was determined.

"Everyone wonders when they're gonna die," Stockton told the
editor. "I know, but I'm powerless to stop it." Their relations had
sometimes soured after publication of his Mecklenburg diary as all it

brought him was grief and revenge. He felt the paper had used him for profit, just as the Patrick County, Virginia, politicians used him for votes. The same as he'd been the paper's inside man at Mecklenburg, he'd alerted it to breaking news in Powhatan. The histoplasmosis epidemic. Willie Lloyd Turner's cell filled with weapons and keys. "To be perfectly honest," he once wrote the editor, "more than once in the years since first hearing from you . . . I've wished I'd thrown that 1984 letter from you in the trash." Yet for all that, he'd never severed ties with the newsman.

As far as the paper's top editors knew, no other Death Row inmate had ever written a daily account of walking toward his execution and published it in a newspaper. It was hard to say no. The deal was on, with caveats. Stockton would be paid a correspondent's fee of $100 per story. It was the first time he'd been paid for his work, and he was overjoyed. The paper also agreed to buy him an electric typewriter. But his journals would not be about his guilt or innocence, nor whether he received a fair trial. They would be about the process of preparing for America's ultimate penalty, starting two months before his scheduled execution and running once a week until the last week, when he'd write one a day. The last would be written on Execution Day. It would be printed the next morning regardless of what happened—execution, pardon or clemency.

He started writing the first column that day.

But first he had to attend to the minutiae of living and dying. Stockton asked Ron Smith, the minister who baptized him that cold day in 1993, to act as his executor. He conferred with his lawyers, Anthony King of the D.C. firm Howrey & Simon, and Steve Rosenfield, a private practitioner from Charlottesville, Virginia. He once figured he'd had more than twenty-five pro bono lawyers during his twelve and a half years fighting the death sentence, a number that was by no means unusual. But he liked Tony and Steve the best, partly because they had stuck by him the longest and knew his case so well. King was black and built like a Redskins defensive back; he rarely seemed ruffled. Once again, Stockton had grown close to a black man. Rosenfield, small and wiry, reminded Stockton of a feist, the small hunting dogs that nipped at the heels of a bear. The two lawyers believed Stockton should get a new trial, but experience argued otherwise. They were also trying to get him transferred anywhere less brutal than M-Building during his final days.

All that remained was choosing the way to die.

Stockton once swore in a moment of angry bravado that he'd pick electrocution since lethal injection was how they put dogs to sleep. But the chair terrified him. Lethal injection seemed cleaner. Less painful. He'd be strapped to a gurney and stare at the ceiling while saline, then poison, dripped into his blood. Virginia officials refused to say what chemical fix they used, but the common brew, going for $70, was made of three drugs: sodium pentothal, used to knock out the inmate; followed by pancuronium bromide, a synthetic curare that stopped breathing by paralyzing the diaphragm; topped off with potassium chloride, which caused cardiac arrest. The procedure was called more humane, but no one really knew what happened once the poison dripped inside. The first inmate executed by lethal injection after 1976 was Charlie Brooks, Jr., in Texas on December 7, 1982. He made a series of apparently involuntary efforts to draw a breath, followed by a churning of the stomach muscles. Sometimes minor surgery had to be performed before an open vein could be located, and in some executions, authorities spent up to forty minutes looking for one. In December 1988, the IV carrying drugs into the arm of Texas Death Row inmate Raymond Landry sprang a leak, spraying technicians and witnesses. In May 1989, also in Texas, an incorrect mix of drugs caused Stephen McCoy to choke and heave.

Lethal injection dated back to 1888, but the method was rejected in favor of electrocution, then considered more humane. The people of the late 1800s were entranced by the harnessing of electricity, but by the mid-1990s medical technology with its dependence on drug therapy was the current "miracle." Oklahoma was the first state to legally adopt lethal injection in 1977, followed the next year by Texas, New Mexico and Idaho. When Virginia made the change in January 1995, the law mandated that the condemned must choose between the needle and the chair. Anyone refusing got the needle by default, and most were relieved to escape the chair. Lethal injection also had "the highest rate of spectator satisfaction," said Michael Radelet, a University of Florida professor who studied America's executions. Witnesses reported that death was more palatable, with no smell of burnt flesh, no smoke or sparks. The execution was even performed with all the hallmarks of modern health care. The condemned was laid on a clean, white sheet, a heart monitor attached to his chest. The doctor swabbed the soon-departed's arm with alcohol, the purpose to kill germs and prevent infection. The condemned wasn't being killed, merely anesthetized.

The introduction of lethal injection happened in the same year that victims' survivors were first allowed to watch the execution. The state called this therapeutic vengeance, allowing the survivors "closure" for their rage and grief. There was some debate whether this actually occurred. For some, injection seemed too peaceful compared with the violent way their loved ones had died. Although critics called opening the executions to survivors a return to public hangings, the strongest argument in its favor seemed to be that continued exclusion made the survivors feel like victims as well.

Stockton wondered whether Kenny Arnder's mother would watch when his turn came.

• • • •

Wilma Arnder wondered the same herself. In some ways, she wished she didn't have to make the choice. She was not a vengeful woman . . . at least not anymore. There'd been a time when it wouldn't have bothered her a bit to stand Dennis Stockton against a pole and shoot him as full of holes as a sifter. But seventeen years after her son's murder, she felt no sense of satisfaction with the coming execution. All she felt was an abiding sense of sadness and maybe the hope that after all these years there'd be some kind of end.

One part of her still didn't believe it would happen. There'd been so many delays. A lawman told her the execution was imminent; she could see herself in the small mirrors hung round the parlor, a small woman with white permed hair and glasses, not really believing him but too polite to say otherwise. It was like she was in prison too. It got worse this year when she turned sixty-five. That meant mandatory retirement from her inspector's job at the nearby chicken plant. Other retirees filled their days with hobbies or travel, but for her it meant more time to dwell on Kenny. She made dollhouse furniture from clothespins, but her fingers worked automatically as she stared into the mirrors or out the window and remembered those terrible days.

Kenny was the second youngest of her six children, a tall boy with long brown hair and an easygoing manner who wrapped her around his finger. She'd raised them all herself after she and her husband split up. Maybe that was part of the problem, that he'd never had a father to lay down the law. Soon he started getting in trouble: he didn't lie to her exactly, but he also didn't tell the whole truth about the tough crowd he ran with. Sometimes he lived at home, other times away. But he always came back when he got in trouble and he'd been in a panic in July 1978 when he thought he'd go to jail for stealing some wheels. He called Stockton from her house for a ride to Kibler Valley, then gave her directions where to pick him up. She never found him that night, and never saw her son again.

Wilma had only seen Stockton two or three times before Kenny's death, but since then he'd been in her thoughts daily. Kenny had idolized his older friend. All during the investigation, she'd hoped police would find that someone else was responsible. It took a cold-blooded killer to murder a friend.

Sometimes she found herself thinking about Stockton's mother. Poor woman, she'd been left by her husband and her son was on Death Row. How could things end so badly that started full of hope? It was sad, Dennis being so intelligent and a good ballplayer and all, yet turning to crime. When she heard Stockton's mother died from cancer, she hoped she found some peace.

Still, she'd always suspected Stockton. When Virginia charged him five years later, she wasn't the least surprised. When Kenny had first gone missing, Dennis called sounding worried. He called again the night Kenny's body was identified. She told him the police were going to identify the body through dental records. He never called again.

She never for a minute believed his pleas of innocence. When during the trial Randy Bowman told of Dennis accepting blood money, she hated him down to her very core. She never believed the tales that Bowman had lied. She talked to him and he was scared, not of Dennis but of Tommy McBride. It was like people knew more than they were saying yet never let on.

Now her family asked if she wanted to watch the execution. Her sister said she'd love to go, but Wilma wasn't so sure. She didn't think watching him die would ease the pain. She'd read how some mothers built up the hate and thought watching would purge it, but that wouldn't bring Kenny back. Nor solve the mystery of why he was killed.

Maybe that was the worst part now—the mystery. After the murder, when the hands were knocked off the stone angel atop Kenny's gravestone, she and her children repaired the damage. Then the hands were knocked off again. By then Stockton had long been in jail. Who was behind it? Why this lingering hate? What could cause such evil? She read every story that came out about Dennis, but there never were any clues.

Now her son lay beneath a flat stone in the back of the shadeless cemetery. It seemed so unreal, carved with praying hands that looked severed themselves. She rarely visited anymore. The last time she went was four or five years back. Sometimes she saw on late movies how people went to grave sites all the time. Hollywood made it bittersweet, like peace waited among the headstones.

But for her, it hurt too much to return.

• • • •

Stockton discovered one of Death Row's hidden laws: time, once moving so slowly, speeds up as an execution nears.

He left M-Building in Powhatan on April 26, 1995. He'd sued the state two years earlier, claiming that his civil rights were being violated as revenge for his diary's publication. Now the guards said to pack his stuff, he was leaving . . . but they didn't say where. The ride was slow, along winding back roads. It had been so long since he'd been out: where there had once been forests, he now saw trailer parks and industrial barns. The right-of-ways along the roads looked overgrown. Virginia used to take pride in her roads, the medians and shoulders clipped lawn-close, but then the prison riots started and the DOC stopped the road gangs. Weeds shot up; ragweed grew high. At fifty-four, he felt like such a relic. Remembering such things made him feel old and tired.

When they turned off Route 386, he knew for sure that his new home would be his old. The van pulled in the sally port gate . . . the same through which Linwood and the others had escaped. He looked up in the tower, now manned, but didn't recognize the guard. They rolled slowly down the gravel, flanked by guards . . . same as on that sweltering day a dozen years earlier. They stopped outside Building One and the doors were thrown open. The smell of new-mown grass drifted from the yard.

The guards walked him to C-Pod, Cell 64. He recognized it as Alton Waye's on the night of the escape. "Welcome back, Dennis!" Tuggle yelled from inside his cell. Tug and he were now the last of the old crowd. His appeals were ending too. Their executions might be back to back. Stockton wondered if they'd be neighbors in the Death House.

The other prisoners watched as Stockton was locked inside his cell. Some of the guards who'd been here forever said he was a snitch, but some of the older cons remembered the diaries and knew of the state's revenge. Stockton glanced out his window, then sat on his bed. A whole generation of killers had come and gone, yet everything seemed frozen in time. The inmates glanced up from their tables but didn't come over. The zombies still stared from behind their doors. C-Pod looked the same, though it sure smelled a lot better than M-Building. More important, his cell was quiet and clean. But as he studied this new generation, he heard the same old lies and poses, the tongues of the lost and the damned.

Yet as his orientation stretched over the next few days, he did note differences. There were now more than fifty condemned men in Mecklenburg, more than double the number when he first arrived in 1983. The races were just about evenly split, a few more blacks than whites. He'd already heard some of the names: the two cop killers, Thomas Royal and Gregory Beavers. Joe Payne was here, professing his innocence. Joseph O'Dell, sentenced for raping and strangling a Virginia Beach woman, now making waves with DNA evidence that seemed to contradict the prosecution's blood tests, conducted in the mid-1980s before DNA was widely used—evidence that made him a cause célèbre in Europe, where anti–death penalty sentiment ran high. O'Dell even took his pleas to the Internet to argue his innocence worldwide. Like Stockton, the men fought for new trials—sometimes in new ways, but almost always with the same lack of success.

Some things changed, others stayed the same. When Stockton first came to Mecklenburg in 1983, only a few executions had occurred nationwide following the revival of the death penalty in 1976, yet within a year the rate would rise dramatically and keep rising. By New Year's Eve 1994, a total of 257 executions had been held in the eighteen years since the death penalty's return. In 1983, there were not yet one thousand prisoners under sentence of death across the nation; by 1994, that number had nearly tripled. In 1983, as now, almost every one of those to die or be sentenced to death were poor defendants relying on court-appointed attorneys. Then, as now, Stockton never encountered a rich defendant on Death Row.

Then, as now, time molded into similar patterns for almost every Death Row case: years of delay and torpor, suddenly exploding into a frenzied paper onslaught, a mountain of legal thrust and parry. By early 1995, the U.S. Department of Justice Statistics calculated the average wait for execution as ten years, two months. The electorate was outraged by the wait—had been for a long time. State and national representatives demanded that the walk to death be shortened, and one way to do this was to limit the scope of federal appeals. In 1992, the U.S. Supreme Court, once considered the "court of last resort," seemed to comply with the popular will. On May 4, 1992, sixteen days before the execution of Roger Coleman, the justices ruled in *Keeney* v. *Tamayo-Reyes* that federal courts were not required to hold evidentiary hearings if state courts did not hold them, despite the fact that federal judges found constitutional errors in 40 percent of the capital murder cases they reviewed. In Virginia, where new evidence was rarely heard by state courts, the federal system of checks and balances on errors by the state virtually ceased to exist.

By 1995, Virginia's appeals courts were known for having the lowest rate in the country for overturning cases. "It's not because Virginia has the best criminal justice system," said George Kendall of the NAACP Legal Defense Fund. "It's because Virginia enforces its twenty-one-day rule religiously." So religiously, in fact, that by 1995 Virginia was still the only one of the nation's top five states for executing prisoners that had not released a single Death Row inmate after reviewing new evidence of innocence. Executive clemency remained the only hope. In the early 1990s, then-governor L. Douglas Wilder granted conditional clemency to three men nearing their executions: Joe Giarratano in 1991, Herbert Bassette in 1992 and Earl Washington in 1994. Wilder freed them from the threat of execution after new evidence, ignored by the courts, cast doubt upon their guilt. But their sentences were merely changed to life in prison. It was up to the state attorney general's office—champion of the twenty-one-day rule—to order new trials for them, but this never happened. They were still in prison in 1995, and remain in prison today.

Another big difference that Stockton now noticed was age. The killers seemed younger, some still in their teens. Virginia's minimum age for death was then fifteen, one of the lowest in the nation, surpassed only by Arkansas, which allowed fourteen-year-olds to go to trial as adults and be subject to adult penalties. In a cell near him was Christopher Douglas Thomas, who was seventeen in 1990 when he killed the sleeping parents of his fourteen-year-old girlfriend. Even younger was Steve Roach, an eighteen-year-old kid from Greene County, north of Charlottesville. He arrived a week after Stockton's return. Dennis wondered if *he'd* looked the same to Bill Broadwell that first time in prison—that same war-orphan look with the hollow-eyed stare.

The kid's crime didn't make sense, but then The World itself made little sense to Stockton anymore. On the night of December 2, 1993, Roach walked to the house of his neighbor, seventy-year-old Mary Ann Hughes, who'd always been friendly and paid the boy well for chores. But this night he took along a shotgun and blew her away. He took $150, some credit cards and her car keys, then drove as far as South Carolina before having a change of heart, so he abandoned her car, thumbed back home and turned himself in. When the cops asked why he did it, the boy shrugged and said he didn't know.

If anything, the kid seemed to want to die. The only thing he really cared about was his three-year-old brother, whose photo he'd taped to the wall. The kid favored him and Stockton kidded: "You sure he's not your son? You sure you didn't get some cute thing in a family way?"

How many times had he seen it: some old con trying to give a youngster a reason to live. Frank Coppola had done so with Giarratano, Bill Broadwell with him. Now he was trying to do the same. Without thinking he gave the boy his most prized possession, a Mickey Mantle card. He told the kid to pass it to his brother. Dreams were for the young.

The kid could barely read or write, so Stockton brought him into the newsletter as a hands-on school. "What's the use, they're gonna kill me anyway," Roach whined in frustration, and Stockton would pin him with the stare that chilled his jury. "You don't think that little brother of yours ain't watching how you handle this?" he answered. "You don't think that's important? You screwed *your* life. Don't screw his."

The psychology seemed to work and the kid came back from the dead. But out of hearing, Tuggle and others would echo: "What's the use, Dennis? The kid's right. He's doomed."

"Maybe," Stockton answered, "but that's how they want you, ready to die." Then he'd quote something he picked up in all his years of reading. He couldn't remember who said it, but he'd hung on to the phrase like glue: *Where there's life, there's hope.*

• • • •

Then something did bring hope, and it seemed to come from the blue.

Since 1994, a reporter working for the Norfolk editor had been investigating Stockton's claims of innocence. Stockton no longer had any idea how many reporters he'd talked to over the years, but this one's father had grown up around "Bloody Harlan" County, Kentucky, and farther back than that were family tales of murder and moonshine. Sometimes during their phone calls, they'd get off Stockton's woes and jaw about the hills of North Carolina and Tennessee. For his part, the reporter strolled gradually into Dennis's life, almost as though crumbs had led him into these thick woods. In 1993, he'd discovered evidence of innocence that had been unfairly withheld from the trial of a young black man in Norfolk who was convicted of murdering a convenience store manager. When the story was published, the original judge ordered a new trial and the man was acquitted. This led to questions about the fairness of other murder trials in Norfolk, and *this* led to the finding that 12 percent of Virginia's death-penalty cases since 1976 had serious claims that favorable evidence had been withheld from trial by prosecutors or police in order to win convictions. Stockton's case was one of these.

By then, Stockton's lawyers had been arguing for years that their man had not gotten a fair trial. At first, the arguments were based on the fact that the man who allegedly hired Stockton to kill Kenny Arnder had never been tried and the statements of those who said they heard Randy Bowman brag about lying in Stockton's trial. Then, in 1990, a letter from Bowman surfaced in which he implied that promises made to him by law enforcement officials for his testimony against Stockton had never been kept. Trial rules require that such deals be made known to the jury; if not, a mistrial can be declared. Writing from prison two weeks before Stockton's trial in March 1983, Bowman groused: "I'm writing to let you know that I'm not going to court unless you can get this 6 or 7 months I've got left cutoff [*sic*] where I don't have to come back to prison." The lawyers also filed affidavits by the former Patrick County sheriff and one of his shift commanders in which they said they had also heard Bowman make these complaints. Both men said Bowman was angry after Stockton's trial because promises made to him were not kept, but nothing about an alleged promise came out during Stockton's trial.

"Go find Bowman," Stockton said to the reporter. "Ask him if he got a secret deal." On April 10, 1994, the reporter drove to Mount Airy, a Southern mill town like so many others he'd seen, with perhaps the difference of the Andy Griffith Playhouse smack in the middle of town. He looked for Randy Bowman, but the big man could not be found. Maybe he was in prison, but when he asked no one seemed to know or want to say. It seemed a common thread among those he interviewed: they seemed worried, or secretive, or scared. But the reporter did find other evidence that intrigued him, bits and pieces that seemed to support Stockton's claims.

The first hint came from Randy Bowman's criminal files. Bowman said during Stockton's trial that he had not received any favorable treatment for his willingness to testify, but court records appeared to show otherwise. Bowman testified in Stockton's preliminary hearing on August 17, 1982, and seventeen days later prosecutors in Surry County, North Carolina, dropped charges against him of obtaining stolen property. Such treatment continued after Stockton was sent to Death Row. In 1981 Bowman had been sentenced to four and a half years in prison on a string of charges, but he was out on parole a few months after testifying in Dennis's trial. For the rest of the decade, Randy was charged with repeat offenses, parole violations that for others often meant a return to prison. But he only spent minimal time in jail.

The second hint that perhaps Stockton was telling the truth came from a statement made to police by Robert Gates, the man who claimed he watched Stockton kill Ronnie Tate and bury him, the witness whose testimony cemented Dennis's "future dangerousness," thus ensuring his trip to Death Row. Gates gave police a detailed account of Tate's killing and burial, but failed miserably when he tried leading them to his body. It was only when Stockton showed them that they found the bones. Stockton repeatedly said that Gates's statement to police was so full of inaccuracies that it proved he had been lying, but no one ever checked these claims.

According to Gates's statement, Ronnie Tate was buried in an abandoned Boy Scout camp between Mount Airy and Winston-Salem on the night of July 2 and 3, 1979. It was between midnight and 12:30 A.M. when he and Stockton rode back from the dirty business, and Stockton was driving. They stopped at the Pinnacle exit off U.S. 52, a lonely place in the middle of nowhere. Gates told police: "I remember that just as plain as day because there was a sandwich shop there and he [Dennis] stopped . . . and they was a couple police cars setting there in the parking lot that night and I remember I looked inside and I seen a black-headed woman running the cash register and Dennis had to write a check."

The shop was the Pinnacle Sandwich Shop. It still stood, a small and friendly diner overlooking U.S. 52, the federal highway linking Mount Airy to Winston-Salem, thirty-seven miles to the southeast. The sandwich shop had been owned since May 14, 1967, by Charles Watson, a quiet, friendly fellow who ran the business with his wife. The reporter found the shop on the night of April 12, 1994; he bought a cup of coffee and showed Gates's statement to Watson and his wife. "That can't be right," Watson answered. "Back then, we closed at ten P.M. week nights, eleven on weekends. We never had a black-haired woman at the cash register." He paused a second and seemed to think. "And July third, we wouldn't have been open anyway. We always closed up for the Fourth of July."

Watson looked through the wide glass windows at the night surrounding his diner. During the day one could see from here the solitary peak of Pilot Mountain, an impressive sight, but now it was dark and there were just shadows and the occasional headlights of a passing car. "Nobody ever came and checked this story till now," Watson told the reporter, sounding troubled. "This is the first I ever heard of it. No Surry County sheriffs, nobody from Patrick County. This was a man's life. It's not that far from Mount Airy. You'd think they'd want to check everything out before they sent some guy to the chair."

The reporter returned to Mount Airy almost exactly one year later, on April 18, 1995, a few days before Stockton's return to Mecklenburg. Maybe he could find Randy Bowman this time, he hoped, and ask about the existence of a deal. This time he got lucky. By April 20, he had tracked Randy to a boardinghouse where he lived with his mother, Stacy Vestal, just a few blocks from the Mount Airy police station. The house's foundation had settled and the entire structure seemed to lean drunkenly to one side. The concrete stoop in front of Bowman's side entrance tipped from erosion; a large gray rat scurried under the house when the reporter walked up and knocked on the door. Stacy Vestal, a small, scared-looking woman wearing a faded housecoat, answered. She glanced to the side when the reporter asked for Randy. "Yeah, I'll talk to him," came a gravelly voice. Randy's mother opened the door wider for the reporter to enter, then disappeared, gone like smoke.

Randy was sitting in an armchair just inside the door, watching Oprah Winfrey. The years had not been kind to the big man. The reporter had seen the pictures from the mid-1980s of Randy, big, bald and barrel-chested, filling up the frame. Now he was forty and his hair and beard had grown out and turned salt-and-pepper. His face was pale and pitted; the pockets beneath his eyes were thin and bruised. Randy's left eye had a tic that spread into his cheek as he talked. The phone rang ten or fifteen times in the nearly empty house, then stopped . . . rang again and stopped. No one ever answered it. The phone rang on and on.

"Nothing good came to me after that trial," he told the reporter, eyes straying to the TV. The reporter asked if he'd ever received deals or special treatment for his testimony. Randy answered, "There never was no promises or deals, nobody ever saying they'd do this or that." He paused. Jobs were hard to find after the trial, he added. "I just got hassle for testifying against Tommy McBride."

The reporter showed Bowman the letter he'd written from prison to Jay Gregory demanding release from prison. Bowman said that although it looked like his handwriting, he'd never written the letter. The reporter asked about his light jail sentences. Bowman swore that, contrary to court records, he had served every day of his time.

That seemed about it, the reporter thought. Just to be sure he had covered every angle, he dragged out Bowman's testimony from a fat folder he'd brought with him into the room. Randy had said on the witness stand that he was at the home of Tommy McBride when he heard Stockton agree to kill Arnder for $1,500. He asked Bowman about it again. Randy repeated his tale about dropping into McBride's one night in 1978 to sell a stolen gun. McBride was angry and wanted Arnder dead for reneging on a Valium deal.

No changes there. But now, Randy said something different. They were talking about McBride's alleged offer of $1,500 for someone to kill Arnder. Randy looked at the reporter and recalled that as soon as he heard the mention of a murder deal, he said, "I'm out of there. I didn't hear Stockton say, 'I'm going to do it. . . .' "

The reporter felt as though the floor had dropped out from under him while Oprah talked on. Had he possibly heard right? This was the exact opposite of what Bowman had said on the stand. He'd testi-

fied then that Stockton butted in and took McBride's offer, saying he
needed the money, then the two went into the back where McBride
kept his cash. Without a witness to the murder deal, there could
never have been a death sentence. The reporter pointed out the
change in his story. "I left," Bowman repeated. "I never heard Dennis
take the deal."

This was strange to the point of being surreal, the reporter thought.
He went over the contradictions two more times with Bowman to
make sure neither of them had misunderstood anything. But every
time, Randy stuck to his guns. "The only thing I was involved in was
such a little bit," Randy asserted, maintaining that his testimony could
not have convicted Stockton. "What I heard wasn't a lot."

The reporter asked how Randy had gotten involved. The big man
shrugged: he was in prison in North Carolina when Surry County officials approached him, he said. "My name came up," he said. "I don't
know how. The way the Surry County official was talking to me, I
got the idea I could be charged, so I told what I knew. It wasn't me
coming to them. They came to me."

Randy leaned forward and his armchair creaked. "I don't believe
nobody knows the whole truth," he said, forehead shiny with sweat.
"I don't know if Dennis got a fair trial." The reporter asked Bowman
if he thought Stockton was guilty. Randy thought a moment, then
answered: "*I* wouldn't pull the switch on him. He might be guilty or
he might not. The cops down here are as crooked as he is. The Surry
County sheriff's department then was crookeder than the crooks.
They just don't go to jail."

The reporter rose to leave. He was trembling with excitement, and
felt like he would explode if he didn't tell someone what he'd just
heard. But he tried to stay calm and not give away his excitement. As
he stuck out his hand to shake Randy's, he noticed that the big man
looked more pale than when the interview started. Throughout the
interview Bowman had seemed certain of himself—almost unconcerned. Now, he noticed that for the first time Bowman appeared
worried, even a little scared. The reporter said, in parting, that he'd
probably call again if there were further questions, and Bowman answered, "No problem." The reporter closed the door behind him and
wondered whether Randy Bowman had the slightest inkling of the
hounds he'd unleashed that day.

• • • •

Stockton's voice trembled when the reporter read Bowman's recantation over the phone. "I've dreamed over the years of Randy Bowman coming forward and saying that he lied," he replied, adding, "Whatever the outcome, it's God's will that'll be done." The state, for its part, said the recantation was not substantiated until they sent their own investigators, while Stockton's lawyers claimed this merely proved what they'd always said: Bowman told authorities what they wanted to hear. But why would he change his story so late in the game?

Guilt and conscience, at least one expert believed. Reverend James McCloskey had seen it before. He made a living from last-minute recantations like this. A businessman turned minister, his Princeton, New Jersey–based Centurion Ministries had collected evidence freeing fifteen innocent men from prison from 1980 to 1995. Of these, fourteen were released after recantations, the most famous being Texas Death Row prisoner Clarence Brandley, released just days before his scheduled execution. Brandley, who was black, was sentenced to die for the 1980 rape and murder of sixteen-year-old high school cheerleader Cheryl Dee Ferguson, who was white. McCloskey and his investigators discovered that prosecutors suppressed evidence and that key witnesses lied. When the girl was murdered, suspicion immediately fell on Brandley, the school's maintenance supervisor, and his other four janitors, all of whom were white. One of the janitors, John Henry Sessums, told McCloskey that a Texas Ranger had developed the theory of Brandley's guilt during a walk-through of the crime scene. "Since you're the nigger, you're elected," Brandley was told. But Sessums knew better and for seven years kept a terrible secret: two other janitors had killed the girl. He'd suffered nightmares ever since, remembering how he'd let the girl be dragged to her death. Nine days before Brandley's trip to the executioner, he made a full confession on video, admitting he'd lied out of fear of the real murderers and the Texas Ranger. "I let one innocent person go to her death," he said. "I couldn't let another."

"These witnesses feel terrible," McCloskey said. In such cases, police would sometimes coerce the witnesses into making the false statements, and it was only when someone outside the case—an investigator or reporter—came knocking that they told the truth after so many years. Yet McCloskey had also seen a danger in such recantations: the witnesses could slip back to the old tale, denying they'd ever recanted, once the state reminded them of the penalties for lying on the witness stand.

Stockton's lawyers petitioned the state and federal courts for a new trial. The whole basis of Stockton's death sentence had been up-ended, they said. The state countered that Bowman had just been confused. Soon two detectives visited his home and he signed a state-ment saying he'd never recanted to the reporter. Stockton's lawyers said they had no doubt the detectives threatened Bowman with a per-jury charge.

A judge set Stockton's execution for September 27, 1995.

Through it all, Stockton's nerves felt like stripped wires. This was a new kind of torture, playing with him ten times worse than any-thing at Powhatan. Once he started crying during meal time in the dayroom and Tuggle and the others stared, bewildered. The Old Man of Death Row was betraying in public the one emotion that never left your cell.

There was no dignity in this, he thought. No control. He felt like the poor spider in his grandfather's sternest sermons, dangled by a thread over flames till his tormentor let go.

There was only one place where he *did* have control.

His first column was published on Sunday, August 8, a week after his execution date was set. He stared off the front page, his black-rimmed glasses by him on the wooden bench, face a pale off-white etched in deep, dark lines. He leaned forward, elbows supporting his weight, hands folded like a prayer. There was no repose in this photo, no plea for mercy. His eyes challenged the camera. This is what you want, he told the reader. Get a good long look. Walk with me:

A Life on Death Row: The Journal of a Condemned Man

Since 1976, when the U.S. Supreme Court gave states the authority to reinstate the death penalty, Texas, Florida and Virginia have led the na-tion in the number of people executed.

If Dennis W. Stockton is put to death as scheduled on Sept. 27, he will be the 27th inmate to die in Virginia in the past two decades. The other 26 counted down the weeks and hours to their executions in relative pri-vacy. Stockton, convicted of murder for hire and sentenced to death in 1983, decided to share with the public the story of his final weeks.

*So beginning today, in diary entries written in his cell, he will tell
what it is like to turn the pages on the calendar and watch the hands on
the clock, knowing the day, the hour and the method of his death.*

JULY 26, 1995: My name is Dennis Stockton, inmate No. 134466.

I'm on death row at Mecklenburg Correctional Center, sentenced to die for a crime I'm not guilty of: murder for hire. I've
been saying this since long before it became fashionable to do so. I
want to be free!

It's 9 P.M. now, the day almost over. And what a day it's been.

My attorneys, Steve Rosenfield and Tony King, visited today
with the news I've been expecting to hear: the state has set a date to
kill me, Sept. 27. A judge will sign the order on Monday. The date
the state has set is one day after the U.S. Supreme Court is scheduled to hear my final appeal. Not a lot of legal leeway there.

No one from the prison or Department of Corrections has let me
know that I have a killing date, but I didn't really expect they
would. From what I have been told, it will happen like this: the
warden will come to the pod and all the other death-row inmates
will be sent to their cells. Then the warden will read me the death
warrant, and guards will take me out to a van for the ride to the
Death House in Greensville County. I'm not sure when this will
happen, or even if it will happen in exactly this manner.

While I wait for whatever the future holds for me, I spend my
days in a cell (22) in a prison (A-Pod, No. 1 Building) within a
prison (Mecklenburg). Mecklenburg is where I began my life on
death row on June 15, 1983. I was removed to a prison in Richmond
on Jan. 31, 1985, and returned here on April 26 of this year. In between, I spent most of my time in M-Building at Powhatan Correctional Center, which houses some of the meanest, scaredest and
craziest prisoners in Virginia.

I am 54 years old. I've been locked up since July 29, 1980, when I
was arrested in my native North Carolina on unrelated charges.
I've been locked up for 15 years and one week. I was charged with
capital murder in summer of 1982. In March of 1983, a jury, after a
2½-day trial, sentenced me to death. From July 1987 through May
1990, during a period my death sentence was temporarily overturned, I was in the general prison population, working in the

prison print shop. After a resentencing hearing in 1990—a hearing demanded by me rather than by the state—I was again sentenced to death and taken straight from the courtroom to M-Building. I was formally resentenced on July 30, 1990, the day after Dale Earnhardt won the Talladega 500 and the day before Nolan Ryan won his 300th major-league baseball game.

Most of my life is spent in this cell. I have a steel bed welded to one wall. The bed has five rows of holes, each about the size of a silver dollar. There are 18 holes to a row, 90 in all. My mattress is 1½ inches thick. It is so thin that when I lie down, I can feel the holes underneath. I have a window covered by a heavy metal screen. A crank allows me to open and close the window. There are nine louvers in the window, which only open partway. If I take four steps from the back of my cell, I will bump into the cell door. I can take two steps from my bed to the wall opposite it. I have a sink with hot and cold water, a commode, a table with a swing-out attached seat, two shelves for storing personal and legal property and a plastic foot locker.

The door to the cell is solid metal and has a tray slot for meals and a 3-inch by 36-inch window for guards making rounds at night to shine a flashlight through and wake me up, should I happen to be asleep. There is a light in the ceiling at the rear of my cell. I have tied an old shoestring to the switch so I can turn the light on and off without having to climb on my bed. The floor is painted gray, the rest of the cell nicotine white. We are no longer permitted to paint our cells.

I have several pictures on my walls. If you look in my door the only one you can see is a large, full-color picture of Dale Earnhardt standing at the back of the 1987 Chevy Monte Carlo he won 11 races in that year. I have many more pictures Dale has autographed and sent me over the years. My cell is also decorated with a *Gallery* centerfold, a calendar, a mountain waterfall scene and a copy of the Ten Commandments. Over my sink is a mirror, which I had to buy.

All in all, conditions here are more livable than they were in M-Building at Powhatan. When I was there, I played music on my radio/tape player constantly to overcome the never-ceasing uproar around me. The state is experiencing budget difficulties that have forced the closing of some mental health facilities. Many people formerly confined to "nut houses" were in the cells around me at Powhatan. Being around these people even unhinged some of the guards, and they only had to be here eight hours a day. A little ditty I composed, called "The Funny Farm," will give you an idea of what I mean:

> I sit here and listen as neighbors holler, bang and scream. They sound just like children waking from a bad dream.
> Most sound incoherent as they rave and rant, and it's doubtful if any know just where they're at.
> At all hours, day and night, their raving can be heard. Many times I've wished I could fly away like a bird.
> Kill, Fuck, Suck and Burn, is all that I hear. From neighbors afar and others quite near.
> Where do they find folks like they lock up these days? Could it be that all of society is crazed?
> If ever I want to find peace of mind, only one way to do so can I seem to find.
> When I hear, "Let's riot and burn down the building," I close the hall door and tune in "All My Children."

My day begins with a period I refer to as my "quiet time," which is when I pray and read from my Bible. The version I like reading best is the Today's English Version. I have a King James and New International version as well. I was baptized on March 1, 1991, while in M-Building.

I eat my meals at tables out in the pod area. I have to walk up seven steps to reach that area. There are three metal tables to sit at, and each table seats four. They are bolted to the floor. All 11 inmates on the pod often show up for meals. I usually eat with Steve Roach of Greene County. As for the food: it's the kind where you don't ask for seconds. The meal I look forward to most is on Saturday, when we get two toasted cheese sandwiches and pinto beans.

There's a color TV in the pod area that's on most of the time. A shower is located at each end of the tier. We get an hour out at breakfast, an hour at dinner (the midday meal) and two hours at supper. Weather permitting, we are allowed two hours of outdoor recreation on Monday, Wednesday and Friday. The rest of the time is spent in our cells.

Hot weather is the worst time on death row. The air is moist and hard to breathe. That's when I am pestered by flies. Can you imagine trying to type with flies buzzing around you and your work? I used to swat them with an old rolled-up newspaper, but then I got hold of a little money and was able to purchase a 39-cent genuine plastic fly swatter from the canteen.

Once, in M-Building, a fly that had been extremely bothersome, one that always hid when I stopped what I was doing and picked up my swatter, came to rest on my typewriter on the "G" key. I was in the process of spelling out the word "guess." That's where he met his end. Trust me on this; it happened.

When the temperature and humidity were way up, I spent a lot of time watching the paint on the walls of my cell at M-Building un-dry. Yes, un-dry. Years ago, while listening to a NASCAR race one Sunday afternoon, I heard Darrell Waltrip make a statement that went something like, "The race was about as exciting as watching paint dry." I understand what he meant. I felt the same way watching paint un-dry.

In 1990, I had to sit in an upstairs holding cell for several hours while waiting for a new coat of pale green paint to dry in my new cell. Later, during the humid days of July and August, I awakened one morning to find that many pictures I had hung on the walls had fallen because the paint was so moist.

Running a fingernail across the paint, I found I could pull the paint off the walls. Not all at once, but in surprisingly large sections. Underneath the green paint, I discovered a layer of light blue. Un-painting the cell further, I discovered a *Playboy* centerfold between the green and light blue layers. Beneath the light blue layer I found a Band-Aid and, of all things, a page from a Bible. When they painted my cell, no one bothered to take down the wall decorations first. They just painted over them!

Underneath the light blue paint was a coat of dark blue. In the following weeks, I "unpainted" to the point that most of the green was gone. It only remained in places I couldn't reach. I found five different colors en route to the bare concrete. Whoever painted the cell got about as much paint on the floor as on the walls and ceiling.

The page from the Bible, covered by two layers of paint, was from the book of Isaiah. I memorized one of the verses, Isaiah 26:3: "He will keep thee in perfect peace whose mind is stayed on thee: because he trusteth in thee."

The response was instantaneous. Virginia is a conservative state and most callers screamed their outrage. Similar letters made their way to Stockton. He got a chuckle. Did these people really think they'd convince him to stop writing? He'd been working toward this point for years, in many more ways than one. Wilma Arnder saw the columns and felt the resurfacing of an old, deep hatred.

Stockton realized his role had changed from the last time his diaries were published. Then he was a spy in the house of chaos, now a travel writer describing a journey all must take. His cruise was just rougher than most. He was also a war correspondent, witness to a struggle between justice and mercy. As he wrote his columns in 1995, more than three thousand people were under sentence of death in America. Twenty-six states had actually held executions since 1976—though thirty-eight states, the federal government and military officially sanctioned them—and the national average was one execution per month. Executions cost the public far more than life imprisonment: precise costs were hard to determine, but in states that had studied the issue, costs ranged from $2.3 to $15 million per execution, compared with $750,000 to $1 million for locking someone up for forty years.

Said one California attorney who'd tried more than one hundred capital cases, "The politics of death is a bottomless pit that sucks everybody in." For every compelling argument for or against the death penalty, there seemed a mirror image that proved just as valid. Who could deny the pain of a mother whose child was slaughtered, who now demanded that society exact retribution? And yet, how many innocent people had been sacrificed to the politics of revenge? An October 1993 report by the U.S. House Judiciary Committee said that forty-eight innocent men had been freed from Death Rows across the nation since 1972. That came to a nearly one-in-six ratio of freed to executed prisoners. Of the forty-eight men, 52 percent "were convicted on the basis of perjured testimony or because the prosecutor improperly withheld exculpatory evidence." The report singled out Roger Coleman's as a case where the courts failed to ensure justice.

But 1993 was also the same year that the U.S. Supreme Court dismissed new evidence of innocence in the case of Texas Death Row inmate Leonel Herrera. In a controversial six to three decision, Chief Justice William Rehnquist declared that it was not unconstitutional to execute an innocent man if all the rules had been upheld. Instead of being heard in clogged federal courts, he wrote, such cases belonged in the hands of governors, where the "deeply rooted" tradition of executive clemency acted as "the fail-safe of our criminal justice system." In his dissent, Justice Harry Blackmun wrote: "The execution of a person who can show that he is innocent comes perilously close to murder."

To Stockton it seemed that Death Row was just the most visible part of a world without mercy, a world that had truly gone mad. In the decade he'd lived in M-Building, a culture of violence had grown around him, a violence of which he'd been part and parcel. The United States now imprisoned a larger proportion of its citizens than any other Western nation. Some estimates held that at least one in every four males had an arrest record. The "monster factory," as Stockton called it, made good business. Alternatives to prison were discouraged; more prisons were built in rural areas over the previous fifteen years than over the past two centuries; the fastest-growing job category in public service was "corrections officer." By 1995, the nation's prison and jail population approached 1.6 million, three times what it had been a dozen years earlier, and the odds of leaving general population were about as slim as leaving The Row. Virginia, like most states, had passed increasingly punitive sentencing until finally the prisons were filled with "eighty-five percenters," inmates who must serve 85 percent of their sentences under new no-parole laws. In the 1960s and 1970s, there had been a recognition that rehabilitation paid off in lower recidivism, but the violence of the crack epidemic led to mandatory minimum sentences and the cry to throw away the keys. In 1994, Congress outlawed Pell Grants for prisoner training and education. The message was clear: once inside, don't bother coming out.

Maybe he was lucky, he thought. At least he had a way out. He was one of the few to find a voice. His next column, appearing August 13, was the most nightmarish of all:

The Macabre Mechanics of Execution

AUG. 8, 1995: The Commonwealth of Virginia will allow me to decide how I want to die. I have two choices. I can be electrocuted or die by lethal injection. Since I'm a dope addict who used to love slipping a needle into my arm and injecting drugs, I'm going to choose lethal injection.

Over the years I've learned a great deal about what goes on during electrocution, and to be perfectly honest, I find it frightening. I read an opinion former Supreme Court Justice Brennan wrote, detailing what took place when someone was being electrocuted. I kept a copy of it. It sounds like something out of a Stephen King novel:

"Witnesses routinely report that, when the switch is thrown, the condemned prisoner cringes, leaps and fights the straps with amazing strength. The hands turn red, then white, and the cords of the neck stand out like steel bands. The prisoner's limbs, fingers, toes and face are severely contorted. The force of the electrical current is so powerful that the prisoner's eyeballs sometimes pop out and rest on his cheeks. The prisoner often defecates, urinates and vomits blood and drool. The body turns bright red as its temperature rises, and the prisoner's flesh swells and his skin stretches to the point of breaking. Sometimes the prisoner catches on fire, particularly if he perspires excessively. Witnesses hear a loud and sustained sound like bacon frying and the sickly sweet smell of burning flesh permeates the chamber. This smell of frying human flesh in the immediate neighborhood of the chair is sometimes bad enough to nauseate the press representatives who are present."

On death row, I seldom think about death or dying. I'm too busy fighting the anger and frustration caused by my surroundings. But when I do think about my situation, it's sometimes in dreams—when I manage to fall asleep.

At least three times I've drifted off and dreamed I was dead. I never dream of how I came to be dead, just that I am . . . and that I'm buried. This seldom varies in detail.

In the dream, I wake up to find myself in a casket, buried underground. I open my eyes, but there's really nothing to see, for all around is blackness. Imagine this by picturing a framed sheet of black paper. Title it, "View from the Grave."

I am aware of the confined quarters, for as I try to sit up I bump my head and learn that, no, sitting isn't permitted.

Next I find I can't roll over to relieve my cramped back. I can't do anything but lie as I am. Never have I experienced such quiet. Absolutely nothing to hear.

Would it be possible to break out of my casket? No, I can't do that, for I can't get any leverage to push upward—and my next thought is of the six feet of packed earth atop the casket I'm in.

Is my casket inside a concrete grave liner? Oh, my, those concrete slabs atop the grave liner are surely sealed. And just how much do they weigh? No, Dennis, you've been buried. Here you are meant to stay! There's no escaping. This is the ultimate escape-proof prison.

I try to open my mouth and find I cannot. The mortician has sewn my lips shut. Realizing that gives rise to another thought: Didn't he do the same to my eyes? I reach up and feel my eyes, one of the few things I can do, and I learn yes, they too are sewn shut.

By now I've made another startling discovery. My face is covered with a full beard, several inches long. I distinctly remember shaving this morning, so how could this be? The beard is most uncomfortable—itchy—and when I try to scratch it, I learn my fingernails are several inches long. Next I learn I can move my feet enough to scratch my ankles with my toes. In doing so, I learn my toenails are also several inches long. This causes me to burst into uncontrollable, hysterical laughter, for a thought has come to mind—of how in the old days cowboys didn't want to die with their boots on. Now I know why!

The flowery funeral-home smell and the darkness are maddening. I know my efforts are useless, but can't help but push against the unyielding casket top. . . . It's always then that I wake up.

I long ago learned that once a man is pronounced dead after an electrocution, the death squad will not touch the body for 30 minutes to an hour. The dead person is simply too hot to touch.

During this "cooldown" period, exhaust fans are on, attempting to rid the chamber of the stench caused by the "microwaving" of a human. Members of the squad had earlier stuffed their nostrils with Vaseline and donned surgical masks.

Once the body has cooled enough to be moved, it is "frozen" in a sitting position. The back, legs and arms have to be broken so the dead person can lie on a gurney and be taken out of the death chamber. Taken out to where? To the office of a medical examiner where, believe it or not, an autopsy is performed to determine the cause of death. Yes, I agree that doesn't make sense, but that is what is done. A bit of "gravy" doctors have legislated themselves into, and which you pay for.

And it gets better. Many times the doctor performing the autopsy will take body parts for further use and/or study.

On one news magazine show, I saw a segment that has me afraid of death by lethal injection. It seems they have drugs that, after injection, leave a person in a death-like state, yet still alive. The show I saw this on said doctors in Haiti pronounced many people dead after they'd been injected with these drugs, only later to find the person up, walking around, very much alive but in a "zombie-like" state. This was attributed to voodoo. In several cases, the one pronounced dead had been buried, the funeral witnessed by many— and later that dead and buried person is up and walking around in public.

I had my dream at least two or three times, long before seeing this report on television. So I find myself so paranoid about how the Commonwealth of Virginia plans to kill (or maybe not) me that I've decided I want my body cremated instead of buried. I simply am not going to chance my dream coming true. A friend of mine promised to scatter my ashes on a high mountain peak in the Great Smoky Mountains on a windy day while the 11½-minute version of Lynyrd Skynyrd's "Free Bird" plays wide open.

If I am killed by the state by lethal injection, then I hope I am indeed dead when they get through with what they do. I'd surely hate to wake up at the time I'm being cremated. If it gets that far, I want to be dead—no pun intended—certain to be dead. I just wish I had a say in the choice of drugs they use in bringing about that condition.

Many people in Mount Airy, N.C., and Patrick County, Va., are outraged that the lethal injection bill became law. Some have gone so far as to say they wanted to pull the switch and watch me fry.

To those I'd just say, "Sorry to disappoint you!"

• • • •

The days marched on. On August 18, a DOC official gave Stockton his death warrant, the state's official document naming the time and place of his execution. It had to be read at least ten days before the execution, after which Stockton could be moved from Death Row in

Mecklenburg to the Death House in Greensville, sixty miles to the east. As he wrote, he realized that all of his experience was being siphoned into the columns. It seemed easier to deal with everything that way:

Death Warrant Brings Numbness, Relief, and Knowledge the Nightmare Will End

FRIDAY, AUG. 18, 1995—About once a week, we get what the menu says is French toast but what I call fried lightbread for breakfast and it so happened that's what was on the menu this morning. That in itself should have told me it wasn't going to be too good a day.

I made do with a half-pint carton of milk and a cup of coffee while out at the table during meals. Anyhow, the hour flew by and before I knew it, "lockup" was being called, meaning it was time for all but two of us to return to our cells. I wiped off the table I sit at during meals, threw all the trash in the trash can and went on to my cell.

I'd already planned my day. Had my typewriter set up, the paper already in it for the first page. My door had hardly shut behind me before it was opening again. I thought perhaps the officer in the control booth had made a mistake and I stepped over to the door to let him know my door was open. About then, I heard my name being called.

Glancing up at the entranceway to the Pod, I saw two people standing out in the hallway—and they wanted to see me. One of them was someone I didn't know and can't recall ever seeing before. He was a small guy with a slight build, dark hair and a Clark Gable moustache. I walked on up to see what the officer and this man I didn't know wanted.

He told me his name and said he had an order from the Circuit Court. Said if I couldn't read, he would read the order to me. I told him I could read and knew what was in the order, so he handed me a copy and left.

It was my death warrant. I'd known sooner or later they were going to bring it to me. I'd known ever since the court had set the day I would be killed.

I went back to my cell and laid the order down on some papers lying atop my footlocker and got busy with what I had planned for the day.

Remember me saying I already had a page in my typewriter? Well, I made a mistake in spelling after doing only seven double-spaced lines. It came to mind I was letting my curiosity about that order interrupt my train of thought and if I didn't want to erase a lot of mistakes, I should stop and read what it said. It don't make sense, I suppose, since I already knew what was in it, but neverthe-less this was what my mind was telling me to do.

I was curious to see what a death warrant looked like. That baby took three pages to say what I already knew! Three pages to tell me I was going to die on Sept. 27. I mean, the Virginia Supreme Court hardly ever needs more than one sentence to deny an appeal and here they needed three pages to give me my killing date.

The whole first page had four lines and the names of all the lawyers involved. The second page had 15 double-spaced lines. The third just had the judge's signature at the top and the signa-tures of all the lawyers involved. They wasted more paper than anything else. Lots of legal language. It said that if I can't read, the warrant will be read to me. And then, there's the point of the whole thing:

"This court hereby orders that the execution of Dennis Waldon Stockton's death sentence be carried out on the date of Sept. 27, 1995, at such time of day as the director of the Department of Cor-rections shall fix."

It was like I didn't feel anything when I read the warrant. Any reactions I'd had came several weeks earlier when my lawyers told me that the date was Sept. 27. I took a sip out of my Pepsi Cola then and said how this wasn't very much time, how there was no way I was going to be able to finish the book I was collaborating on with another death row man, Steve Roach.

Still, knowing the date of my killing was a relief. Now I slept better, knowing that this nightmare was going to be over soon. Even my prison psychiatrist agreed that I seemed relieved.

That piece of paper means the state's machinery, waiting to kill me, is finally set in motion. By law, the warrant has to be read at least 10 days before an execution. Anytime afterward, a van will come and take me from Mecklenburg to Greensville, where the Death House is. I have no idea when that will happen. There won't be any warning. Even my lawyers don't know.

I try not to think about it these days.

Anyhow, once my curiosity was satisfied I stuck the death warrant in an envelope with some other papers. Only then was I able to turn this machine back on and get my work done.

I was on the phone quite a bit during the remainder of the day. Had to call my lawyer and several friends. I've used the phone more in the last three weeks than I have in the last three months. And I can tell you right now I don't like talking on the phone so much. Seems I'm saying the same things over and over and over. Seems a lot of people are worrying about me and I have to do a lot of reassuring and consoling. And that's really a drag, because it seems to me that if anyone should be worrying right now, it should be me. But I'm not, for Jesus is doing that for me, like He promised to do. And that gives me time to do what I like best—write fiction, set in the Smoky Mountains, where my characters are free to do what they please.

One more thing. A friend of mine here in the Pod, another death row inmate, asked to see the death warrant. He wanted to see what one looked like. I gave it to him.

He looked it over, then gave it back. He looked sad, like he didn't know what to say for fear of saying the wrong thing.

I understood. I'd been in the same position myself back in September 1993, when talking over the phone to my friend Joe Wise. Joe was in the Death House, awaiting execution. Forty-eight hours later, he was electrocuted.

So I changed the subject.

On September 11, the guards told him to pack—it was time to go. He was being moved to Greensville, home of the death chamber. He tucked his legal folder under his arm and two packs of cigarettes in his pockets. He looked at the box containing his typewriter and asked the watch commander if they'd let him take that along.

"After Turner?" the white shirt said. "Whatta *you* think?"

"I admit it's a dumb question," Stockton said.

They shackled his hands and led him from his cell. The others were shut in their cells and watched the ritual through the glass strips of their doors. He experienced a weird displacement, as if watching himself through their eyes. They nodded solemnly as he passed. Even Steve Roach couldn't speak. Dennis felt dizzy in the silence and remembered the time he had been watching like Steve, helpless and silent as Joe Wise was led away. He suddenly remembered his other

Death Row friendships—Linwood, Roger Coleman, Tuggle—and how in this world all friendships seemed doomed. *Say something!* he wanted to scream to Steve and all the others as the sally port closed behind him, but kept his silence. Somehow, it seemed expected of him, a role he had to play out, a silence he accepted as well.

They took him to a segregation unit in Greensville, gave him new clothes, a handbook of rules, a daily five-milligram dose of Valium. The next evening, three officers escorted him to the watch commander's office. A lieutenant told him he had a choice of executions: the chair or lethal injection. He chose the latter, and the lieutenant had him sign a form.

Stockton smiled. "I'm an old addict, Lieutenant," he said. "Load that baby down with methamphetamine."

The guards started laughing. Stockton joined in.

He discovered that he wasn't alone in the segregation unit. Lem Tuggle was in a cell nearby. Lem had an execution scheduled before Stockton, and had been moved to here from Mecklenburg a few days prior to Dennis. But Lem also expected a stay, and the move hadn't been as somber. Now their cells were directly opposite. They talked, but had to be careful since the prisoners in the segregation unit were famous for dropping "kites," prison slang for notes, to DOC officials in hopes of getting favorable treatment.

One day as they talked, Dennis had an idea. He'd been interviewed a million times by journalists. Why not conduct an interview himself? Hell, he wrote for the newspaper now; besides, he'd been interviewed so much himself he could do it blindfolded. Tuggle would make a perfect subject. He mentioned a Q and A to Lem, who loved the idea. On September 19, Stockton's interview with Tuggle appeared as part of his column in the newspaper:

Q. Tug, how old are you and how long have you been locked up?
A. I am 43 and was first locked up on Sept. 14, 1971. I was given parole in June of 1981 and was sent back to prison in May of 1982 for crossing the state line to find work. I made parole again Feb. 14, 1983, and was arrested again in May of '83.
Q. Try to think back to your early years and tell readers something positive about that time in your life.
A. When I was 10 years old, living in Smyth County, I met an old man living alone that everybody else was afraid of. But I walked up to him and

260 | *Dead Run*

began talking to him and we became best friends. His name was Sam.
I took him a birthday cake and he was so happy he cried.

Q. What is your favorite TV show?

A. "America's Funniest Home Videos."

Q. What are your hobbies in prison?

A. Building churches from matches.

Q. What is your favorite book of fiction and nonfiction?

A. "Clan of the Cave Bear" and the Holy Bible.

Q. Do you believe in God and the Second Coming of Christ?

A. Yes.

Q. Has it been difficult handling the notoriety you attained because of the
   1984 breakout?

A. The notoriety from my death-row escape has been difficult to handle
   at times. Any time something happens, guards and people on The
   Outside think I'm part of it.

Q. What are your favorite sports?

A. Car racing, and Kyle Petty is my favorite driver.

Q. If you were freed today, what would you do?

A. My girlfriend and I would go as far from Virginia as we could, to a
   place where we could live out the remainder of our lives in peace.

On September 16, Stockton was moved to the Death House, his
permanent address until Execution Day. There were three cells in L
Building and he was in Number 2, the middle one made famous by
Turner and his typewriter. The cells were four times larger than normal—it seemed an enormous amount of space and he stretched his
arms just for the joy of not brushing his knuckles against a wall. Facing his cell was a table at which a guard sat at all times. Hanging on
the wall above him was a clock; above that, a TV mounted on a rack.
A telephone hung next to the guard and another sat on his desk.
Stockton's small bed was pushed against the cell's right side; a toilet
was on the opposite wall in the far corner. No partition screened the
commode. Everything he did was lit by fluorescent lights in the high
ceiling that stayed on night and day; everything he did, including
using the commode, was noted by the guard in a log. There were no
windows, just twenty-foot-high cinder-block walls painted a bland
pastel that no one ever seemed to remember. No natural light crept
into the room, no moon or stars. Just endless, artificial day.

• • • •

Eight days before his execution, Stockton's lawyers lobbed another bomb into court. They filed three affidavits by people close to Bowman. All three said he'd bragged to them of murder. Two of the three swore he boasted that *he,* not Stockton, killed Arnder.

Stockton stood in the Death House, numbed by the news. The floor seemed to drop away from him. Now, witnesses were alleging he'd spent the last twelve years on Death Row due to the false testimony of the real killer. The affidavits were explicit. The first was from Bowman's ex-wife, Patricia McHone. In the summer of 1978, she said, she rode with Randy to Tommy McBride's house and waited outside in the car while he tried selling McBride a stolen rifle. Soon he came out and said Tommy offered him money to kill Arnder but Dennis Stockton butted in. "However, within a short time of that visit," she said, "Randy came home one evening and told me that he had just killed Kenny Arnder." He threatened to kill her too if she ever told a soul.

The second affidavit was from Kathy Carreon, a former friend of Bowman's. "I was good friends with Randy Bowman, spending much time with him," she said. In October 1994, "Randy told me that he killed Kenny Arnder with the help of two friends."

The third affidavit was from Timothy Crabtree, Bowman's oldest son by Pat McHone. After their parents divorced, Tim and his younger brother became wards of the state, shuffled between foster homes until adopted by James Crabtree, a businessman in the eastern part of the state. From December 1994 to April 1995, Tim, then sixteen, went to live with Bowman against the advice of Crabtree. During that time, his father enlisted him in several burglary schemes, he said, including the alleged break-in of his adoptive father's Laundromat near Lumberton, North Carolina. Unlike McHone and Carreon, Tim did not specifically say that Randy bragged of killing Arnder. Instead, he "told me many stories about people he beat up or about people he killed," the boy said. "I also read about the people he hurt from a journal he kept in a composition book. He never mentioned names. He told me of one incident where he killed a boy and disposed of the body with the help of some friends. He showed me where they left the body and I remember it was near a stream in or near Mt. Airy, N.C. He said this happened before I was born."

The state branded the affidavits "uncorroborated statements," calling them suspect for appearing so late in the game. Bowman denied it all. But according to Stockton's lawyers, the three lived in fear of Bowman. "They know about other murders," Rosenfield told the press. "They know he will seek revenge."

These fears were reflected in their statements and in interviews. Timothy Crabtree said: "Randy's reputation for violence is well deserved. He is feared by many people that I met while I lived with him. I have concerns for my own safety in light of signing this affidavit." Kathy Carreon said she lived in fear for her life, while McHone's statement was an extended narration of terror. "I am frightened that [Randy] or a family member may try to kill me for the information I am giving," she said. "I am terribly frightened of Randy, but I am also upset at the possibility that an innocent man will be executed."

From the beginning, Randy Bowman had been the heart of the state's case against Stockton. He now became the heart of appeals to save him. Throughout, the big man's career had been a litany of stolen guns, threats, escape, drugs, forgery and petty theft. Between convictions, he spent time in jail, though rarely as long as his crimes seemed to warrant. Now the affidavits and their allegations of murder put it all in a colder light.

Bowman married Patricia Anne McHone on March 3, 1978. She was his second wife: court records showed he had not yet divorced his first, a situation soon remedied. McHone quickly learned she had married into violence. She watched as Randy beat his mom, then turned on her. She was eight months pregnant with Timothy when one such beating induced labor. After the birth, Randy was on the run from police with his wife and new son in tow. She remembered the day Timmy wouldn't stop crying and Randy made her put him in the bathtub. The crying still didn't stop, so Randy grabbed his gun. He put it to the baby's head and screamed: "If you don't shut this kid up, I'm gonna shoot him right here." She grabbed for the barrel but miraculously Timmy went to sleep, as if some basic survival instinct had kicked in, she said.

The marriage lasted eight years. Pat told relatives of her ordeal, two of whom later corroborated her affidavit. "He struck me countless times, some requiring hospitalization," she said in her affidavit. "He threatened to kill our child if I did not do what he wanted. . . .

He threatened to kill me a number of times if I failed to help him or if I ever revealed his criminal acts." Randy supported the family by theft, stealing regularly from cars and homes, Pat said. His specialty was handguns and rifles. When caught, he would pull what she called "stunts" to keep from going to court. "He had someone drive a car over his leg, trying to break it, so that he could be in the hospital on the day he was due in court. He once shot himself in the shoulder to avoid a court appearance. He used these tricks to avoid court in order to obtain a favorable outcome from the court and prosecutor. At least, that was what he told me."

McHone said she was home alone in bed the night Randy burst in bragging how he had killed Arnder. It was a year or two after Arnder's murder in 1978; Randy had been drinking and as soon as he made the admission seemed to realize what he had done. He said he'd kill her if she ever repeated his words and over the years reminded her of that promise, McHone related. There were other stories too, particularly of revenge. An acquaintance had ratted on him, so one day he visited his house and found him working under his jacked-up car. She said Randy laughed when he told of kicking away the jack and of the man's screams as the car came down, crushing him to death. He could do anything to anybody, she said he bragged.

When Pat finally broke away, he threatened to kill her if he ever found her, she said. Now Randy lived alone, but someone apparently looked after him after he testified in Stockton's trial. His jail times were usually short, and even when in prison the living was good. It was during this time that he befriended Kathy Carreon, and he bragged to her how well he was treated behind bars. "Randy said there was a guy in prison [who] covered for him—a big drug man," she said. "When he went to prison, that guy made sure he didn't want for nothing: money, protection, anything." When the two got out and the drug man moved north, he told Randy to come up too. Randy often daydreamed of going: it would be Fat City.

The boasts and threats continued as the years reeled by. Court records showed that in July 1986, Bowman threatened from jail to "kill anybody who ratted on him." He told Kathy Carreon that "if you needed someone knocked off, he knew someone who could do it."

By August 1994, Bowman lived with his mother, Stacy Vestal, in a boardinghouse at the edge of Mount Airy. Carreon lived in a trailer out back. During the day he drank beer and downed his mother's nerve pills, she said. By night, he'd be drunk and high, a combination that made him mean. He threatened to kill the landlord several times and dreamed up get-rich-quick schemes. Carreon and neighbors alleged that he made his living selling hot guns. "He asked me to go buy guns in other cities," Carreon remembered. "He wanted me to buy pistols in pawn shops; he said there was nothing illegal about it. Then he sanded the serial numbers off" and sold them as untraceable weapons in Winston-Salem and other towns. Easy money, he allegedly bragged, failing to add it was also a federal crime. Neighbors called police about him to no effect.

In 1994, he allegedly hatched a scheme to rob an old man who owned a convenience store and gas station near the Ararat River. "Randy tried to talk me into helping him rob the old man," Carreon recalled. "He said, 'I've watched him awhile. I know what he does. He counts his money on Sunday, puts it in a bank bag then walks up the hill behind the station to his house. There're no lights there, it's dark. We'd rob him then, hit him in the head. He'd never know who did it.'

"I said, uh-uh. It was when he started talking that crazy stuff that I stayed away."

On August 18, 1994, Randy chased his mom to Carreon's trailer behind the boardinghouse while threatening to kill her. He screamed, "You'd better get out of this house or you will die." Then he stood outside the trailer and threatened both his mother and friend. "If you don't come outside, I am going to shoot up your house," he yelled. "I'm going to get more bullets, but I will be back." The two terrified women called police. He was charged with trespassing and making threats, found guilty in lower court and sentenced to nearly fifteen months in jail, one of the stiffest sentences he'd drawn since Stockton's trial. But he appealed the verdict in superior court, and in March 1995 accepted a plea agreement. Bowman pleaded guilty to trespassing and was given thirty days in jail in exchange for prosecutors dropping the threat charges. In eleven days, he was out.

By now, Tim Crabtree had entered the scene. "In the fall of 1994, I expressed my desire to get to know my biological father," he said in his affidavit. "My adopted father expressed his concerns and voiced his objections, but I went."

It was the first time in ten years that he'd seen his real father. He stayed with Randy and Stacy Vestal from December 1994 to April 1995, leaving shortly before Bowman recanted his testimony to the reporter. "During that time, Randy said I did not have to go to school, so I did not," his affidavit said. "Randy told me that it would do me no good to go to school. He did not have a job, but instead he got money from stealing and selling property. He wanted me to help him and I refused for a long time. I finally did help him commit burglaries."

One of the first schemes Bowman allegedly floated past the boy was that of robbing the old man near the river, the same one he'd allegedly pitched to Carreon. "He told Timmy to wait in a raft downriver, near the convenience store," James Crabtree later said. "He would rob the old man of the bag of money, then they would take the bag in the raft downriver, leaving no trail." But Tim refused.

Meanwhile, Tim discovered how violent his father could be. He watched as his grandmother, Stacy Vestal, was beaten by Randy, her son. He listened as Randy told tales of people he'd hurt and killed. One day his dad went out, so he entered his bedroom and found a wire-bound composition book containing a list of things Bowman had allegedly done to people. It went into detail—pages and pages. One story that struck him most was the time he allegedly raped a girl then killed her boyfriend. Tim put the book back before his father returned.

Tim was sick with fear and conscience, a sickness that grew worse when he heard of the man on Death Row. When he came back to his adoptive father's home outside Lumberton that April, Jim Crabtree could tell that Tim was troubled. Finally, the truth spilled out. Tim admitted he was terrified of Randy. But he also feared that his silence would help doom an innocent man.

Timothy's affidavit was notarized on September 15. The next day, Rosenfield contacted North Carolina state investigator Ron Perry, who had been involved since the beginning in the Arnder case. Rosenfield told Perry about the affidavits and asked for a search warrant of Bowman's residence to find the composition book. But Perry told the lawyer the case was closed, so Rosenfield asked the Surry County sheriff's department to issue a warrant and they too refused. On September 18, he faxed a search warrant request to the director of the state's Bureau of Investigation in Raleigh, North Carolina, but was told by a deputy chief that the agency had no jurisdiction unless invited by Virginia officials. He called Patrick County's chief prosecutor, who refused. In the end, he was stunned, recalling Stockton's tales of sinister doings in the little town.

Stockton's lawyers filed the affidavits on the afternoon of September 19. The next day, the story was published in the Norfolk paper the editor and reporter worked for, and soon after that in other area papers across Virginia and in parts of North Carolina. Law enforcement officials in both states answered the story and others that followed only with silence. If a chance ever existed to solve some mysteries, it was lost. Randy Bowman's journal was never found.

• • • •

Many now assumed the courts would take heed of this fresh round of new evidence and grant Stockton a hearing. The newspaper in Norfolk and its sister publication across the state in Roanoke editorialized in favor of a new trial as the execution neared. On Friday, September 22—five days before the execution—the Virginia supreme court denied without comment his plea. On Monday, September 25, a federal judge in Richmond issued a sixty-day stay of execution during which a hearing would be scheduled to review the new evidence, but this brief triumph was overturned by the federal court of appeals on the very next day.

Stockton wrote about the disappointment in his column, the penultimate before the one he was scheduled to write on Execution Day:

A Day That Began Badly Brings Devastating Legal News
"But I had nearly lost confidence; my faith was almost gone because I was jealous of the proud when I saw that things go well for the wicked."—Psalm 73, 2–3.

TUESDAY, SEPT. 26—After another night on bits and pieces of sleep, I woke up this morning to find a breakfast tray filled with diced raw potatoes with a smattering of gravy. The fancy menu they show the news media would describe it as hash-brown potatoes and creamed beef. I slung the tray and its contents out into the hallway in front of the cell.

Within a few minutes, an officer and his superior, Capt. Gibbons, showed up. Gibbons is head of Virginia's legal killing squad.

On the morning Lem Tuggle got his stay last week, Gibbons and three others played poker all night around a table outside Tug's cell. I told him it was remarkable the taxpayers of Virginia were paying him and three other officers to play poker all night. Then I said, "I know I'll be seeing you again."

Seeing that breakfast, then Gibbons, was a tipoff that this wasn't going to be one of my better days.

The killing team, a group of between six and eight officers, has been marching by, looking real mean, scowling. I saw them go into the death chamber and heard them turn the power to the electric chair off and on—even though I have chosen to die by lethal injection. Russ Ford, my spiritual adviser, explained that they were also practicing subduing people by force.

My attorneys met with Gov. Allen at noon today about my clemency petition, and one of them, Steve Rosenfield, is coming down to see me tonight. I'm expecting two other visitors today: Russ Ford and Ron Smith, the executor of my estate.

At 12:05 P.M., I looked up and the Rev. Henry Garrard from Richmond was at my door. He drug up a chair and I drug up mine. The time with him flew by. He's been ministering to prisoners since forever. It's a blessing to have someone like him as a brother and friend. We talked about the Lord and how he tends to help people in my situation in times such as this. He remarked on how well I had been taking things.

At 12:30 P.M., I was still waiting to hear about a request I put in on one of the countless forms they use here. I want a typewriter to type one page of my will. The form came back with a box checked that said it wasn't an emergency—even though it's my will and they're planning to kill me tomorrow. I wonder what they consider an emergency?

I don't know if it's a good sign or not, but I didn't see any of the death squad for several hours after seeing Officer Sharp at 9:40 A.M. But that could be because the hit team is resting, getting ready for action.

Just after lunch, Russ and Ron showed up. They pulled their chairs up to the door and we had a pleasant visit. While we were talking, here came the hit team again.

I called my lawyer Steve's office at 4 P.M. His secretary patched me through to Richmond, where he and my other lawyer, Tony

268 | *Dead Run*

King, were meeting with the governor. When Steve left to come here, Tony headed for Washington on the chance he has to file something with the U.S. Supreme Court. This has been a hectic day for everybody.

Late this evening I got the word that a federal appeals court overturned a stay of execution that a judge had issued just yesterday.

After the news reached here, the first member of the hit team arrived about 8:45 P.M. His name was Lynch. At 9, the second member arrived. His name was Healey. They're eyeing me now like a dog eating dinner; by the time my visitors leave, they will all be replaced by the state's hired killers.

It had all come down to this, he mused. The affidavits, the recantation—none of that mattered. As always, the state's ban on introducing new evidence twenty-one days after conviction took precedence. "Last minute stays . . . represent an interference with the orderly processes of justice which should be avoided in all but the most extraordinary cases," the federal judges said when rescinding his stay. They questioned the credibility of McHone, Crabtree and Carreon, not because of inconsistencies in their statements but because they had never been cross-examined on a witness stand. Because they came so late in the game. "This last minute attempt to replicate a state trial setting through affidavits and federal evidentiary hearings twelve years after the fact of conviction bears little relationship to the orderly and deliberate manner in which justice should proceed," the judges complained.

Stockton nodded his head, resigned. He'd seen it too many times with so many men.

There are levels beyond sadness, depths beyond resignation where you accept the limits of justice and prepare yourself for the end. How you met it mattered, Dennis thought: if not to others, at least to yourself. He thought of a question Ron Smith once asked. "Dennis, did you kill that boy?" He asked it with real discomfort. "Because if you did and you've been saying all along that you're innocent, you're not right with God."

He'd looked at Ron a long time. There would always be that question, no matter how many times he explained. "I was with him the night they said he died," Stockton said. "There was a party and some pretty heavy use of drugs. But I left the party around midnight and it was still in full swing. When I left, Kenny was alive."

"But do you know who did it? It's always like you've been holding something back. Wouldn't that have saved you?"

For a second, the old look of hatred returned, the one the minister had tried to expunge all these years. "They know who did it, and it never mattered," Stockton answered. He sighed and his shoulders slumped. "I wasn't part of the murder, Ron. Why would I do that? Kenny Arnder was my friend."

There was still an interview scheduled with a Washington, D.C., TV station. There'd been so many interviews lately, so many people interested in his columns and his case that it was hard to keep them straight. They asked the same questions, over and over, and it made him tired. But there were occasional moments when everything seemed to fall together and he caught a glimpse of light. When he could say to himself that no matter what happened, he'd done as old Bill Broadwell taught so long ago. He'd stood up straight when all was said and done.

"Dennis," the TV reporter asked, "if you had a minute alone with the governor, what would you say?"

Stockton turned to his lawyers and asked, "Can I answer how I want?"

A startled glance passed between Steve Rosenfield and Tony King. "However you want, Dennis," one of them said.

He smiled at their surprise. He thought of all these years. This was the third governor to serve since he'd been sentenced to death—first Robb, then Wilder, now George Allen, Jr., son of football legend George Allen, who with fellow coach Vince Lombardi proclaimed the cult of victory. The governor had been a young man of twenty-five or twenty-six when the murder occurred. Stockton thought of all the courts, lawyers and judges . . . all the times his pleas had fallen on deaf ears. He was innocent of Kenny's murder, but wasn't he guilty as well? Hadn't he chosen this route the moment he'd toyed with evil? Hadn't he helped shape this river of betrayal and rage that swept them all up, guard and prisoner alike, killer and governor, the voters crying for vengeance, the system answering their cries? He smiled again at the TV reporter and cameraman, at his lawyers, all watching, mystified by the delay. We all drown in it, Stockton thought, but it doesn't need to be that way. He remembered the joke Linwood told him when he first arrived at Mecklenburg, how the only redemption for the men on Death Row was execution, but the long march had reshaped him just as it had Willie Turner and Joe Wise, as it had Roger Coleman and Wilbert Evans, Joe Giarratano and Linwood, though he still had his doubts about JB.

He nodded that he was ready, then looked straight into the TV camera, finally making contact with all those who thought he should die simply because The Law said it was the right thing to do. "I'd say this," he said. "Governor, go ahead and kill me. I'm fifty-five years old by now and my life's done wasted. Let Steve Roach go free in my place. He's a young man on Death Row who has a boy at home," a younger brother who needed a father figure to teach him how to fish and play ball. In the end that was all that mattered, he thought: the only way to overcome the monster factory was by ensuring that a kid never entered at all. When he'd passed on his Mickey Mantle card, he'd passed with it a tiny bit of an old left-handed pitcher's dreams.

"That's what I'd say." There was silence for a second. One of the TV people cleared his throat. "Well," one of his lawyers breathed.

Stockton cocked his head and looked at the TV reporter, who was straightening his notes. "Now you'll run that, won't you?"

"Oh, yes, don't worry," the reporter said.

Execution
Day

The road to Virginia's death chamber is not well marked. The Old Dominion's executions are always held at night, so a newcomer approaches the turnoff in darkness, traveling south from Richmond or due north from Emporia on old federal highway 301. The way runs past darkened road houses mysteriously circled by parked cars, pay-by-the-hour motels, cleared stands of timber where tobacco struggles to grow. A small sign, forest green and nondescript, points west, and if the driver doesn't miss the sudden turn, he bumps over railroad tracks and creeps through swampland until cresting a slight rise and spotting for the first time the stark guard towers and coiled razor wire of Greensville Correctional Center. And there the blacktop ends.

Witnesses to state executions are chosen long before Execution Day. They will be chauffeured over this route, meeting early at a state police station in nearby Jarratt, though some—journalists, the condemned man's lawyers and ministers—must find their own way. The DOC is rarely at a loss for witnesses and has not had to solicit applications for the past several years. Witnesses' reasons for wanting to view death are as varied as their backgrounds. A prosecutor asked to attend because he might someday request the death penalty and wished to see the consequences. A twenty-eight-year-old mortgage loan officer wanted details for a novel. A computer operator, skeptical that executions were actually carried out, came away believing they should be televised. One witness said that in rural Emporia many people applied. "It's something to do," he said, "like shooting deer."

Except for the journalists, tonight's witnesses would all be private citizens, unusual because police usually predominated. They included a property manager, an auto mechanic, a retired navy shore patrolman. As they woke that morning in their beds, they thought of what the night would bring. Some had read the condemned's dispatches chronicling his last days. Some had followed the controversy over whether the state was sending an innocent man to death. Some saw him as a symbol for all the ironies and absurdities of the death penalty, while others considered him an ice-cold killer using the media in a last-ditch attempt to escape justice.

They rose and washed their faces. It was September 27, 1995, and a slight chill was in the air. All would congregate tonight to watch the execution of Prisoner No. 134466, Dennis Waldon Stockton: America's three hundredth Death Row inmate to be executed since the nation reinstated the ultimate penalty in 1976.

• • • •

Stockton slept well that night—a deep, dreamless sleep. He slid into consciousness and opened his eyes. The guard noticed his awakening and recorded it in his log.

A member of the Death Squad came through the door and stood before his cell. "Stockton," he said, his face impassive, "you know what day it is."

"Kinda hard to forget," Stockton replied.

The guard told him they would inventory his stuff and package it in boxes. "After that, you can have as much tranquilizer today as you want."

"Better give me a mild dose, then."

The first of those allowed to spend the day with him arrived shortly after 9:30 A.M. It was Rosenfield. Stockton wasn't surprised: Steve never could keep still. He'd spent the night in a hotel in Richmond and rose early, the fields and abandoned silos a blur as he drove. Wednesday, September 27, was overcast, sky the color of lead. He felt so bizarre the closer he drew to the Death House. He felt displaced from himself, floating, the way Dennis sometimes said he did.

Stockton was in the middle cell. He seemed upbeat, which was a huge relief to Rosenfield, who felt like an exposed ganglion, a twitching clump of nerves. A table was set before his cell with a phone and an ashtray, partially filled. A Marlboro hung from Stockton's lips.

"Don't smoke that, it'll kill you," Rosenfield said, the first comment he'd make every time they met. "I'll remember that," Stockton said.

Ron Smith and Russ Ford, the Death Row ministers, arrived soon afterward, followed in midmorning by Tony King. The members of his personal death watch were all here. The four dressed casually for the vigil, agreeing beforehand it was proper attire for what they considered murder. Stockton wore a clean white T-shirt and white boxers. An orange prison jumpsuit was folded on the table. They talked of where they'd spent the night, who had called about the case, the weather. The post guard sat quietly, marking in the log. The TV aired soap operas. A couple of guards passed through. King related what he'd filed with the U.S. Supreme Court, and they speculated on when they might hear.

The cell to Stockton's left was occupied by Herman Barnes, a young man sentenced for the robbery and murder of a seventy-three-year-old grocer in 1985. He was officially scheduled to die today too, but everyone expected a stay. Soon it was granted and Barnes was taken from his cell for the return trip to Mecklenburg. He was all smiles, then remembered Stockton and grew tongue-tied.

The newspaper editor called to see if he could meet with his old friend one last time. He wanted to get into the Death House, but when he arrived at 1:45 P.M., prison officials would not allow him inside. It was the same old story, one that he'd encountered during every interview with Stockton—the DOC would not allow the media into areas where the condemned actually lived. The last meeting between the editor and Stockton would take place in a small, brightly lit room in the Death House. When the editor entered the interview room, Rosenfield was seated by the wall. A thin, intense man, he looked haggard. The editor and Rosenfield exchanged pleasantries. Because the editor had not been allowed to bring a notebook and pen to the meeting—this was a personal meeting, not an interview, the DOC said—he borrowed Rosenfield's. The lawyer asked if he could stay in the room during the interview, and the editor agreed.

Stockton was wearing an orange jumpsuit when he appeared on the other side of the Plexiglas plate. The editor and inmate smiled greetings at each other. It had been eleven years since the two men had first met. This would be their last meeting, the editor knew, and just like on that warm June day in 1984, they would sit facing each other through a glass wall, talking by telephone.

During the 1984 meeting, the man who sat across from the editor was gaunt and unsmiling. On this, the day of their last meeting, Stockton wore horn-rimmed glasses and smiled frequently. They made small talk. They chatted about baseball, about how Stockton's boyhood idol, Mickey Mantle, had died the same month Stockton was scheduled to be executed. Stockton smiled and noted that, unless a last-minute reprieve came, he would not know how the 1995 baseball season ended. Oh, what the hell, he said, his Yankees were out of the pennant race anyway.

"What they really needed," he told the editor, "was a good left-handed relief pitcher out there in the bull pen." And who better than an old lefty named Dennis Stockton?

As they talked, the editor got angry. He had read the transcript of Stockton's trial and hundreds of pages of appeals briefs; he had interviewed dozens of people familiar with the case. He would never know for sure if Stockton had committed the crime that put him in this room on this day, but he did know this: the justice system had failed Stockton. There were questions about the credibility of the key witness against Stockton, the only person whose testimony had made this a capital-murder case, and those questions would never be answered in a courtroom. The editor knew the chance that Stockton's life would be spared by the governor or the U.S. Supreme Court was almost nonexistent. As he studied the man who had become his friend, the man whose writings he had edited for more than a decade, his anger grew.

Now it was time for him to act as Stockton's editor one last time. Stockton would have to dictate to the editor his final diary entry, the one that would run in the newspaper the next day. The editor felt a chill. He was jotting down the words that, barring a miracle, would be the words of a dead man when they appeared in print the next day. Using the borrowed pencil and notebook, he began to jot notes as Stockton spoke . . . "WEDNESDAY, Sept. 27—I got the best night's sleep since I arrived here at the Death House. A deep, dreamless sleep . . ." When he finished, Stockton told the editor he would call the newspaper and dictate a final statement or any last thoughts.

The interview lasted about an hour. When the guard knocked at the door, signaling that the interview was over, the editor realized that Stockton had done most of the talking. It suddenly grew eerie and uncomfortable. Rosenfield wondered what right he had to witness something this private. There was silence, then Stockton pressed his left hand to the glass. The editor pressed his right hand on his side. "I want to thank you for giving me the opportunity to become a published writer," Stockton said. "But most of all, I want to thank you for being my friend."

Their eyes met and they rose. The editor turned to Rosenfield, his eyes stricken. Stockton cleared his throat and turned away.

The rest of the afternoon passed uneventfully. There were other calls, a TV reporter from Roanoke. But mostly, Stockton and his watchers tried to fill the time. Their conversation revolved around his past, books, family, friends and his funeral. Stockton wanted to be cremated, his ashes sprinkled somewhere nice. The silences became longer. They tried not to glance at the clock. Stockton said he'd read about the death-watch beetle, how it made a sound like a ticking watch and was believed to portend death. He'd have liked to have had one for a pet. Once he excused himself and sat on the toilet. The four turned away awkwardly to give him a modest amount of privacy. The guard noted it in his log.

Once during the afternoon, they got to talking about baseball. Stockton told how he had been scouted by the Yankees and had remained a die-hard Yankees' fan. "You were a lefty, right?" Rosenfield said. "Did you have a pickoff move to first?" With that, Stockton rose and took his stance. The guard's station was first base. Stockton and the guard had talked baseball in their long hours together, and the guard had seen this move. He inched from the desk as if to steal second. Stockton watched, unconcerned. He went into his stretch, then suddenly pivoted toward the invisible first baseman. But he didn't throw because the guard got back in time. Stockton had a cold Pepsi in triumph. His lawyers and ministers were howling. The guard shook his head when the watch captain peeked in.

They talked of Hollywood. This would make a great Hitchcock thriller, they agreed. The clock ticks toward an innocent man's execution while the real killer goes free. They started imagining which actors would portray them. They laughed so hard trying to pick the right actors that they nearly cried.

It was time for his last meal. He ordered six toasted cheese sandwiches, six Coke Classics, french fries and ketchup. He got through a couple of the sandwiches, then his appetite waned. He insisted that the others help him, especially Rosenfield, knowing that the wiry lawyer avoided greasy food like the plague. But Rosenfield hadn't eaten for seven hours, so he patted the sandwiches and fries with several napkins and dove in.

By now, his final column needed an ending. They all knew what would be coming soon. At 6:55, the telephone above the guard rang for the first time that day. He answered and told them it was the Supreme Court. Rosenfield took the call. A deputy clerk informed him that the court had declined to intervene.

Everyone rose, watching as he listened, knowing from his face what was said. Only Stockton stayed seated, his eyes glued to Rosenfield. The clerk was saddened at having to be the messenger; Rosenfield comforted him. He hung up the phone and gazed straight at his client as he told them the news. Stockton half grinned, a strange, stiff rictus, then all returned to their seats.

That left the governor. Although the Supreme Court had dubbed executive clemency a safety valve for the judicial process, clemency was inherently a matter of grace. But grace and politics rarely mixed. Wide popular support for the death penalty had made commutation an unpopular political move. At 7:45, the phone rang again. Tony King took this call. "Governor Allen has concluded that there is no reasonable factual basis for intervening," Allen's deputy said.

They were all standing now, nobody knowing quite what to do or say. Execution was little more than an hour away. Stockton cleared his throat and sat down. Everyone else followed suit. There was a numbing sense of horror in each of them: the sense that this had to be some cosmic screwup. Things couldn't get this far in the world they thought they knew. The calvary always rode over the hill; justice prevailed. This reality was too hard to bear. Rosenfield felt the anger well inside him like a geyser and gripped his chair back tightly to fight it down. Ron Smith, who'd baptized Stockton and believed that God would be just, began to cry.

"Dammit, the last hours of my life I'm not going to do this," Stockton snapped. "I want you to be strong!" He looked at each man and said how much they meant to him. He extended his hands for prayer and asked that strength be given to all.

"I guess I can end this column now," he said, trying to make a joke, then scribbled a line or two on the paper he'd been provided by the Death Squad. He asked the guard to dial the newspaper's number, then spoke to a female reporter he'd never talked to before. He told her of the decisions of the Supreme Court, and said he had nothing to add to the column.

It was the second reporter from the Norfolk paper that he'd talked to in two days. It seemed he couldn't get away from the place, he thought with a soft chuckle. The night before, he'd talked to the reporter who'd investigated his claims of innocence and taken the recantation from Bowman. But, of course, he was calling them now, unlike all those years when they'd called on him.

The phone call to the reporter who'd investigated his claims of innocence had not been easy. The reporter had been sitting at his desk at the newspaper, finishing up the story about the overturned stay, when the phone rang. He'd been dreading the call. He'd been assigned by his editor to witness Stockton's execution—he would write background and quotes prior to leaving for Greensville, then phone his observations of the execution back to a colleague at Norfolk to top off the story, which would appear the morning after Stockton's scheduled execution, no matter what happened. The reporter had been through a lot during his dozen years at the paper, but he'd never had to tell a man that he was going to watch him die. How do you do it? He'd seen death before, he'd even been a suicide counselor, but nothing had prepared him for this. As a police reporter, he'd seen plenty of bodies: the guilty and the innocent, shot, stabbed and drowned. In 1991, he'd watched as a Russian tank rolled over a Lithuanian freedom fighter, crushing him beneath its treads. The trick was to keep taking notes, like raising a professional shield. But witnessing an execution was like entering another country. It was planned, and by watching he became part of the design.

The reporter had even witnessed an execution before, an electrocution in Greensville in 1993 of a man sentenced for killing two women ten years apart. He'd never even talked to that condemned man, but the day of the execution dawned. So strange. As the time of the execution neared, he found himself unconsciously focusing on small details: the texture of leather beneath his fingers; the cold smell of the air; the dark puffs of cloud passing overhead. It dawned on him that he was treating it like *his* last day, trying to absorb as much life as possible. If he was going through this, he wondered with a slight twinge of guilt, what about the condemned man?

All these things rolled through the reporter's mind as the call came in from Dennis Stockton the night before his scheduled execution. He'd spent the day looking through his notes, thinking perhaps there was one more piece of evidence he'd overlooked, something that would make the court reconsider its decision, a key to the whole mystery. But he'd included in his stories everything he'd found. Now Dennis was calling one last time and the reporter told him he'd been assigned to attend his execution. "I won't if you don't want me to," he said, cradling the receiver.

"I'd be honored," Stockton answered, his voice growing quiet. "I always said I wished you'd investigated my case back when I was tried, back when it would've mattered and the courts would've had to listen."

"I'm sorry, Dennis," the reporter answered, voice shaking. "I guess it wasn't enough." There was silence, then Stockton said good-bye and hung up. The reporter sat quietly at his desk, flipping through his notes, but could find nothing new.

Now Stockton talked to the female reporter at the newspaper. She sounded young and friendly, and Dennis wondered who she was. In his younger days, when he was free, he might have tried to get to know her, but those days were long gone. "When will this column run?" he asked her, and heard her voice turn sad when she said the next day, September 28. He suggested a headline, WRAPPING UP LIFE'S LOOSE ENDS:

WEDNESDAY, SEPT. 27—I got the best night's sleep since I arrived here at the death house. A deep, dreamless sleep. I had asked God for a good night's rest and he obliged.

Barring a miracle, it will be my last night's sleep in this life. Today is my execution day.

I started keeping a diary on June 20, 1983, shortly after I arrived on Death Row. This, I suppose, will be the final entry.

Right after breakfast today, the officer in charge came in with all my property for me to go through, item by item. There was my typewriter, my manuscripts, six cartons of cigarettes, three or four bottles of Prell shampoo and so on.

We packed it all into boxes to be given and sent to different people—one for my friend Steve Roach on Death Row, one for Steve's father, one for my brother.

I guess you'd call this tying up the loose ends of one's lifetime.

I talked to a TV reporter from Roanoke today. She said she had spoken with Governor Allen's office and the governor said he wouldn't allow an innocent man to die. We'll see.

If I could have one minute with the governor, this is what I would tell him:

"Governor, go ahead and kill me. I'm 55 years old and my life is over. Let Steve Roach go free. He's a young man who has a boy at home, a boy who needs a father to learn him how to fish and play ball."

I spoke to Steve on the phone today. When I got ready to hang up, I could hear him crying. I told him, "Damn it, don't you go and cry on me."

They came around today and told me about my last meal. There are no more special "last meals" anymore. That all ended, along with typewriters in the Death House, with Willie Lloyd Turner.

I got to circle something from the regular menu. I asked for six melted cheese sandwiches, an extremely large order of french fries and six Coca-Cola Classics. That's in case my lawyers and my minister join me.

I've been following my beloved New York Yankees and it looks like they're fading in the stretch run. They could sure use me in the bullpen—a ninth-inning closer. Of course, I won't know how it all comes out.

Since I won't be around to do it anymore, Steve Roach is keeping up the tradition of putting out the prison newsletter I started, "Passin' Thoughts." In the first issue, I noticed he had misspelled the word Thursday and I was going to correct him but I didn't. He's going to have to learn the same way I did.

What would I do if I were suddenly a free man?

I'd get in a car with my friend Ron Smith and we'd drive to the airport, then fly to his home in Florida. Ron has a job for me down there working with his son in the construction business.

I'd probably go swimming in Ron's pool, then walk over to the trailer he has for me to live in. Then I'd put some paper in the typewriter and start on a new manuscript.

I'm a man of few needs. Just a typewriter with a new ribbon and some Bugler tobacco to roll my own cigarettes.

Well, we got the word late this evening that first the Supreme Court and then Governor Allen ruled against me.

It won't be long now before they come to get me. That's when Steve Roach and some of my other friends on Death Row at Mecklenburg crank up their cassette players.

They'll be playing Lynyrd Skynyrd's "Free Bird" wide open at 9 P.M. The live 11½-minute version.

When the last strains of that song fade away, one way or another I'll be free . . . free as a bird.

On the other side of the prison, David Bass—the DOC's regional administrator, brother of the Mecklenburg warden who'd been reassigned after the Great Escape—was briefing witnesses on the mechanics of execution. Bass was a softspoken man, radiating peace and calm in both dress and demeanor. The reporter was among the witnesses, listening as Bass talked, somehow reminded of a moderate Southern Baptist preacher who exuded quiet confidence that all would go according to God's plan.

Bass ended his talk with a call for questions. There was the uneasy silence of people who, perhaps for the first time, were about to confront mortality. The reporter watched as one man uncertainly raised his hand.

"Has the state ever executed somebody they later found to be innocent?" he asked.

Bass was taken aback, a rarity. He hesitated a minute, tugged briefly at his navy blue tie.

"I don't know how to answer that," he finally responded. "That's for a court to decide."

• • • •

Time now grew short. Shortly after eight, Stockton's visitors were asked to leave so he could shower. They returned five minutes later and he wore his orange prison jumpsuit with Velcro snaps, presumably to make things easier for the coroner. He'd been moved from the middle cell to the one closest to the death chamber. The guard's desk had been placed perpendicular to the cell. Stockton talked about his will and handed out some effects. He gave Rosenfield his remaining Marlboros and started laughing because he knew the lawyer didn't smoke. He also gave him one of his Coke Classics. Each visitor promised to honor his final requests; he asked again about his remains and Smith promised he'd sprinkle his ashes over a waterfall in the Blue Ridge Mountains.

He started work on a final statement, but the words wouldn't come. Simply to survive, he'd learned to submerge his feelings. Now, with death near, he couldn't dredge them up. For the first time that day, he lost his composure, frustrated at this final failure.

"Dennis," Smith said quietly, "why don't you let one of your fictional characters do the speaking for you?"

Stockton's eyes lit up and he covered the white page with words. His final statement was in the words of Danny Revels, one of his fictional alter-egos, a voice of reason and wisdom that Stockton possibly wished he'd become. He said good-bye to his friends and family, then added: "To those that don't know Dennis like I do, well, Dennis is a victim of crime in the worst kinda way. May God not hold the feelings of his enemies toward him to their charge." He ended: "To y'all that don't know the *real* Dennis, I wish you did."

Now he was ready. Members of the Death Squad came to the cell block and stood at parade rest. Smith looked at his friend. Stockton loathed these black-suited guards, men he considered small cogs in the system who reveled in the fear they inspired. They always watched him like vultures, drawing sustenance from the least sign of weakness. One or two had made comments about his diaries and the fellow guards who'd been fired. At times Smith found himself hating them too, though he tried to fight it down. Surely they weren't always like this. Surely it was the job that made them this way, reflections of what the larger system had become.

As if on cue, Stockton gripped his cell bars. "I bear you no ill will," he said to the men in black. "I know you're just doing your jobs. I forgive you." They didn't speak, but answered his statement with a tilt of the chin on faces chiseled from stone.

The warden arrived at 8:45. His approach was heralded by a nod from the guard at the desk. The nod seemed understood by all. They stood as the warden walked in, flanked by other dark-suited officials. They unconsciously stood at attention as he stopped before the cell and read from the death warrant.

Rosenfield and King looked at each other. What was their duty at a time like this? they wondered. Should they object? On what grounds? That the ritual seemed unseemly, insensitive? Stockton stood attentive, showing no emotion. The cell door rolled open and stopped with a click and he grimaced, then stared straight ahead as two guards, one on each side, entered the cell.

This was The Walk they had all dreaded. Stockton and his escort stepped from the cell. The death chamber door opened magically. They'd always heard it took eight steps down the short hall, but it took them only six. Somehow they felt cheated. They passed the threshold and entered the chamber, the destination they'd heard of so often but now saw for themselves.

The witnesses, including the reporter, had already arrived. Thirty minutes earlier, accompanied by David Bass, they quietly squeezed into a prison van and rolled through the double gates, then around the perimeter of towers and billowing wire. They stopped behind L-Building, home of Greensville's worst inmates. The Death House, a windowless, one-story bunker, hunched in its shadow. As they stepped from the van, taunts and obscenities greeted them from the unseen prisoners overhead. "You're next!" one yelled. "Motherfuckers, hope ya like it!!" another cried.

They were herded through a chain-link pen the size of a dog run, through another set of double doors and into a tiered witness room with white plastic chairs and two glass walls. A blue and white sign hanging by their chairs commanded: ALL PERSONS MUST REMAIN SEATED AT ALL TIMES. Through the front window, they could see the chamber's gray walls, its gray linoleum floor. Two phones hung on the wall—a red one, with an open line linked only to the governor's office, and a black one, a line to the rest of the prison. The corrections' chief huddled over the red phone, the receiver to his ear. The black phone, a step away, was left unattended.

Through the side window, the witnesses could see another room— this one for the victim's family. The blinds were open but the glass was smoked so no one could see inside. Wilma Arnder was there with members of her family. She'd never believed the stories about Bowman's recantation or the affidavits. All were lawyers' tricks. "There's no doubt whatsoever that Stockton is the killer," she told a journalist a day earlier. "He's a cold-blooded killer who has no conscience." Now, she hoped, her son would have justice and it all would finally end.

At 8:54, the witnesses saw Stockton for the first time. He walked in, hands shackled in front, flanked by the Death Squad. His lawyers and ministers trailed behind. His dark hair was slicked across his forehead; he wore heavy, dark-rimmed glasses. His skin was almost transluscent, a sickly fish-white. They were struck by how old he looked. They hadn't known they'd be watching the execution of an old man.

Stockton hesitated inside the door, looking at the white-sheeted gurney centered in the room. A ceiling-high, blue-vinyl curtain hung immediately behind it, dividing the front of the chamber from the back. The medical staff responsible for the injection stood behind this screen, blocked from the view of the witnesses. The apparatus for administering the poison—the vials and plungers and stopcocks—were also blocked from view; in fact, all that could be seen of the actual killing equipment were intravenous lines and the sensor for the heart monitor that dangled from a pocket in the curtain. The base of the electric chair peeked underneath where the curtain did not quite touch the floor. The gurney's head was turned toward the heavy curtain, with its foot toward the witnesses. The arms stuck out straight, like a cross; black straps hung from the waist, ankles and arms.

Stockton scooted onto the gurney and the guards moved toward him, but Rosenfield stepped forward to take his glasses, breaking the practiced flow of their drill. The interruption made them angry. Rosenfield and Stockton had discussed this part because Stockton needed his glasses to get to the chamber without stumbling. Two guards moved quickly, blocking Rosenfield. "I just want to give these to my lawyer," Stockton said, but Rosenfield said he would get them later. The warden looked irritated that his ceremony had been disturbed.

The guards swarmed over Stockton, strapping him down. Russ Ford left by a side door marked "13" while Ron Smith stepped back into the hall separating the witness rooms. The attorneys were shown to the witness booth; they climbed the raised platforms and sat in the back row. One was white with anger, the other sniffing back tears. The room was dark, but the windows were high and the theater brightly illuminated. They could see everything clearly. Stockton was now strapped to the gurney, arms stretched out, legs straight ahead. Rosenfield wondered if the resemblance to a crucifixion was lost on any of the witnesses. A curtain was drawn over the window. The witnesses could not see the medical staff insert the needles into Stockton's veins.

The gallery was quiet and still. A journalist with the Associated Press turned to David Bass and asked: "What is that curtain made of?" The question seemed unnecessarily cold, and the reporter who'd investigated Stockton's claims of innocence caught himself leaning away from the man and thinking, This is why people hate the press. In the reflection of the glass, he could see the two lawyers tense at the question, then roll their eyes. Another journalist from a Southside paper asked what Stockton was wearing on his feet. Bass quietly answered, "Shower thongs."

Finally, the curtain before the witness booth was opened. Stockton lay as before, an IV inserted in each arm. One was a backup in case the primary line clogged. The black straps holding his arms and legs seemed more apparent. Rosenfield stared at his client's face, trying to read his expression. Stockton gazed at the ceiling. He seemed calm.

Suddenly, the black phone rang.

The witnesses jumped. The prison officials stared at it, alarmed. Stockton craned his head to watch as a black-suited official hurried to answer. Rosenfield felt a surge of hope. Had the governor decided to grant clemency at the last second? Just as in a movie? He knew Dennis felt the same. The official picked up the receiver.

"No, this is the Death House," he said.

Wrong number.

Stockton dropped his head.

The warden nodded to someone standing near a wall, and a tape recorder and microphone were taken to Stockton. The official leaned over and asked if he had any last words.

Stockton recited from Scripture, Isaiah 26:3. "Thou will keep him in perfect peace whose mind is stayed on thee, because he trusteth in thee." It was the verse he found on his wall as he stripped away layers of paint, the forgotten line that leapt at him like a message from the dead.

It was 9:04.

The phone rang again. The same official hurried to the phone and snatched up the receiver. "No, this is a wrong number," he said louder, more irritated.

In the days to follow, word leaked from the prison that the calls were no accident. Stockton's diaries had exposed incompetence and corruption on many levels of the prison hierarchy. Many people suffered for his revelations. It was rumored that the calls were a final, cruel joke. Someone wanted revenge.

The warden nodded again. The IV lines began to twitch, meaning that the poisons had been released and were running into Stockton's veins. What if there's a mistake? Rosenfield thought in horror. What should I do? His eyes could not leave his client's face. Dennis stared at the ceiling. His eyes closed like shutters. At 9:08, there were ripples in his chest, probably spasms caused by the blood's terminal acidity, the body's last primitive protest. The spasms ended, and it was apparent Stockton would not move again.

The blue curtain was drawn. The journalist from the Southside paper turned and told Stockton's lawyers he was sorry. The kind words were appreciated. Rosenfield and King were allowed to hang back as the witnesses were led outside in silence. The unseen prisoners above them raged.

• • • •

Stockton's attorneys had time to compose themselves before facing the assembled reporters. They were shaken in a way they had not foreseen. They felt empty, as if wrapped in the arms of a dream. It was a fine illusion the state had created: death that did not seem like death, just a peaceful slide into sleep. Stockton was killed in the easiest way possible. Their visceral responses to death seemed deadened as well.

They walked outside the chamber together, and the fresh air felt mercifully crisp and good. They could not help but think how lucky they were to be alive, how any misstep could end that gift. With that, the collected rage and frustration of the past few days began to turn to grief under the stars. They awaited the van's return and talked in hushed tones. They wondered if the condemned men played "Free Bird" at nine o'clock as Dennis asked. They later learned some had.

The driver deposited them near the TV trucks topped with satellite dishes, their logos identifying them from Richmond, Norfolk, Roanoke, North Carolina and Washington, D.C. They were massed outside Greensville's administration building, ready for the live feed to the eleven o'clock news. The two attorneys stepped into a pool of lights. King said there was no reason to rush to judgment like this for a man who had made a convincing claim of innocence. He turned the podium over to his partner and stepped away. Rosenfield's voice cracked with sadness and anger as he noted one of the many ironies in his client's life and death: the same judicial system that refused to grant Stockton a new trial because the evidence came too late also refused to appoint him investigators in the beginning when the evidence could have been found and would have been heard. "It's hard to understand why the state is in such a hurry after this length of time," he said. "Maybe it wanted to save a few bucks at the cost of innocent lives, and Dennis Stockton is one."

A TV reporter asked a final question: "Mr. Rosenfield, do you think Stockton was innocent?"

Rosenfield looked up from the podium and spotted the ambulance bearing Stockton's body to the coroner. He recalled a conversation between Dennis and one of his ministers about whether there was an afterlife, whether we ever found a place of justice far beyond revenge. The conversation had irritated Rosenfield. Death was death, he wanted to tell them. The rest was speculation.

Now as Rosenfield watched the ambulance leave the prison gates, he wished he hadn't rushed to judgment about that conversation between Stockton and the minister. The vehicle glided down the road, past the swamps, into darkness. Dennis will learn the truth now, won't he? Rosenfield thought. As shall we all some day.

He looked back up at the lights and remembered the time his client fantasized escaping with the others that night in 1984. He wouldn't have been recaptured, he said. "I wouldn't've made their mistakes." Then Dennis paused and laughed. "Of course, I made the biggest mistake of all. I trusted the system." Rosenfield thought about a society that fostered such trust and betrayed it. Then he answered the TV reporter's question:

"There's no doubt in my mind they got the wrong man."

Epilogue

The next day, a North Carolina man would call Rosenfield's office. He had just read the story in the local paper about Stockton's execution and he was crying. He had proof that Stockton didn't kill Arnder, he said, but he'd thought the federal court would allow the evidentiary hearing and the truth would come out. He hadn't heard until after the execution that the stay had been overruled. He felt responsible for Stockton's death.

He was also afraid. When the lawyers tried to convince him to go public, he refused. The real killers were still free, he said, and he had a family. Could the lawyers provide them round-the-clock protection for untold years? The lawyers conceded they couldn't.

In the days that followed, those who believed in Stockton's innocence dispersed to their own private shells to come to grips with what seemed to them another moment of indifferent evil in the century that made it commonplace. Pat McHone and Kathy Carreon went into hiding, frightened for their lives. Timothy Crabtree despaired of fitting into an adult society where power seemed more important than truth. Steve Roach and the other condemned men saw their futures.

The fifty-six men put to death in America in 1995 represented the most executions in a year since 1957, when sixty-five were executed. In 1995, executions were held in sixteen states, with Virginia tied with five others for third-most executions. By the end of the year, 313 inmates had been executed since the reinstatement of the death penalty in 1976. Another 3,054 awaited their own final walks, but these figures did not include the other casualties: the murder victims themselves; their survivors, drawn into a wait that by then averaged eleven years and two months; the lawyers, ministers, guards or prison administrators caught in a system they could sometimes barely reconcile with their beliefs.

Five months after Execution Day, the United Nations reported that governments around the world continued to violate the right to life and cited Stockton's execution as one of six cases in 1995 where the United States imposed the death penalty despite doubts about the condemned's guilt. This special investigation by the UN Commission on Human Rights raised concerns that many death sentences in the United States "continue to be handed down after trials which fell short of international guarantees of a fair trial."

More than a year after Stockton's execution, witnesses watched the death of Lem Tuggle, the last player in the Great Escape. On December 12, 1996, he entered the chamber in typical Tuggle fashion, looking at the witness booth and crying "Merry Christmas!" before the poison dripped into his blood. That year a new generation of condemned inmates tried unsuccessfully to get evidence entered in court, almost always without success. That year, Virginia rose in the ranks of killing states to second, trailing only Texas.

By November 1998, the number of Death Row inmates across America had swelled to 3,517, and 486 prisoners had been executed since 1976. Also that November, a conference at Northwestern University's law school in Chicago focused on the seventy-five men and women who had been freed from the nation's Death Rows in the twenty-two years since the Supreme Court reinstated the death penalty. Such "wrongful convictions," accounting for a one-in-six ratio of releases to executions, raised the strong likelihood that those released were about to be executed for crimes they had not committed.

In 1996, the year after Stockton's execution, Randy Bowman offered to tell Rosenfield and King "the real story" of Arnder's murder for $1,000. Worried about a conflict of interest, the lawyers did not pay but tried to find backers in the media. A German film company, interested in Stockton's story for German public television, agreed to cover part of the cost, but no American medium—broadcast or print—was interested. After *Dead Run*'s publication in November 1999, the North Carolina man who cried while telling Rosenfield of Stockton's innocence considered going public with his evidence, but ultimately stayed silent for fear of his family's safety. Then, a second man came forward. On March 24, 2000, William Shaw of High Point, North Carolina, told Rosenfield, Tony King, the editor and the reporter that Arnder had not been killed in Virginia after all, but in a small house on the outskirts of Mount Airy. It was a claim that echoed Bob Day's words to Stockton in Mecklenburg in October 1983. Shaw, who described himself as Tommy McBride's former lieutenant, said that a man came to him soon after Arnder's murder and told of going to a local drug dealer's house off South Franklin Road in Mount Airy during the time Arnder was missing in July 1978. He had only meant to purchase some marijuana, but when he stepped inside the house "he sees Arnder tied up in the kitchen and tortured" by the dealer and his two nephews, Shaw claimed. Shaw recalled the man saying: "I got out of there quick . . . it's something I wish I'd never seen." Shaw was adamant about the man's confession and allowed himself to be taped, yet the details and players in his version were different than in that told tearfully to Rosenfield the day after Stockton's execution.

In the end, who could tell the truth from the lies? There remains something ill-starred and Gothic about Mount Airy, a town where the bodies of unnamed victims were reportedly dumped in a well off the side of the road, where armed drug dealers got drunk, cursed God and for a few short years thought they were bigger than life and the law. Each new "truth" uncovered a contrasting truth, so that in the end, the only certainty was that the true story surrounding the murder of Kenny Arnder that warm July night in 1978 might never be revealed. The law's purpose had shifted from the search for truth to the triumph of procedure. The lawyers argued law, and society looked away.

Five years after Stockton's execution, the death penalty debate assumed a new urgency. Crime was down, but the annual total of executions in America continued to climb. On January 31, 2000, Governor George Ryan of Illinois imposed a moratorium on capital punishment after thirteen wrongly convicted men were released from his state's death row, more than had been executed since the reinstatement of capital punishment in 1976. Across the nation, eighty-seven condemned inmates had been released after unearthed or previously suppressed evidence proved their innocence. The new debate focused on the use of DNA testing to establish a "doubtless" guilt or innocence before someone was executed. But DNA was never a factor in Stockton's journey. His fate—like that of many others on death row—hinged on the testimony of a single witness, a fact that would have made him ineligible for death in the Bible ("At the mouth of one witness he shall not be put to death"—Deuteronomy 17:6). If he'd lived to see the millennium, the debate—like the law—would have done him little good.

Albert Camus captured the plight thirty years earlier: "Long in advance the condemned man knows that he is going to be killed and that the only thing that can save him is a reprieve, rather similar, for him, to the decrees of heaven," he wrote. "Everything goes on outside of him. He is no longer a man but a thing waiting to be handled by the executioners. He is kept as if he were inert matter, but he still has a consciousness which is his chief enemy."

Stockton never read Camus but knew the cost of waiting. It was the greatest revenge of all, one from which there was no escape or reprieve. Even so, he found himself. He created his own small triumph. He was forced back on himself and found a voice. The voice gave him dignity.

Ron Smith thought of this as he sprinkled Stockton's ashes over a waterfall splashing down the lee face of the Blue Ridge Mountains. Four days after Stockton's execution, he and two church members hiked to a small stream bubbling over some rocks. It was beautiful that day, the leaves ablaze in autumnal reds and yellows, the air fresh in the spray. The only sound was that of the water and some acorns dropping from the oak trees. Smith read the burial passage from the Scriptures then sprinkled Dennis's ashes on the water. Dennis had saved two candy bars and a can of Classic Coke for them to share after the ceremony—a kind of farewell. This stream flowed into others, all eventually forming the James River, meandering through the state, east through the Piedmont, past the gray walls of Powhatan. It would be nice if his ashes traveled that far, Dennis once told him. Like Dennis did, Ron Smith let his mind drift, imagining that final watery journey from the land of slavery into the sea.

Smith watched the ashes swirl, then wash away.

Notes

Chapter 1

9   *"A forty dollar ounce . . . more than he makes from the state."* Daryl Cumber Dance, *Long Gone: The Mecklenburg Six and the Theme of Escape in Black Folklore.* Knoxville, Tenn.: The University of Tennessee Press, 1987, p. 13.

Chapter 2

19   *"For example . . . until he just knew you'd be there."* Dance, *Long Gone,* p. 43.

27   *Stockton could tell the guy was nuts . . . his high, weird way.* In addition to news accounts and Stockton's notes, the character and history of Morris Mason was taken from Joseph B. Ingle, *Last Rights: 13 Fatal Encounters with the State's Justice.* Nashville, Tenn.: Abingdon Press, 1990, pp. 248–251. Especially helpful was "Morris Mason as I Knew Him," by fellow Death Row inmate Joe Giarratano.

Chapter 3

42   *"It is possible . . . capable of carrying out real violence."* Richard E. Nisbett and Dov Cohen, *Culture of Honor: The Psychology of Violence in the South.* Boulder, Co.: Westview Press, 1996, p. 72.

44   *Of them, 125 were hanged.* David Hackett Fischer, *Albion's Seed: Four British Folkways in America.* New York: Warner Books, Inc., 1984, p. 400.

44   *Literate criminals. . . . The poor and illiterate went to the gallows.* Fischer, *Albion's Seed,* p. 399.

46   *"a society of . . . anyone who stood in their way."* Fischer, *Albion's Seed,* p. 687.

59   *"Follow vandals . . . takes humiliation and turns it into rage."* Jack Katz, *Seductions of Crime: Moral and Sensual Attractions of Doing Evil.* New York: Basic Books, Inc., 1988, pp. 312–313.

Chapter 5

90   *"As our society grows more mobile . . . murderous fantasies grows apace."* Robert K. Ressler and Tom Shachtman, *Whoever Fights Monsters.* New York: St. Martin's Press, 1992, pp. 150–151.

91   *"He had told all those lies in order to have fun . . ."* Ressler and Shachtman, *Whoever Fights Monsters,* p. 228.

Chapter 8

159   *"Guards told . . . but no one was killed."* Dance, *Long Gone,* p. 76.

Chapter 9

184   "Linwood," by James Briley, in *FYSK* magazine, 13 (Winter 1984), p. 18, reprinted in Dance, *Long Gone,* p. 131.

184   Linwood Briley's note to his minister, reprinted in Dance, *Long Gone,* p. 134.

Chapter 10

207   *"They made excuses . . . and prayed to them every day with perverse devotion."* Gabriel Garcia Marquez, *News of a Kidnapping.* New York: Penguin Books, 1996, p. 60.

Chapter 11

220   *"When he felt his resolve weaken . . . his wife would ask."* Peter Boyer, "The Genius of Death Row," *The New Yorker,* Dec. 4, 1995, p. 66.

221   *He wrote in his memoirs ... all mention of it faded into thin air.* Paraphrased from Turner's memoirs, in Boyer, "The Genius of Death Row," p. 73. *The New Yorker* obtained the rights to Turner's unpublished memoirs after his execution in 1995; at first, the magazine planned to publish them, but then decided against that option due to problems verifying some of the statements in Turner's manuscript. Instead, Boyer used the memoirs as the basis for his excellent psychological profile of Turner.

222   *"As I walked in ... the smell of death."* Quoted from Turner's memoirs, in Boyer, "The Genius of Death Row," p. 75.

Epilogue

289   *"Long in advance ... his chief enemy."* Albert Camus, "Reflections on the Guillotine," in *Resistance, Rebellion and Death,* trans. Justin O'Brien. New York: Vintage Books, 1974, p. 201.

Sources and Acknowledgments

Stories like this have as much to do with the hope and pain of those whose lives briefly intersect Death Row as with any one man or woman's quest for justice. Most seek justice as they see it, or at least do their best to make the system work in admittedly hard circumstances. When that system does not work, some find themselves reappraising their beliefs, while others, without knowing quite what happened, find that they too have become casualties.

Writing a book like this presents its own special challenges. Although the authors attempted to contact as many principals as they could, it was not always possible. The decades passed, people moved, grew old or died. Some slipped into anonymity, as Stockton said his siblings did to protect themselves from harassment; others possessing knowledge of the events that resulted in Stockton's death sentence did not come forward, or, doing so, went back into hiding for fear of their lives. The main characters in this story, of course, were Stockton's contemporaries on Virginia's Death Row, and almost every one of them had been executed by 1996. Yet much has been written about the events occurring on The Row from 1983 to 1995, and with the help of letters, diaries, memoirs, interviews, newspaper and magazine articles, Daryl Cumber Dance's *Long Gone: The Mecklenburg Six and the Theme of Escape of Black Folklore,* and our own personal experience, the authors have tried to reconstruct life on Death Row and to faithfully portray the thoughts, words and deeds of prisoners, guards and others who worked, lived or died in that world.

The primary source for Stockton's tale comes from Dennis's writings over the years. These include his letters from Virginia's Death Row to *The Virginian-Pilot,* diaries and journals, unpublished works (specifically his autobiography, *The Daybook,* but also a novel and collection of other writings), newsletters and columns that were published in *The Virginian-Pilot* prior to and after his execution. A lot of what could be called traditional journalism went into this work. Most of the events described herein appeared over the years in the pages of the Norfolk newspaper, as well as in other Virginia newspapers. Bill Burke was the story editor during each of these periods: 1984, when a team of reporters verified Stockton's diary entries concerning the escape and his tales about himself; 1986, when Stockton first faced execution and was even then claiming innocence; 1994, when Stockton's tale was part of a larger newspaper package about legal problems with Virginia's Death Row cases; and 1995, when Stockton wrote his columns about approaching an execution, Randy Bowman recanted and three people gave affidavits about Bowman's alleged statements of involvement in the Kenny Arnder murder. Joe Jackson was the lead reporter in 1994 and 1995 and thus took the recantation from Bowman, interviewed Wilman Arnder, Jay Gregory, Tommy McBride, Robert Gates and other players in the drama, and researched court records.

We found over the years that Stockton was surprisingly reliable concerning details. In his description of his pitching before New York Yankee scout Tommy Byrne, he remembered the make of Byrne's car and other details of the game, which Byrne later verified. His tales of drug dealing by Death Row guards were verified by a state police investigator in 1984; the investigator said that Stockton was accurate in 90 percent of his details, and, later, there were drug charges filed against one guard, whose name is not given in this book. Stockton said that there was evidence that Bowman had accepted a deal for his testimony in Stockton's trial, something prosecutors denied, and then in 1990 Bowman's letter from 1983 surfaced, the one that demanded favorable treatment before his court appearance. Stockton discounted Robert Gates's version of the killing and burial of Ronnie Tate, and then in 1994 the owner of the sandwich shop mentioned by Gates independently disputed Gates's version, too. Stockton said he didn't kill Arnder, and there were the affidavits by two prisoners saying they heard Bowman brag about lying at the trial, as well as an affidavit quoting the words of Junior Danley, who said he was present at the murder but that Stockton wasn't there. Weeks before Stockton's execution, the three affidavits implicating Bowman in the murder were filed in court. These are just a few of the instances when Stockton's claims were independently verified.

Stockton also proved to be a reliable source for information that didn't specifically have to do with his case. He was the first to alert *The Virginian-Pilot* to the histoplasmosis epidemic that swept through Powhatan Correctional Center in 1994; his descriptions of the numbers of guards and inmates affected and the fear that swept M-Building, were all verified. He was also the first to tell the authors about the discovery of Willie Lloyd Turner's homemade keys and weapons cache at Powhatan, and about the DOC "suits and ties" who stood outside Turner's cell and using a racial epithet said, "He sure is a smart little nigger. Musta took him years to do all those things." One thing that was not verified was Stockton's account of Willie's gun in Powhatan, but considering the more famous gun that was later discovered in Willie's typewriter in the Death House, Stockton's account is at least plausible.

Stockton's account of his childhood comes from his autobiography and was verified in part by a long project published by *The Mount Airy News* in 1986. Stockton's version of the 1984 escape (in his diaries and autobiography) was largely verified by accounts of hostages and other prisoners involved in the planning. Information gleaned from Darryl Cumber Dance's *Long Gone* is cited in the Notes. Everything about Randy Bowman comes from court records or interviews. Bowman's criminal history comes from files in the Surry County and Patrick County courts. The quotes from Pat McHone come from her affidavit and phone interviews; the quotes from Kathy Carreon come from personal interviews and her affidavit; the quotes from Timothy Crabtree come from his affidavit. As mentioned in the story, Bowman denied the allegations made by McHone, Carreon and his son.

The chapter concerning Willie Lloyd Turner came from court records, Stockton's tales of Turner, interviews and original reporting in *The Pilot*, but it also draws heavily on Peter Boyer's "The Genius of Death Row" in *The New Yorker*, cited in the Notes. The account of the discovery of Turner's gun in the typewriter comes from original reporting by two other reporters in *The Pilot,* Laura Lafay and June Arney.

The account of Stockton's last day draws heavily on a long letter from Steve Rosenfield. The account of Stockton's execution was first-hand, since Joe Jackson was a witness.

One can see, therefore, that Stockton's story took years to resolve itself, long before anyone knew that it would be written into a book. But even then, many people sensed that the tale was an extraordinary one. It could never have been told without the effort of all the reporters, photographers, editors and researchers at *The Virginian-Pilot* who contributed over the years. It also would not have been possible without the aid of Ron Smith, Stockton's minister and executor, who allowed us use of Stockton's letters, diaries and unpublished writings, and of Steve Rosenfield and Anthony King, Stockton's attorneys in his last years. Other lawyers were also helpful, including Gerald Zerkin of Richmond and Stockton's pro bono lawyers at the Washington, D.C., firm of Arnold & Porter. Marie Deans seemed at times a one-woman crusade to ensure fair representation for the condemned, while Russ Ford, the Death Row chaplain, probably saw farther into the hearts of the condemned than anyone. Meanwhile, a small army of defense attorneys, state officials and investigators were instrumental in making sense of the other Death Row cases that played out while Stockton was on The Row.

One private investigator who deserves special mention is G. R. "Ronnie" Cheek of High Point, North Carolina. After Bowman's recantation to the reporter, Stockton's lawyers hired Cheek to find Pat McHone and others who might have witnesseed evidence that corroborated and explained this sudden about-face. What Cheek found instead took the case in an unbelievably new direction. Cheek tracked Pat McHone to a mobile home in rural North Carolina; although McHone said she was terrified of her former husband's revenge, she also could not bear to think that her silence might allow an innocent man to be executed. She agreed to a videotaped interview, but only if Cheek were present: her fear shows on the tape, and she looks as if at any second she might flee. Through McHone, Cheek found Timothy Crabtree, and later found Kathy Carreon hiding in a tiny trailer outside Mount Airy. "Am I that easy to find?" she asked before giving her own affidavit. As all three made their allegations of Bowman's boasts of killing Kenny Arnder and others, "I could feel their fear vividly," Cheek recalled. It takes a good detective to track down those who have gone into hiding, and an even better psychologist to gain their confidence. In the process, Cheek became convinced of Stockton's innocence and even today, he says, "the case stays in my mind daily."

Others also played their parts outside the walls of Virginia's prisons. Tom Joyce of *The Mount Airy News* guided us through the murky waters of politics and law enforcement in both Mount Airy, North Carolina, and Patrick County, Virginia. Jim McCloskey, director of Centurion Ministries, gave valuable insight into the souls of witnesses who recant. Jim Crabtree expertly balanced concerns for his adopted son, Timothy, and the desires of both that an innocent man should not die. Tony Giorno and Jay Gregory were both convinced that Stockton was guilty, and were forthright in their explanations why. Wilma Arnder, too, found herself in a storm not of her own making, and as Stockton's final days progressed, that storm just got worse. We can only hope that should we ever find ourselves in a similar situation, we face it with as much grace and honesty. And there were those who believed Stockton was innocent and talked about it, but feared for their own safety or that of their children should their names ever be used.

Finally, this story would not have been published without a little help from New York. Noah Lukeman, our literary agent, believed in the story when others didn't. Bill Thompson, former editor of Delphinium Press, believed also and directed us toward Noah. Philip Turner, our editor at Times Books, made the words shine with intelligence and precision. All have our gratitude.

About the Authors

From 1985 to 1997, JOE JACKSON was an investigative reporter for *The Virginian-Pilot* of Norfolk, for which he covered police, state and federal courts, and jails and prisons. He investigated Dennis Stockton's claims of innocence and took the recantation of the state's main witness during Stockton's trial. His stories resulted in the acquittal of a man wrongly convicted of murder and a federal investigation of the Norfolk jail after sixteen prisoners died through the years, primarily of medical neglect; he was nominated three times for the Pulitzer Prize.

WILLIAM F. BURKE, JR., has been an editor at *The Virginian-Pilot* since 1980. During his tenure, stories he has edited have received four Pulitzer Prize nominations. He contacted Death Row inmates at the Mecklenburg Correctional Center following the notorious mass escape in 1984, obtained Dennis Stockton's diaries, edited news stories based on these writings and published Stockton's columns from Death Row, including one on the day after his execution.

Both Jackson and Burke live in Virginia Beach, Virginia.